D1566382

9·17

STYLES FOR WRITING

A BRIEF RHETORIC

STYLES FOR WRITING

A BRIEF RHETORIC

GERALD LEVIN
THE UNIVERSITY OF AKRON

HARCOURT BRACE JOVANOVICH, INC.
NEW YORK / CHICAGO / SAN FRANCISCO / ATLANTA

ACKNOWLEDGMENTS

The author wishes to thank the publishers, agents, and individuals who have given permission for reprinting the following copyrighted material.

EDWARD ARNOLD LTD., for material from "What I Believe," by E. M. Forster. Reprinted from his volume *Two Cheers for Democracy*, published by Edward Arnold Publishers Ltd.

ATHENEUM PUBLISHERS, INC., for material from *A Sad Heart at the Supermarket* by Randall Jarrell. Copyright © 1960, 1962 by Randall Jarrell. Reprinted by permission of Atheneum Publishers.

BLACKWELL & MOTT, LTD., for quotations from *The Nature of the Universe* by Fred Hoyle.

Miss Sonia Brownell for extracts from *The Lion and the Unicorn*, by George Orwell, Secker & Warburg.

CHATTO AND WINDUS LTD., for material from *Brave New World Revisited* by Aldous Huxley, and from *Eminent Victorians* by Lytton Strachey.

Northrop Frye, for the essay "The Keys to Dreamland," from *The Educated Imagination*.

HARCOURT BRACE JOVANOVICH, INC., for material from "What I Believe," copyright, 1939, © 1967 by E. M. Forster. Reprinted from his volume *Two Cheers for Democracy* by permission of Harcourt Brace Jovanovich, Inc. For material from "England, Your England," in *Such, Such Were the Joys* by George Orwell, copyright, 1945, 1952, 1953, by Sonia Brownell Orwell. Reprinted by permission of Harcourt Brace Jovanovich, Inc. For material from *A History of Western Morals*, © 1959 by Crane Brinton. Reprinted by permission of Harcourt Brace Jovanovich, Inc.

HARPER & ROW, PUBLISHERS, INC., for excerpts from pp. 84–6, 88, 90 in (hardbound Ed.) of *The Nature of the Universe*, Rev. Ed. by Fred Hoyle. Copyright, 1950, 1960 by Fred Hoyle; for excerpts from pp. 60–62 in *Brave New World Revisited* by Aldous Huxley. Copyright © 1958 by Aldous Huxley; for about 850 words as scattered quotes from "Letter from Birmingham Jail," April 16, 1963, in *Why We Can't Wait* by Martin Luther King, Jr.; for excerpt from p. 196 in *The Points of My Compass* by E. B. White. Copyright © 1960 by E. B. White. Originally appeared in *The New Yorker*. Reprinted by permission of Harper & Row, Publishers, Inc.

HARVARD UNIVERSITY PRESS, for Chapter V, "Daniel Boone: Empire Builder or Philosopher of Primitivism?" from Henry Nash Smith, *Virgin Land: The American West as Symbol and Myth*. Copyright, 1950, by the Presi...

A. M. HEATH & COMPANY LTD., for extracts from *The Lion and the Unicorn*, by George Orwell, Secker & Warburg, Publishers.

HORIZON PRESS, PUBLISHERS, for material reprinted from *Politics and the Novel* by Irving Howe, copyright 1957, by permission of the publisher, Horizon Press, New York.

HOUGHTON MIFFLIN COMPANY for material from *Parkinson's Law* by C. N. Parkinson, published by Houghton Mifflin Company.

Mrs. Laura Huxley for extracts from *Brave New World Revisited* by Aldous Huxley, Chatto and Windus Ltd.

INDIANA UNIVERSITY PRESS for "The Keys to Dreamland," from *The Educated Imagination* by Northrop Frye. Copyright © 1964 by Indiana University Press. Reprinted by permission of the publisher.

LITTLE, BROWN AND COMPANY, PUBLISHERS for material from *The Late George Apley* by John P. Marquand. Copyright 1936, 1937 by John P. Marquand; copyright renewed 1964, 1965 by John P. Marquand, Jr. and Christina M. Welch.

THE MACMILLAN COMPANY, for excerpts from *Science and the Modern World* by Alfred North Whitehead. Copyright, 1925, by The Macmillan Company.

M. I. T. PRESS, for material reprinted from *Language, Thought, and Reality* by Benjamin Lee Whorf by permission of the M I T Press, Cambridge, Massachusetts. Copyright © 1956 by the Massachusetts Institute of Technology.

MC GRAW-HILL BOOK COMPANY, for material from *Robert Benchley* by Nathaniel Benchley. Copyright © 1955 by Nathaniel Benchley. Copyright 1947, 1948, 1954 by Nathaniel Benchley. Copyright 1954, 1955 by the Curtis Publishing Company, Inc. Used with permission of McGraw-Hill Book Company; for material from *Present Tense* by Norman Cousins, copyright © 1967 by Norman Cousins. Used with permission of McGraw-Hill Book Company.

THE NEW YORKER, for selection from "The Sporting Scene" by Roger Angell. Reprinted by permission; © 1964 The New Yorker Magazine, Inc.

G. P. PUTNAM'S SONS for material from *Eminent Victorians* by Lytton Strachey.

RANDOM HOUSE, INC., ALFRED A. KNOPF, INC., for excerpts from *The Way of Zen* by Alan W. Watts. Copyright © 1957 by Pantheon Books, Inc., a Division of Random House, Inc. Reprinted by permission of the publisher; for excerpts from *A Mencken Chrestomathy*, by H. L. Mencken. Copyright 1949 by Alfred A. Knopf, Inc. Reprinted by permission.

CHARLES SCRIBNER'S SONS for material from *Ford* by Allan Nevins, Charles Scribner's Sons, 1954.

SIMON & SCHUSTER, INC., for material from *America As A Civilization* by Max Lerner, copyright © 1957 by Max Lerner. Reprinted by permission of Simon and Schuster.

Mrs. A. S. Strachey for material from *Eminent Victorians* by Lytton Strachey, Chatto and Windus Ltd.

Mrs. James Thurber for material copr. © 1957 James Thurber. From "The Psychosemanticist Will See You Now, Mr. Thurber," in *Alarms and Diversions*, published by Harper and Row. Originally printed in *The New Yorker*.

THE UNIVERSITY OF CHICAGO PRESS, for material from *The Professional Thief* by Edwin H. Sutherland, copyright 1937 by The University of Chicago.

THE VIKING PRESS, INC., for material from *Eichmann in Jerusalem: A Report on the Banality of Evil* by Hannah Arendt. Copyright © 1963 by Hannah Arendt. Reprinted by permission of the Viking Press, Inc.

YALE UNIVERSITY PRESS, for material from *The American Mind* by Henry S. Commager, published by Yale University Press, 1950.

A. WATKINS, INC., for "The Holborn" by Arturo Vivante. © 1968 Arturo Vivante. First published in the New Yorker Magazine, September 14, 1968.

PREFACE

Styles for Writing is designed primarily to cultivate in the student an understanding of many prose styles. It is a basic text for the composition course, offering help in such matters as fused sentences, comma faults, and dangling modifiers, and containing a glossary of usage. The topics of classical rhetoric stand behind the book but do not dominate it; the language and presentation are directed to the beginning student who has had little or no training in these ideas. I have used much of the material and methods of presentation with my freshman classes during the past eleven years.

Styles for Writing builds from a study of the structure of the paragraph and the sentence to matters of diction, the rhetoric and logic of the essay, and the research paper. The treatment of rhetoric and logic covers the methods of developing ideas in exposition and argument; the parts of the essay, with discussion of the introduction, confirmation, refutation, and conclusion; and deduction, induction, and logical fallacies. All of these are illustrated with examples of style by contemporary writers who are concerned with issues of current importance. Four complete essays—by Norman Cousins, Northrop Frye, Arturo Vivante, and Henry Nash Smith—illustrate the argumentative, expository, autobiographical, and documented essay, respectively. These four essays are analyzed for the student, reviewing topics discussed in the particular chapter. I have tried throughout to avoid a prescriptive tone. The usual student errors are discussed in the context of cogent writing. The emphasis is on writing effective sentences, not merely grammatically correct ones, and the student is given a basis for determining what is effective.

Styles for Writing contains material from my *Brief Handbook of Rhetoric* (1966), but it is almost entirely a new book. It would be impossible to name here the many writers on rhetoric and logic from whom I have learned, but I do wish to mention Professor Edward P. J. Corbett, on whose masterful exposition of the common topics

I have drawn, and to thank Professor Paul B. Davis of the University of New Mexico, who read the manuscript and made helpful suggestions. I wish also to thank my wife, Lillian Levin, for her assistance and encouragement, as well as Dorothy Mott of Harcourt Brace Jovanovich. This book is dedicated to a fine teacher and warm friend, John R. Hull, of the University of Akron, whose death occurred at the time the manuscript was being completed.

GERALD LEVIN

CONTENTS

THE RESEARCH PAPER   209

INDEX   237

THE WRITER AND HIS AUDIENCE

"Ought I not to look at the sunset rather than write this?"—
VIRGINIA WOOLF

THE AUDIENCE OF ONE

The English novelist Virginia Woolf wrote in her diary: "And this shall be written for my own pleasure. But that phrase inhibits me; for if one writes only for one's own pleasure, I don't know what it is that happens. I suppose the convention of writing is destroyed: therefore one does not write at all."[1]

You may have asked yourself a question much like Mrs. Woolf's: "If I did not have to write this paper for this course at this time, would I write at all?"

Outside the classroom you may write for yourself. If you keep a diary or a journal or write stories or verse that no one else sees; if this writing pleases you—you are writing for an audience of one. But suppose you are dissatisfied with what you have written; suppose you

---

[1] *A Writer's Diary* (New York: Harcourt Brace Jovanovich, 1953), pp. 339, 132.

feel you have not expressed your thoughts and feelings truly. In judging your own writing you have become a different person from the writer; you have become writer and critic. You have—perhaps without realizing it—become an audience of two.

THE AUDIENCE OF TWO

We are not always willing to become judge and critic of our own writing, in part because we tend to think well of what we have written. But when we are writing for others, who will judge our writing and be persuaded or unpersuaded by it, the situation changes. You may be writing your congressman to persuade him to take action on a bill, or writing your college newspaper or a national magazine to explain your views on pollution or on war or poverty. You may be trying to persuade your parents or friends to share your beliefs or actions. You may be writing a love letter. In these situations you are necessarily more aware of how you have expressed your thoughts and feelings. You are writer and critic.

Mortimer J. Adler, the philosopher, suggests that readers of love letters "read for all they are worth." Adler explains what happens:

> They read every word three ways; they read between the lines and in the margins; they read the whole in terms of the parts, and each part in terms of the whole; they grow sensitive to context and ambiguity, to insinuation and implication; they perceive the color of words, the odor of phrases, and the weight of sentences. They may even take the punctuation into account.
>
> —*How to Read a Book* (New York: Simon and Schuster, 1940), p. 14.

We may extend the comment to suggest that writers of love letters write for all they are worth. They draw upon the means of composition available to them as fully as they can; they employ a rhetoric and a logic. They become writer and critic simultaneously and become eager to increase their power of expression. Their thoughts are fixed on a single purpose and that purpose determines each aspect of their process of composition. T. S. Eliot wrote of "the intolerable wrestle with words and meanings," the experience of each writer as he seeks to express his feelings not only to himself but to others.

THE AUDIENCE OF THREE

We have been talking, really, about an audience of three. If we include our composition instructor, then we have an audience of four.

Or if we include our classmates who may have to listen to our composition, then perhaps our audience has increased to twenty or thirty. In short, what we choose to say and how we choose to say it are usually determined by circumstances more complex than the simple situation of the audience of one or two that we began with. The choices we make—the decisions about our audience and our purposes —before and as we write are decisive to the success or failure of our writing in its final form. This success or failure is measured by more than the immediate gratification we feel in the act of writing.

INTENTION AND SELF-UNDERSTANDING

If you write to your parents that you wish to remain in school and you really do not wish to stay, you may write a letter that will displease your parents so that they will not wish to help you further. Or you may be angry with your representative or with the general public and, perhaps unconsciously, attempt to anger or insult them, even though your real interest might be better served by persuading them to accept your beliefs or feelings.

It is simple to say that effective writing depends on self-understanding and a clear sense of purpose—and, we should add, an awareness of our resources as writers. In practice, however, we are seldom fully aware of or deeply concerned with these matters. This is not to say that when you write your congressman you do not consider your style; you do consider the way you write, probably choosing a more formal manner than that which you would use in writing to your family or friends. What you choose to do will depend on what you think you must do. But if you want to make your writing effective— right for your audience and for your real purpose—then you will need all the resources of rhetoric, that is, the art of persuasive speech and writing, that practice and a continuously developing knowledge of the immense number of possibilities available to the writer can give you.

CHOICES AND POSSIBILITIES

Obviously the writer who seeks to conciliate his audience and promote common interests will approach the act of writing differently from the writer who wishes merely to create a favorable impression of himself, perhaps widen the area of disagreement, or even impress on his audience their ignorance and incapacity to judge important issues. The former writer may be more aware of his intentions than the latter writer. However, he may not be aware that certain ways of writing that are logical or that he may think will conciliate his audience may have exactly the opposite effect or prove to be ineffective because of the nature of the audience.

For instance, suppose a speaker addresses a group of Canadian lawyers who are making a study of pending legislation in the United States Congress and wishes to convince them of its benefits. Traditional rhetoric prescribes different orders of confirming arguments in that part of the oration in which the speaker defends his ideas. One of these orders begins with a relatively strong argument, proceeds to a relatively weak one, and concludes with the strongest possible argument. Another arranges the arguments according to their logical strength. Both orders would be appropriate, given the purpose of the speaker, because the audience is not manifestly hostile to the legislation, their attitudes ranging from indifference to mild and strong interest.

But suppose the audience consists of American taxpayers organized to oppose the legislation. For this audience the logically strongest argument may possibly be the least persuasive; the logically weakest argument might be the one best suited to winning their good will and cooperation. In this instance, the rhetorical consideration is seen to be as important as the logical. Attention to rhetoric cannot assure the quality of the writing, but it is a necessary consideration. All good writing at least is organized to secure an effect. One of the prime marks of bad writing is writing organized to no effect.

Other considerations may not occur to the unpracticed writer, yet are important to his success. One of these is the knowledge he shares with his audience. There may be a reason to tell the audience what they know, if only to remind them of facts crucial to the argument; it would be useless to tell them everything known about the subject. Yet this is exactly what the unpracticed writer tries to do. And if he fails in an essay of moderate length to limit his subject properly—for instance, if he tries to examine the history of pollution control in the United States rather than local laws designed to control pollution—his essay is certain to be no more than a sprawl of information directed to no purpose. A precise limitation of the topic is indispensable to the success of any essay.

The practiced writer, having determined the interests and knowledge of his audience, selects his detail in exposition on the basis of what his audience does not know and his examples on the basis of what it does know. In an exposition of his city's current effort to control air pollution, he may provide detail on existing statutes before commenting on their efficacy; he may explain one or two of these statutes through familiar examples of their application. If, in an argument, he tells his audience only what they know and believe in an effort to conciliate them, he may win their good will but not their intellectual assent. His problem is how to earn good will without saying what he does not believe or pretending that significant differences in viewpoint and thought do not exist. He may decide on a frank exposition of significant similarities in viewpoint and thought, followed by an equally frank exposition of differences. Withholding important facts or failing to indicate critical differences may alienate the audience; on the other hand, the persuasiveness of the argument may depend on delaying discussion of these differences. If ideas are unfamiliar or hard to grasp, it will prove ineffective to begin with them. It is effective to approach them through a series of examples.

A closely related rhetorical consideration has to do with the presentation of conclusions. Do you state your belief at the beginning? Or do you present your evidence systematically to lead to your conclusion? Again, you must assess your audience for the answer. If you are writing a deductive essay, in which general truths or assumptions (in logic called premises) lead necessarily to other conclusions, your assessment of the audience may suggest that the usual procedure of working from premises to conclusion be reversed and the conclusion be presented first and repeated at the end. The reason for this change may be that the conclusion probably will be less controversial than one or more of the premises. Thus a particular audience may disagree less with the conclusion that pollution laws need revision than with the writer's premise that the federal government must assume the major responsibility for legislation and enforcement. How an audience reacts to a statement will depend, too, on the attitude of the writer toward himself as well as toward his audience. Broad authoritative generalizations may be fitting at the beginning of magisterial histories or general studies (for example, the opening sentence of Charles E. Silberman's Crisis in the Classroom, "Ours is an age of crisis," or that of Johan Huizinga's The Waning of the Middle Ages, "To the world when it was half a thousand years younger, the outlines of all things seemed more clearly marked than to us"). But if they occur in essays by amateurs in a subject, they may provoke skepticism or laughter.

There are good reasons for proceeding cautiously; the truly modest writer knows his knowledge is limited and he avoids dogmatism. There are bad reasons, too, one of the worst being timidity. The excellent advice of the British scholar R. B. McKerrow is worth quoting: "In the first place, unless you yourself believe in what you are doing, you will certainly not do good work, and, secondly, if your reader suspects for a moment that you do not set the very highest value on your work yourself he will set no value on it at all."

There is no "best" kind of introduction, but an effective introduction reassures the reader that he will be treated as the equal of the writer and not as a sounding board for ill-conceived and ill-expressed ideas. Remember, too, that in all one's writing it is as easy to bore your reader as it is to bore your partner in conversation. And it is easier for the reader to shut a dull book than it is for the listener to leave a dull conversationalist.

THE PURPOSE OF THIS BOOK

The study of rhetoric is the study of choices. We have examined a few of these briefly above. The chapters that follow give you examples of many styles of modern prose; these examples illustrate choices made by respected writers. The examples and the accompanying text and exercises should help you to increase and strengthen your own resources in rhetoric and logic.

Our study begins with the paragraph because the many kinds of paragraph development introduce the many kinds of organization in the whole essay; a mastery of the topic sentence of the paragraph is preliminary to the mastery of the thesis statement of the essay. The succeeding discussions of the sentence, punctuation, and diction develop numerous and related points about rhetoric that bear, too, upon the whole essay and are developed in the chapter on the rhetoric of the essay. The discussion of logic in the following chapter shows that the rhetorical and logical development of paragraphs as well as the whole essay are twin, and sometimes inseparable, considerations. The concluding chapter, on the research paper, draws on earlier discussions of evidence and deductive and inductive arguments.

The chapter on the rhetoric of the essay includes three complete essays representing autobiographical writing, exposition, and argument. These illustrate various principles of organization. The concluding chapter contains a documented essay on Daniel Boone.

Styles for Writing, then, offers a continuous discussion of the process of composition; each chapter builds on the preceding discussion, though you will be able to study the chapters separately if you wish. The book is in no sense exhaustive of the many kinds of paragraph and sentence development or organization of ideas in modern writing; a single volume would not be sufficient to cover these. Nor does it presume neutrality; it does make judgments and recommendations about effective style. Above all it encourages you to become increasingly aware of the prose styles you may command as well as the personal accent you will learn through practice to give them.

As you study these examples, you may discover that a minimum test of good style is the absence of qualities likely to disturb your reader—thus the attention in this book to common sentence and punctuation errors. But more important will be the discovery that an increasing knowledge of, and command over, the many resources of language and rhetoric can give you a mode of expression that will reflect more accurately and more effectively your interests, your intellectual attitudes, your personality.

THE
PARAGRAPH

Though many paragraphs are merely transitional and therefore are likely to consist of a few sentences, most paragraphs are like short essays: they have a beginning, a middle, and an end. A mastery of the paragraph is an important step to the mastery of the whole essay. We will consider, first, the uses various writers make of the beginning, middle, and end; and second, the characteristics of good paragraphs—a clear guiding topic idea, a clear ordering of main and subordinate ideas, brief necessary transitions, and a clear point of view. These are also characteristics of well-constructed essays, as are the characteristics of paragraph organization, our third consideration—definition, division and classification, comparison and contrast, cause and effect, among others. The numerous examples will familiarize you with the differing practices of respected writers, who shape their paragraphs according to their style of thought, yet usually agree on certain basic procedures.

THE EXPOSITORY PARAGRAPH

Newspaper columns often consist of paragraphs of one or two short sentences. In paragraphs of this modest length, ideas are not developed; this kind of paragraphing is nothing more than a special kind of punctuation that calls attention to single ideas and brief supporting detail. Introductory and concluding paragraphs may consist of a few sentences only; the ideas they present are developed in the body of the essay, in expository paragraphs.

The expository paragraph is a unit of thought larger than the sentence; it develops in different ways one idea or related ideas and has a beginning, a middle, and an end. The end of many paragraphs is often the most emphatic part. Though no two paragraphs are constructed in the same way, in part because they function differently, there are a few basic patterns from which individual paragraphs vary. In one basic pattern, the first sentence introduces the central idea or perhaps states it fully; the middle sentences develop and possibly introduce related ideas; the concluding sentences restate the idea or complete the train of thought.

TOPIC SENTENCE

The topic sentence states the topic idea—the controlling idea of the paragraph. It may be the first or second sentence, depending on the preparation the reader needs for the idea. At the beginning of the paragraph the topic sentence will receive natural emphasis; it will receive emphasis at the end if the idea is restated. The following paragraph describes a native of New Guinea:

> Woluklek is a wild-eyed man with an enchanted smile, and he is almost always by himself. Like Apeore, Tuesike, and Asikanalek, he is a solitary. But while Apeore and Asikanalek go their way alone because they like it, and Tuesike seems cut off from others out of shyness, Woluklek is alone because he is unique, and his solitude, though marked, is his condition. Unlike the others, he is not a respected warrior, but neither is he kepu, in the sense of cowardice. In war Woluklek is very often at the fore, but his activity is distracted, aimless, as if he had wandered across the battle lines on his way elsewhere and remained within the range of death out of bemusement. Yet he is not simple. It is as if, on the sunny paths of childhood, he had strayed out of his world into a dream and allowed the dream to waft him where it would, his life or death a matter of indifference.
>
> —PETER MATTHIESSEN, *Under the Mountain Wall*

The first sentence states the topic idea; each succeeding sentence develops or explains how and why Woluklek is a solitary. The last two sentences give a reason for the particular kind of solitude he exhibits: Woluklek is a dreamer.

The topic sentence need not state the topic idea completely; for its purpose is to guide the reader through the paragraph. The reader needs an indication of how ideas will be organized; the details need a frame. Some paragraphs build to a statement of the topic idea at the end, or dispense with a statement altogether. The writer may be presenting impressions unified by a mood or a point of view—much like a camera moving across a horizon and taking in details as they enter its range. The following paragraph is unified by a point of view (a pool in central Australia observed before dusk) and a dominant mood (rising excitement followed by quiet):

> On the ground the timid little coots that have been hiding in the reeds all day emerge into the open and come nervously down to the water to drink. The slightest disturbance is enough to make them scuttle back into cover again, and with their black feathers and red beaks they look like frightened chickens as they run. Now everywhere the trees are alive with parrots and cockatoos—the mulgas skimming by in green flocks, the parrot-cockatoos in grey, the Major Mitchells in pink—and it is not possible for the eye to follow all the arrivals and departures, the plovers, the eagles, crows, the harlequin colors of the bluebonnets, the little waxbills, the ring-necks and the herons. Sometimes there are black swans on the pool, and the pelicans, with their curious undulating flight—a series of upward flaps and a down-glide—descend in line, each bird braking himself for his landing on the water by putting out his webbed feet before him. As the light fades the color of the pool turns to gold, and this is the moment when the galahs, two by two, come in to drink from the bank, anxiously jerking up their heads to look around between each sip, and the bright pink of their breast feathers is reflected in the gold. With darkness silence and stillness return, but then some idiot corella falls off the rotten twig on which it has perched and the whole white flock wheels screeching into the air again. One can expect this to happen half a dozen times but in the end all is quiet. —ALAN MOOREHEAD, Cooper's Creek

The sentence that introduces the succeeding paragraph, "These evenings are the reward for the hot day, and it is possible on Cooper's Creek for the traveller to have a sense of great contentment, at any rate for an hour or two," states a topic idea—a reflection to which the details contribute.

Moorehead builds to his generalization through an accumulation of detail. The following paragraph occurring toward the middle of an essay on sport is more complex in structure. The opening sentence is transitional and serves to introduce details that build to a wholly new idea:

> In England, the obsession with sport is bad enough, but even fiercer passions are aroused in young countries where games-

playing and nationalism are both recent developments. In countries like India and Burma, it is necessary at football matches to have strong cordons of police to keep the crowd from invading the field. In Burma, I have seen the supporters of one side break through the police and disable the goalkeeper of the opposing side at a critical moment. The first big football match that was played in Spain, about fifteen years ago, led to an uncontrollable riot. As soon as strong feelings of rivalry are aroused, the notion of playing the game according to the rules always vanishes. People want to see one side on top and the other side humiliated and they forget that victory gained through cheating or through the intervention of the crowd is meaningless. Even when the spectators don't intervene physically they try to influence the game by cheering their own side and "rattling" opposing players with boos and insults. Serious sport has nothing to do with fair play. It is bound up with hatred, jealousy, boastfulness, disregard of all rules and sadistic pleasure in witnessing violence: in other words it is war minus the shooting.

—GEORGE ORWELL, "The Sporting Spirit"

The opening sentence of Orwell's paragraph is merely an indication of the topic—the fierce passions aroused by sports in young countries. The concluding sentences state the specific idea which the detail of the paragraph develops. Like Orwell, the writer of the following paragraph moves from the specific to the general, but with a difference. His opening sentence—a generalization about American farmers—is directly related to the generalization that concludes the paragraph:

The American farmer is perhaps rather less philosophical than the urban investor. He thinks he has a right to expect not a good living or a good cash income but a permanent and certain increase in the selling value of his land. It is this expectation that makes him hold on through drought and storm flood and tornado. On this expectation he borrows money and, as a permanent borrower, he has no fear of inflation; like the small boy in the story, far from being troubled by the thought, he simply loves it. He knows, in a general, intellectual way, that somebody will have to be the last buyer, but he hopes and trusts that it won't be he. He will be living off the profits, perhaps invested in new lands, perhaps taken out in mortgages or in a rent that takes full account of the presumed value of the land, future as well as present. And the American absentee owner is not necessarily somebody like the late Lord Clanricarde, celebrated miser, tyrant, and last chief of the elder line of the Burkes, but a mild, modest ex-farmer living in decent comfort in the neighborhood of Los

Angeles, raising the moral tone of the neighborhood and swelling the crowds at Iowa picnics. He may be simply a resident in a small Iowa town, able to afford a trip to St. Petersburg to pitch horseshoes in the winter sun of Florida. Or he may be like the Vermont farmer who, when asked by a scornful Midwestern visitor what crops were raised on those stony hills, replied: "The chief crop is those good five per cent Iowa mortgages we hold." The web of speculation, of optimism, of boosting is cast over all the nation.

—D. W. BROGAN, *The American Character*

The first two sentences of Brogan's paragraph constitute a specific idea that the detail following it develops; the concluding sentence relates this detail to the American character. The paragraph moves from one generalization and its supporting detail to a more encompassing generalization.

The topic idea may be developed by *continual restatement* and *intensification*, as in this opening paragraph of a eulogy of President Kennedy:

The thing about him was the extraordinary sense he gave to being alive: This makes his death so grotesque and unbelievable. No one had such vitality of personality—a vitality so superbly disciplined that it sometimes left the impression of cool detachment, but imbuing everything he thought or did with an intense concentration and power. He was life-affirming, life-enhancing. When he entered the room, the temperature changed; and he quickened the sensibilities of everyone around him. His curiosity was unlimited. The restless thrust of his mind never abated. He noticed everything, responded to everything, forgot nothing. He lived his life so intensely that in retrospect it almost seems he must have known it would be short, and that he had no time to waste. Or perhaps it was that, having lived closely to death ever since he swam those lonely, terrible hours along Ferguson Passage in 1943, ever since he nearly died after the operation on his back in 1955, he was determined to savor everything of life.

—ARTHUR M. SCHLESINGER, JR.,
"A Eulogy: John Fitzgerald Kennedy"

Though a single point (stated in the first sentence) is being made, the restatements give us important details about Kennedy's habits and life. The details build in intensity—ending with Kennedy's ordeal in Ferguson Passage and his experience on the operating table. The economy of the paragraph contributes to its power.

Paragraphs do not stand alone; an introductory general statement or a limited or more specific statement relating to the topic idea may have occurred at the end of the preceding paragraph or may occur at the beginning of the next. As a unit of thought, however, the paragraph usually will be a development, through specific detail or subordinate ideas, of a topic idea appearing at the beginning, and perhaps restated in the course of the paragraph or at the end; or a development of an idea that first appears at the end.

MAIN AND SUBORDINATE IDEAS

You may wish to develop your topic idea and also introduce subordinate ideas, not in themselves of equal importance, and either loosely or closely related. You may introduce your main idea at the beginning of the paragraph—one emphatic part—or at the end—another emphatic part—or you may restate it for special emphasis. In addition, transitional words and phrases can be used if they are needed.

In the following paragraph E. M. Forster keeps his main idea before his reader by referring back to it. He uses prominent transitions to distinguish his subordinate ideas:

> [1] I believe in aristocracy, though—if that is the right word, and if a democrat may use it. [2] **Not an aristocracy of power, based upon rank and influence, but an aristocracy of the sensitive, the considerate and the plucky.** [3] Its members are to be found in all nations and classes, and all through the ages, and there is a secret understanding between them when they meet. [4] They represent the true human tradition, the one permanent victory of our queer race over cruelty and chaos. [5] Thousands of them perish in obscurity, a few are great names. [6] **They are sensitive for others as well as for themselves, they are considerate without being fussy, their pluck is not swankiness but the power to endure, and they can take a joke.** [7] I give no examples—it is risky to do that—but the reader may as well consider whether this is the type of person he would like to meet and to be, and whether (going farther with me) he would prefer that this type should *not* be an ascetic one. [8] I am against asceticism myself. [9] I am with the old Scotsman who wanted less chastity and more delicacy. [10] I do not feel that my aristocrats are a real aristocracy if they thwart their bodies, since bodies are the instruments through which we register and enjoy the world. [11] Still, I do not insist. [12] This is not a major point. [13] **It is clearly possible to be sensitive, considerate and plucky and yet be an ascetic too; if anyone possesses the first three qualities, I will let him in!** [14] On they go—an invincible army, yet not a victorious one. [15] The aristocrats, the elect, the chosen, the Best People—all

the words that describe them are false, and all attempts to organize them fail. [16] Again and again Authority, seeing their value, has tried to net them and to utilize them as the Egyptian Priesthood or the Christian Church or the Chinese Civil Service or the Group Movement, or some other worthy stunt. **[17] But they slip through the net and are gone; when the door is shut, they are no longer in the room; their temple, as one of them remarked, is the Holiness of the Heart's Affection, and their kingdom, though they never possess it, is the wide-open world.** —"What I Believe"

The main idea here is the second sentence, which defines "aristocracy." Forster repeats the idea not once but twice: in the sixth sentence, where he expands on the words "sensitive," considerate," and "plucky," and in the thirteenth sentence ("It is clearly possible to be sensitive, considerate and plucky"). The final sentence restates and expands the idea by defining "aristocracy" further. A second idea— Forster's view of asceticism—is developed at some length, but it is clearly subordinate: "Still, I do not insist. This is not a major point."

UNITY

Unity means one idea at a time developed so that your reader is not left with a sense of loose ends, so that he sees how your ideas cohere. One major cause of incoherence—the failure of sentences in a paragraph to form a whole—is the writer's failure to distinguish main ideas from subordinate ideas. Another, as we will see, is the writer's failure to provide needed transitions. Though you can see the unity of your ideas, your reader may not. The solution is to unify the paragraph through a principle of order. You may begin with the simpler of a series of ideas and end with the more complex, you may arrange details chronologically or according to their interest or liveliness, or you may introduce your reasons in the order of their credibility. The accomplished writer, of course, does this without much deliberation; organization is part of his craft, and he has learned through experience to keep his audience in mind as he develops his ideas.

The following paragraph, describing the conditions in a hospital for British soldiers in Turkey during the Crimean War, gains its effectiveness through a careful ordering of details that fall into a number of patterns:

Lasciate ogni speranza, voi ch'entrate: the delusive doors bore no such inscription; and yet behind them Hell yawned. Want, neglect, confusion, misery—in every shape and in every degree of intensity—filled the endless corridors and the vast apartments of the gigantic barrack-house, which, without forethought or preparation, had been hurriedly set aside as the chief shelter for the victims of the war. The very building itself was radically defective. Huge sewers underlay it, and cesspools loaded with filth wafted their poison into the upper rooms. The floors were in so rotten a condition that many of them could not be scrubbed; the walls were thick with dirt; incredible multitudes of vermin swarmed everywhere. And, enormous as the building was, it was yet too small. It contained four miles of beds, crushed together so close that there was just room to pass between them. Under such conditions, the most elaborate system of ventilation might well have been at fault; but here there was no ventilation. The stench was indescribable. "I have been well acquainted," said Miss Nightingale, "with the dwellings of the worst parts of most of the great cities in Europe, but have never been in any atmosphere which I could compare with that of the Barrack Hospital at night." The structural defects were equaled by the deficiencies in the commonest objects of hospital use. There were not enough bedsteads; the sheets were of canvas, and so coarse that the wounded men recoiled from them, begging to be left in their blankets; there was no bedroom furniture of any kind, and empty beer bottles were used for candlesticks. There were no basins, no towels, no soap, no brooms, no mops, no trays, no plates; there were neither slippers nor scissors, neither shoe-brushes nor blacking; there were no knives or forks or spoons. The supply of fuel was constantly deficient. The cooking arrangements were preposterously inadequate, and the laundry was a farce. As for purely medical materials, the tale was no better. Stretchers, splints, bandages —all were lacking; and so were the most ordinary drugs.

—LYTTON STRACHEY, *Eminent Victorians*

Strachey begins his description of the building with the sewers; moves to the floor; the walls; the building itself. The poor ventilation is one consequence of the inadequate size of the building in relation to the number of patients it housed. The second part of the paragraph turns from the defects of the building to those of its contents. The ideas of the paragraph would be disunified if Strachey had moved from the condition of the floors to the bedsteads and sheets, then to the ventilation.

Details of this sort may be related directly to a series of conclusions that constitute a single idea:

The member of the Nazi hierarchy most gifted at solving problems of conscience was Himmler. He coined slogans, like the famous watchword of the S.S., taken from a Hitler speech before the S.S. in 1931, "My Honor is my Loyalty" —catch phrases which Eichmann called "winged words" and the judges "empty talk"—and issued them, as Eichmann recalled, "around the turn of the year," presumably along with a Christmas bonus. Eichmann remembered only one of them and kept repeating it: "These are battles which future generations will not have to fight again," alluding to the "battles" against women, children, old people and other "useless mouths." Other such phrases, taken from speeches Himmler made to the commanders of the *Einsatzgruppen* and the Higher S.S. and Police Leaders, were: "To have stuck it out and, apart from exceptions caused by human weakness, to have remained decent, that is what has made us hard. This is a page of glory in our history which has never been written and is never to be written." Or: "The order to solve the Jewish question, this was the most frightening order an organization could ever receive." Or: We realize that what we are expecting from you is "superhuman," to be "superhumanly inhuman." All one can say is that their expectations were not disappointed. It is noteworthy, however, that Himmler hardly ever attempted to justify in ideological terms, and if he did, it was apparently quickly forgotten. What stuck in the minds of these men who had become murderers was simply the notion of being involved in something historic, grandiose, unique ("a great task that occurs once in two thousand years"), which must therefore be difficult to bear. This was important, because the murderers were not sadists or killers by nature; on the contrary, a systematic effort was made to weed out all those who derived physical pleasure from what they did. The troops of the *Einsatzgruppen* had been drafted from the Armed S.S., a military unit with hardly more crimes in its record than any ordinary unit of the German Army, and their commanders had been chosen by Heydrich from the S.S. élite with academic degrees. Hence the problem was how to overcome not so much their conscience as the animal pity by which all normal men are affected in the presence of physical suffering. The trick used by Himmler —who apparently was rather strongly afflicted with these instinctive reactions himself—was very simple and probably very effective; it consisted in turning these instincts around, as it were, in directing them toward the self. So that instead of saying: What horrible things I did to people!, the murderers would be able to say: What horrible things I had to watch in the pursuance of my duties, how heavily the task weighed upon my shoulders!

—HANNAH ARENDT, *Eichmann in Jerusalem*

This paragraph opens with a series of illustrations of Himmler's gift for solving problems. The generalization drawn from these illustrations—"Himmler hardly ever attempted to justify in ideological terms"—is explored in relation to the method he used to inspirit the death squads and in relation to the character of the men. The concluding sentences, which relate Himmler's method to his character and to that of the men, shed light on the opening illustrations. The paragraph moves from these illustrations to their analysis because the details of Himmler's method must be understood before their significance can be stated. Miss Arendt moves to increasingly complex ideas throughout the paragraph.

TRANSITIONS

You will need transitional words and phrases (*thus, moreover, indeed, nevertheless, on the contrary, in fact*) to connect ideas whose relationship is not immediately clear. Some writers use no such transitions, others many. Forster, in his long paragraph, uses a few:

> I believe in aristocracy, *though*—if that is the right word. . . .
> *Still*, I do not insist.

One of his sentences is transitional:

> I give no examples . . . but the reader may as well consider whether this is the type of person he would like to meet and to be, and whether (going farther with me) he would prefer that this type should *not* be an ascetic one.

These transitions do not crowd the paragraph, obscuring the important ideas. Forster does not announce at length how he intends to proceed to the next idea. You will find that your paragraphs increase in clarity when you read what you have written and strike out needless or repetitious *however*'s and *therefore*'s that aided your thinking in the process of composition but merely clutter the finished paragraph.

A paragraph that develops one idea seldom needs elaborate transitions. Goodman's transitions in the following paragraph are brief and unobtrusive and ease the movement from one idea to another.

> People use machines that they do not understand and cannot repair. **For instance,** the electric motors: one cannot imagine anything more beautiful and educative than such motors, **yet** there may be three or four in a house, cased and out of sight; and when they blow they are taken away to be repaired. Their influence is **then** retarding, **for** what the child sees is that competence does not exist in ordinary people, but in the system

of interlocking specialties. This is unavailable to the child, it is too abstract. Children go shopping with Mama; **but** supermarket shopping for cellophane packages is less knowledgeable and bargainable than the older shopping, as well as providing tasteless Texas fruit and vegetables bred for non-perishability and appearance rather than for eating. Cooking is more prefabricated. Few clothes are sewn. Fire and heat are not made. Among poor people there used to be more sweated domestic industry, which didn't do the adults any good but taught something to small children. Now, **on the contrary,** the man and perhaps the woman of the house work in distant offices and factories, increasingly on parts and processes that don't mean anything to a child. A child might not **even** know what work his daddy does. Shop talk will be, almost invariably, griping about interpersonal relations. If the kid has less confidence that he can make or fix anything, his parents can't either; and what they do work at is beyond his grasp.

—PAUL GOODMAN, *Growing Up Absurd*

In paragraphs that develop several ideas, elaborate transitions still may not be necessary if key words and phrases are repeated in parallel order:

This house on wheels has developed in the past half century from a fussy, crotchety, unreliable contraption to a miracle of engineering which starts easily, shifts automatically, drives smoothly at high rates of speed, develops enormous power (although it is often driven by women and even elderly people), and comes in various shades and combinations of color to suit every taste and sometimes even to match the clothes of the owner's wife or daughter. **It can be paid for** on the installment plan, but it becomes quickly obsolete and is "turned in" and replaced frequently by a new one or by a better "secondhand" one. A congeries of revolutions were needed —in manufacture, quick-drying paint, macadam roads, engine power, car design, mass production, and the assembly line— to produce the end product of the American car. **It congests the cities and the roads,** and in the hands of the amateurs, the "hot rod" enthusiasts, and the neurotics it becomes a lethal instrument of grisly death and decimates the population. **It has made** the filling station, the parkway, the four-lane highway, the quick-service roadside hot-dog stand or restaurant, the "motel," the used-car lot, the trailer camp, the giant freight truck, the motor bus, the parking lot, the shopping center, the Friday-to-Sunday traffic jam, and the urban parking maze the most obtrusive features of the American landscape. **It has made necessary** a continual renewing of road construction, which has laid across the country a labyrinthine network of auto and truck roads, some of them toll turnpike roads financed by private bondowners, the rest financed by Federal and state funds, all of them as essential to the poor as to the rich. **It has brought about** a counter-railroad revolution, making freight traffic and daily travel independent of the railroad station and the commuter train, shifting factory sites and farm values, and spawning new suburbs where the family disperses every morning and reassembles every evening via the automobile. And **it has made** the seaside or mountain holiday and the fishing and camping vacation the routine adventure of the middle classes and even of workers' families.

—MAX LERNER, *America as a Civilization*

If your paragraph contains a large number of main and subordinate ideas, transitions are essential. But these should be the fewest number possible.

Qualification	**But** here it is worth noticing a minor English trait which is extremely well marked though not often commented on, and that is a love
Unobtrusive reference back to *love*	of flowers. **This** is one of the first things that one notices when one reaches England from abroad, especially if one is coming from
Transitional question	southern Europe. **Does it not contradict the English indifference to the arts?** Not really, because it is found in people who have no
Contrast and qualification	aesthetic feelings whatever. **What it does link up with, however,** is another English characteristic which is so much a part of us that we barely notice it, and that is the addiction to hobbies and spare-time occupations, the *privateness* of English life. We are a nation of flower-lovers but also a nation of stamp-collectors, pigeon-fanciers, amateur carpenters, coupon-snippers, darts-players, crossword-puzzle fans. All the culture that is most
No transition needed	truly native centers round things which even when they are communal are not official— the pub, the football match, the back garden, the fireside and the "nice cup of tea." The liberty of the individual is still believed in,
Qualification again	almost as in the nineteenth century. **But** this has nothing to do with economic liberty, the right to exploit others for profit. It is the liberty to have a home of your own, to do what you like in your spare time, to choose your

own amusements instead of having them chosen for you from above. The most hateful of all names in an English ear is Nosey Parker. It is obvious, **of course,** that even this purely private liberty is a lost cause. Like all other modern peoples, the English are in process of being numbered, labeled, conscripted, "coordinated." **But** the pull of their impulses is in the other direction, and the kind of regimentation that can be imposed on them will be modified in consequence. No party rallies, no Youth Movements, no colored shirts, no Jew-baiting or "spontaneous" demonstrations. No Gestapo either, in all probability.

—GEORGE ORWELL, *The Lion and the Unicorn*

Of course to indicate that what follows is reflection. This transition is needed.

Qualification

Here is a partial list of transitional words and phrases:

Qualification: but, however, except for, unless
Comparison: similarly, likewise, in the same way
Contrast: by contrast, on the other hand, unlike, instead, whereas
Illustration: for example, for instance, thus
Consequence: consequently, as a result, thus, hence, therefore, so, finally
Concession: admittedly, of course, although, no doubt, to be sure
Explanation: thus, for, since, because
Amplification: moreover, in fact, furthermore, in addition, for, even
Emphasis: indeed, certainly, above all, surely
Summation: all in all, finally, in summary

We repeat that the more you rely on the natural transitions provided by parallel development of ideas (as in Lerner's paragraph) or the order of climax (to be discussed next) the greater vigor your paragraphs will have.

CLIMAX

Wherever a paragraph—or, as we shall see later, a sentence—includes some ideas that you consider of greater interest or importance than others, you must use climax—the arrangement of ideas that builds from the less to the more important.

Manuel walked toward him with the muleta. He stopped and shook it. The bull did not respond. He passed it right and left, left and right before the bull's muzzle. The bull's eyes watched it and turned with the swing, but he would not charge. He was waiting for Manuel.

—ERNEST HEMINGWAY, "The Undefeated"

Hemingway gains suspense here by saving for the end the statement that the bull was waiting for Manuel. Notice how the suspense is shifted to another action when this statement is introduced earlier.

> Manuel walked toward him with the muleta. He stopped and shook it. The bull did not respond. He passed it right and left, left and right before the bull's muzzle. The bull was waiting for Manuel. The bull's eyes watched the muleta and turned with the swing, but he would not charge.

Getting ideas in the most effective order is not always so easy a process, in part because, as Hemingway's paragraph shows, one idea is not *inherently* more interesting or important than another. It is your arrangement of ideas, as well as your choice of words and sentence construction, that tells your reader what you consider interesting and important. How would you arrange the following sentences?

> The problems now affecting the public schools and the colleges and universities are both urgent and important, involving as they do the most basic conflicts over purpose, structure, and power. Sociologists like to distinguish between "important" problems—the sometimes undramatic and usually intractable problems that persist for some time—and those that are merely "urgent," catching the headlines of the moment but giving way fairly rapidly to some newer concern.

You possibly sense that the sentences are out of order, but are not certain why. The key word is *both*; you would use *both* only if you were referring to a previous idea. Here is the original paragraph:

> Sociologists like to distinguish between "important" problems —the sometimes undramatic and usually intractable problems that persist for some time—and those that are merely "urgent," catching the headlines of the moment but giving way fairly rapidly to some newer concern. The problems now affecting the public schools and the colleges and universities are both urgent and important, involving as they do the most basic conflicts over purpose, structure, and power.
>
> —CHARLES E. SILBERMAN, *Crisis in the Classroom*

You may build to a climax by restating and intensifying your main idea and constructing your sentences so that they suggest an increasing tension of ideas as Schlesinger does in the paragraph on page 11. Here is a more complex paragraph, developing not one but several ideas:

Literature is one of the central continuing experiences of the race. It is no cultural ornament. It is as discrete a method of knowledge as is science, and the kind of knowledge literature makes available is not approachable by scientific method. Through literature, the voices of mankind's most searching imaginations remain alive to all time. No man is half-civilized until those voices have sounded within him. A savage, after all, is simply a human organism that has not received enough news from the human race. Literature is one most fundamental part of that news. One needs to hear Job lift his question into the wind; it is, after all, every man's question at some time. One needs to stand by Oedipus and to hold the knife of his own most terrible resolution. One needs to come out of his own Hell with Dante and to hear that voice of joy hailing the sight of his own stars returned to. One needs to run with Falstaff, roaring in his own appetites and weeping into his own pathos. What one learns from those voices is his own humanity. He learns what it is to carry about within mortal meat a bulb of brain wired to a bush of dendrites. Until he has heard those voices deeply within himself, what man can have any sizable idea of himself?

—JOHN CIARDI, "Literature Undefended"

Ciardi's first sentence presents the main idea. The fourth and fifth sentences restate the idea differently and fully: literature is "one of the central continuing experiences of the race" because through it "the voices of mankind's most searching imaginations remain alive to all time" and civilize man. The examples following describe that experience and intensify the main idea. The last three sentences repeat the fifth sentence, partly through a vivid image—"a bulb of brain wired to a bush of dendrites"—and through a final question that recaps the paragraph. Ciardi never allows the pace to flag: the paragraph moves quickly (and almost entirely without transitions) from one idea to another. Notice how the four sentences discussing Job, Oedipus, Dante, and Falstaff are bound by their opening words.

POINT OF VIEW

Point of view refers to the physical angle from which an object is viewed and described or to a dominant mood or attitude. The opening sentence of Bernard De Voto's essay "Seed Corn and Mistletoe," "No one can approach through winter darkness a house from whose windows light shines out on the snow without feeling quieted and heartened," establishes a point of view in all of the senses indicated: we are given a precise angle of vision, a dominant mood (the feeling of being quieted and heartened), an attitude toward Christmas (the suggestion of an attitude at least), an impression too of the writer's personality. In the course of writing, you may find it necessary to restate the angle of vision or indicate a change of mood or attitude. If a shift in point of view does occur and you have not prepared your reader for it or indicated plainly that a shift has occurred, your essay may become incoherent.

In his biography of Robert Benchley, Nathaniel Benchley characterizes his father through a description of his suite of rooms in a New York hotel:

> It all started when he first saw the place, which, even in the glaring nudity of a semifurnished hotel room, looked Victorian. The walls were a deep cream color, with dark mahogany baseboards and trim, and the windows were cross-latticed, so that each pane was diamond-shaped.
>
> "Oh, so they think they're Victorian," he said. "I'll show them something Victorian, if that's the way they want to play."
>
> His first move was to get a dark red rug, and red drapes to cover the windows and shut out all the light. Then he put a red-velvet, tasseled cover on the fumed-oak table in the middle of the living room (it was a two-room suite), and placed brass student lamps, with green shades, around at various strategic spots. Bookcases were installed on all four walls, and three pictures of Queen Victoria, one of them framed in red velvet, were hung between the windows. He covered the walls with every kind of picture he could find, and as time passed, his family and friends contributed enough so that there was practically no bare space showing.
>
> You entered the room through a small hall, so small as to be almost square, which soon became filled with trunks, stacks of old newspapers and foreign magazines, bound volumes of The New Yorker, overcoats, canes, a sword, and other items not often used. A shelf in this hall contained bills, telephone messages, and a deer skull.
>
> The primary color of the room itself was red, although the green student lamps gave it an atmosphere of well-lighted darkness like that in a sleeping car at night. To the left, as you entered, was a blue couch, sometimes called "The Track," because when he wanted to take a nap on it he would say, "Well, I guess I'll do a couple of laps around the track," and then lie down. The other name for it was the "Wirephoto Couch," because it had a rough, corduroylike covering, and when a person woke up from a nap his face was streaked in horizontal lines, like the early wirephotos. —Robert Benchley

Benchley organizes his detail according to a consistent point of view. After indicating what his father did to make the rooms look Victorian, he lets the reader see the room as it would be seen as one entered through the stuffed hall. Notice that Benchley does not describe the hall from ceiling to floor, but instead limits himself to describing what the hall contained. Like Strachey in his description of the hospital ward, Benchley selects an angle of vision just as a photographer does, to exclude some of the background and concentrate on the foreground. He enjoys, however, this advantage over the photographer: he need include only that detail which he considers important to his central impression. In fact, he need not include *any* background.

The larger room contains many objects, too, and Benchley soon focuses on one of them—the blue couch—which he describes carefully because it exhibits so well his father's sense of humor. Consider the effect the passage would make if the detail were omitted:

> It all started when he first saw the place, which looked Victorian. The walls and windows looked fancy. His first move was to get a rug and drapes for the windows to shut out the light. Then he put a cover on the table in the middle of one room and put lamps around. Bookcases were installed and pictures of Queen Victoria and many others hung. You entered the room through a small, cluttered hall.

Altered in this way, the passage loses its point. You do not see what made the room look overstuffed and ornate: you get merely the *outline* of an impression—and a disunified impression at that.

In the following paragraph the writer selects his detail carefully to convey an impression of the environment of an American railroad town in the last century. In contrast to the paragraph by Nathaniel Benchley, the point of view here is that of an *imagined* observer:

> But the visitor who hired a buckboard and drove out along a country road soon found himself in a different world; a world where ten miles was a great distance, where for long seasons every family was practically farm-bound, and where social isolation wrapped men and women in cobwebs. If the weather was wet the buckboard lurched over ruts, hummocks and mudholes, careening as one wheel tilted up on a grassy bank while another dropped into a slough, or coming almost to a stop in thick mire. Napoleon had said of Poland that "God, out of water, air, earth, and fire, has created a fifth element, mud"—*la boue*; but Poland never saw mud worse than the red clay of Virginia or the viscid gumbo of Illinois. Culverts with approaches washed away would threaten to smash a wheel; deep gullies at the roadside would offer constant risk of an overturn. At a township line the traveller might find the

road either much better or much worse, and at a county boundary it might disappear altogether; for roadbuilding was entirely a matter for local authorities, who often ignored each other. In winter, barns all along the road would be stuffed with crops awaiting a firm surface. The wayfarer, gazing at them, realized that when dry weather came, all the farmers would fetch their crops to market at once. Prices would sag; a famine of freight cars would ensue; much of the product would be wasted. Everybody knew, too, that when roads were in good shape, it often cost the Western farmer as much to take his grain ten miles to railroad as to ship it thence all the way to New York.   —ALLAN NEVINS, *Ford*

The purpose of the above paragraph is to develop the following idea, occurring in the subsequent paragraph:

Thus the very force that had led in the expansion of settlement and in the growth of American industry at central points was exerting a deterrent and even a destructive influence on large regions of the country which its tracks did not reach. The railroad ministered well only to such population as was established within a dozen miles of its stations.

The effectiveness of the paragraph depends on its precise focus and its avoidance of extraneous detail.

Mood can be an essential part of view. Disturbing it unnecessarily is as obtrusive as awkwardly shifting the physical point of view. Note the importance of mood in John Bartlow Martin's description of Columbus State Hospital, a mental institution in Ohio:

The drive curves up the breast of the hill, lined by old trees, marked with a sign, 20 MILES PER HOUR. The grounds embrace 333 acres. The lawn is well kept, burnt brown now in September. It looks like a park, cool, quiet, shady. One would think nothing ever happened here. Two old men, patients, are sitting together on a bench, staring out at the traffic on Broad Street. On a big boulder is a fat old man: He sits there every day, barefoot, painstakingly examining his dirty worn-out socks and wetting one finger and washing his feet. A legless emaciated man rides by in a wheelchair, propelling himself rapidly. A young man alone suddenly arises, takes two steps forward, and stands stiffly at attention; he is making a speech, you can see his lips move, his hands are tense, his body quivers, his features work passionately, but no sound comes forth. Finished at length, he slumps and wearily sits again. A woman visiting her husband is eating lunch with him out of a paper bag. An old man, stooped and dressed in sweater and coat though the day is hot, is carefully stuffing paper into a hole in the bole of a tree. Near him an old man sits with a leaf shielding his bald head. In a circle of benches under a tree where the grass is all worn away, sit thirty old men, talking, shoulders hunched, leaning forward, breaking up sticks that have fallen from trees. The leaves are coming down, winter is not far away, when the old men cannot sit out here. Far off across the landscape at the rim of the hill a young patient is striding rapidly along. In the distance beyond the trees rise the towers of Columbus.   —*The Pane of Glass*

Here the mood is one of seeming torpor and boredom. Though the world of the hospital seems to be a silent one, much is happening. The young man quivers and gestures without making any sounds, and the old men sit talking and breaking up sticks. The description tells us something important about the mentally sick and also creates a mood that prepares us for what is to follow.

The mood is developed through concrete detail presented from a consistently maintained point of view. Martin does not tell us merely that an old man is sitting on a boulder: he provides just enough detail to help us see the man, then concentrates on what the man is doing. The actions of the young man who rises suddenly are described more carefully. The detail of the whole paragraph creates a pattern of futility and aimlessness—a pattern completed, yet also qualified at the end, by the young patient who is "striding rapidly along." To where? Martin says only that the towers of Columbus rise in the distance. The images ironically suggest the separation of the two worlds—that of the hospital and that of the city beyond. The observer is standing where he can see not only the people but also the towers of the city. The focus never veers.

The matters we have so far discussed directly concern the rhetoric of the paragraph–the effective means of clarifying and communicating your ideas. In writing your own paragraphs, you have become aware that such matters as the topic sentence and paragraph unity must be thought through. Even when you have become practiced in writing many kinds of paragraphs, you will always need to revise if only to strike out unnecessary transitional words. One advantage of studying the paragraphs of practiced writers is that you discover procedures of economy and effective organization. To quote James Sledd, "Nobody ever learned to write without reading."

We turn now to the chief methods of developing the topic idea of the paragraph. Most of our examples are of single paragraph development; however the topic idea is often developed in more than one way in a single paragraph, as our concluding section shows.

DEFINITION

Paragraphs of definition are indispensable in exposition and logical analysis. There are at least five basic kinds of definition, used singly or together. The first of these, *etymological*, traces the original meaning of a word to illuminate its current meanings, not to indicate that the word must have that meaning only. For example, the word *silly* derives from a very old word meaning *happy*; in earlier centuries it also meant *poor*, *simple*, and *ignorant*. Consequently, when Milton wrote concerning shepherds, in his "On the Morning of Christ's Nativity"

> Perhaps their loves; or else their sheep,
> Was all that did their silly thoughts so busy keep

he meant *plain*—not *foolish*—thoughts. Obviously, it would be foolish to begin using *silly* with these former meanings. In a satirical novel by Mary McCarthy, a woman who thinks of herself as a purist in language pretends to assume that a person described as *sinister* is left-handed because she knows *sinister* originally meant *left-handed*. Some writers, however, do make a case for restoring an original meaning in order to clarify an idea. In the following passage the writer introduces the etymology of *symbol* to clarify a current meaning of the word:

> The Greek word *symballein*, from which "symbol" derives, means: "to bring together," or, "to come together." The symbolic *sign* brings together, the symbolic *representation* is a coming together, to the point of complete fusion, of the concrete and the spiritual, the specific and the general.
> —ERICH KAHLER, "The Nature of the Symbol"

Kahler's distinction between *sign* and *representation* shows that the word *symbol* has gained refinements in meaning.

Real definitions, unlike etymological ones, are concerned with current meanings, with the present reality a word represents. Like etymological definitions, these may be formal or informal. A formal definition, such as the following from the *Standard College Dictionary*, first relates a word to a genus, or class of objects or ideas:

> jayhawker: a guerrilla raider

then indicates how the word differs from all other members of its class:

> a guerrilla raider/of the Civil War period in Kansas

In some definitions the genus may be given without any more specific difference:

any freebooting guerrilla

It may also be extremely broad:

Geography is the science that describes . . .

or extremely narrow:

> [An isogloss is] a line on a map, as in a dialect atlas, delimiting an area or areas in which a certain linguistic feature, as pronunciation, vocabulary, or syntax, is found.
> —Standard College Dictionary

As a rule, the narrower the genus, the more useful the definition. The limitation depends on how much the reader of the essay can be assumed to know. The definition is for *his* benefit; it should not create difficulties.

All of the essential characteristics of the thing being defined must, of course, be indicated. It would not be sufficient to define a fountain pen as a writing implement that uses ink; quill pens also use ink. And the definition must not be circular; that is, it must not use part of the word being defined:

A fountain pen is a pen that . . .

A complete definition would be:

> A fountain pen is a writing implement in which ink, contained in a reservoir, flows to a metal point [or other kinds of point, if these exist].

Dictionaries may, however, use *pen* in the definition if the genus is well known and is defined elsewhere.

A paragraph may define a word formally, then expand on either the genus or the specific difference or both. Sometimes it is impossible to explain a complex idea in so relatively simple a way. The following exposition of saltiness might be reduced to a statement of genus and specific difference, but the explanation would still be necessary:

> "Salty" is a much more mysterious quality. It too comes from ions, such as the sodium ions and chloride ions formed when table salt (sodium chloride) dissociates in water. Both the positively charged sodium ions and the negatively charged chloride ions contribute toward the saltiness we detect, but each of these ions is merely the most effective member of a whole series. All members of both series induce a salty flavor, although they differ slightly in ways we cannot describe unless they stimulate the bitter sense as well. The other "salty" positive ions are potassium, lithium, ammonium and mag-

nesium. The "salty" negative ions, in addition to chloride, are bromide, iodide, fluoride, nitrate, sulfate, carbonate and tartrate. Almost any combination of these two series, such as sodium tartrate or ammonium chloride will free ions into water and give us a salty sensation.

—LORUS J. and MARGERY MILNE,
The Senses of Animals and Men

Informal definitions concern the associations people make with a word—its auras of meaning. These are its *connotations*, as distinguished from its *denotation* or formal definition. Such definitions may range from the extremely impressionistic to the relatively precise, as these two definitions reveal:

The word "idea" is a very vague term for what we really mean when we talk of the composer's creative imagination. The German word *Einfall* is the perfect expression needed in our situation. *Einfall*, from the verb *einfallen*, to drop in, describes beautifully the strange spontaneity that we associate with artistic ideas in general and with musical creation in particular. Something—you know not what—drops into your mind—you know not whence—and there it grows—you know not how—into some form—you know not why. This seems to be the general opinion, and we cannot blame the layman if he is unable to find rational explanations for so strange an occurrence. —PAUL HINDEMITH, *A Composer's World*

Generally speaking, the word *culture* is used in a sense which approaches the honorific. When we look at a people in the degree of abstraction which the idea of culture implies, we cannot but be touched and impressed by what we see, we cannot help being awed by something mysterious at work, some creative power which seems to transcend any particular act or habit or quality that may be observed. To make a coherent life, to confront the terrors of the outer and the inner world, to establish the ritual and art, the pieties and duties which make possible the life of the group and the individual—these are culture, and to contemplate these various enterprises which constitute a culture is inevitably moving.

—LIONEL TRILLING, *Beyond Culture*

Both writers are concerned with actual usage; they are not insisting that the words defined always have the meanings they attribute to them, or indeed should have them. Hindemith, in fact, is doing something more than suggesting connotations: he is *stipulating* that the German word *Einfall* be used for the experience he describes. The usefulness of stipulative definitions depends on this accuracy in describing experience; if enough people agree that the definition is a useful one, it may be adopted into the language.

If the stipulative definition proposes a theory of some sort (as Hindemith's suggests a theory of creative imagination), the definition is *theoretical* as well. The American philosopher William James provided a theoretical definition of the word *pragmatism*, introduced into philosophical language by Charles Pierce in 1878. James was proposing a new conception of philosophy, distinguishing it from empiricism:

> A pragmatist turns his back resolutely and once for all upon a lot of inveterate habits dear to professional philosophers. He turns away from abstraction and insufficiency, from verbal solutions, from bad *a priori* reasons, from fixed principles, closed systems, and pretended absolutes and origins. He turns towards concreteness and adequacy, towards facts, towards action and towards power. That means the empiricist temper regnant and the rationalist temper sincerely given up. It means the open air and possibilities of nature, as against dogma, artificiality, and the pretence of finality in truth.
>
> —*Pragmatism* (1907)

Since the word had only recently been used in this sense (and only by Pierce whose definition James popularized), James is not proposing a more precise usage than had been customary. A definition that does call for this more specific usage is called *precising*:

> I have been using the term "powerful expression" very vaguely and freely but I think it can be given more precision. I have suggested that the power of an expression of the sublime kind is at least largely due to its inducing a sharp shift in, or a crystallization of, the habitual somewhat empty or vague general concepts and attendant feelings and impulses with which the reader confronts experience. The power is heightened by the fact that the sublime expression doesn't spell out the changes in mental habits that it requires, but packs them in as a presupposed punch, so that they are manifest in the consciousness of the victim rather as an unidentified sense or feeling of portentous implications than as recognized invitations to change his modes of thought.
>
> —R. MEAGER, "The Sublime and the Obscene"

Such definitions are common in legal opinions which offer new interpretations of existing statutes. Of course, definitions may combine any or all of these methods.

DIVISION AND CLASSIFICATION

In exposition and argument a class of objects—a large or narrow one—may be divided according to one of many possible principles: which principle is used depends on the purpose of the analysis. Thus, hammers may be divided according to their use (bricklayer's, upholsterer's, machinist's, blacksmith's, and tinner's hammers, among others), then subdivided according to their source of power, if there is more than one source. The source of power may be the major principle of division: (1) the hand: straight-peen and claw hammers, among others that are held in the hand; (2) a spring or trigger mechanism: the hammer part of a gunlock; (3) electricity or engine power: any electrically driven or engine-driven machine that acts like a hammer. The objects in each grouping must be logically equivalent. If the analysis requires, each of these divisions can include any hammer-like objects whose source of power is the same: an auctioneer's mallet, which is held in the hand, can be put with straight-peen and claw hammers. Each division and subdivision should be consistent and, if necessary, exhaustive. If the division is not exhaustive, the context should indicate this fact in some way.

Dividing an abstract idea, such as government or work, is a more complex process because the process of division depends in part on value-judgment and opinion as well as on factual knowledge. In his *Politics*, Aristotle divides government on the basis of who rules:

> Of forms of government in which one rules, we call that which regards the common interests, kingship or royalty; that in which more than one, but not many, rule, aristocracy; and it is so called, either because the rulers are the best men, or because they have at heart the best interests of the state and of the citizens. But when the citizens at large administer the state for the common interest, the government is called by the generic name—a constitution.

Aristotle then divides these forms on the basis of true and perverted forms, depending on whether the rulers govern for the common interest or merely for their own. In dividing and subdividing, Aristotle is careful to distinguish his principle.

In the following passage, a noted ecologist uses *division* to explain the problem of describing "the environmental system in a way that may help us understand the present crisis." Commoner explains at the end of the passage that the total view of the environment comprises separate views, each of which offers a partial and therefore somewhat distorted idea of the "complex whole." The opening phrase, "the numerous ways of thinking about the environment," indicates the idea that Commoner proceeds to divide:

Consider the numerous ways of thinking about the environment. First, there is its spatial complexity: How can we encompass in a unifying idea the existence, as a stable, continuing entity, of the richly populated, kaleidoscopic ambience of a tropical jungle and the seemingly dead, unchanging desert? Then there is the multiplicity of living things in the environment: What common features can explain the environmental behavior of a mouse, a hawk, a trout, an earthworm, an ant, the bacteria of the human intestine, and the algae that color Lake Erie green? Then there is the variety of biochemical processes that not only are internal to every living thing but also mediate its interactions with other living things and with the environment: How can we hold within a single set of ideas photosynthesis, the fermentative decay of organic matter, oxygen-requiring combustion, and the intricate chemical dependence of one organism on another that leads to parasitism? Each of these questions, representing a separate view of the environmental system, is only a narrow slice through the complex whole. While each can illuminate some features of the whole system, the picture it yields is necessarily false to some degree. For in looking at one set of relationships we inevitably ignore a good deal of the rest, yet in the real world everything in the environment is connected to everything else.

—BARRY COMMONER, *The Closing Circle*

Classification is closely related to division; it differs only in beginning with objects themselves or smaller, logically equivalent entities that can be arranged in or fitted to a class. Thus hammers, screwdrivers, and wrenches can be classified as household tools and their uses distinguished; farce, burlesque, and travesty can be classified as comedy and their individual humor distinguished. In the following paragraph, George Orwell describes the "different forms" of patriotism found among the English and distinguishes the "connecting thread" that runs through nearly all of them:

In England patriotism takes different forms in different classes, but it runs like a connecting thread through nearly all of them. Only the Europeanized intelligentsia are really immune to it. As a positive emotion it is stronger in the middle class than in the upper class—the cheap public schools, for instance, are more given to patriotic demonstrations than the expensive ones—but the number of definitely treacherous rich men, the Laval-Quisling type, is probably very small. In the working class patriotism is profound, but it is unconscious. The working man's heart does not leap when he sees a Union Jack. But the famous "insularity" and "xenophobia" of the English is far stronger in the working class than in the bourgeoisie. In all countries the poor are more national than the rich, but the English working class are outstanding in their abhorrence of foreign habits. Even when they are obliged to live abroad for years they refuse either to accustom themselves to foreign food or to learn foreign languages. Nearly every Englishman of working-class origin considers it effeminate to pronounce a foreign word correctly. During the war of 1914–18 the English working class were in contact with foreigners to an extent that is rarely possible. The sole result was that they brought back a hatred of all Europeans, except the Germans, whose courage they admired. In four years on French soil they did not even acquire a liking for wine. The insularity of the English, their refusal to take foreigners seriously, is a folly that has to be paid for very heavily from time to time. But it plays its part in the English *mystique*, and the intellectuals who have tried to break it down have generally done more harm than good. At bottom it is the same quality in the English character that repels the tourist and keeps out the invader.

—*The Lion and the Unicorn*

Orwell shows differences among classes (he points out, for example, that xenophobia is stronger in the working class than in the middle class), but he also shows what unites them. The "connecting thread" is a "positive emotion" more obvious in the upper and middle classes, and unconscious though profound in the working class. And Orwell cites evidence—patriotic demonstrations in the schools, the working class abhorrence of foreign habits. Then he defines this "positive emotion" more precisely: it is the notorious insularity and xenophobia of the English. The rest of the paragraph comments in detail on this trait.

COMPARISON AND CONTRAST

If we were comparing two Presidents of the United States to show how they conducted their personal diplomacy, we might want to compare them in *other* respects to illuminate our central idea. The purpose of the comparison might be to arrive at a *relative estimate* of the two men; we would not be comparing merely for the sake of comparison. The points of comparison would be arranged to arrive at the central idea. Thus, if we were comparing and contrasting their sense of humor, their way of dealing with political opponents, their way of rewarding their supporters, and their personal diplomacy, we could present these similarities and differences in this order and indicate, first, how their sense of humor became a political weapon; then, how they dealt with their opponents in such a way that they benefited their friends; and finally, how they carried these methods into their personal diplomacy.

There are two basic ways of developing paragraphs of comparison and contrast. The first is evident in this relative estimate of Jefferson and John Adams:

> In character and in talents, Jefferson and Adams were complements. Each was strong in what the other lacked. Adams was a single-minded man, of great directness and tenacity, possessing little tact and no guile. His uningratiating manners were notorious even in New England, where good manners were seldom seen and little appreciated. He was no politician, and an indifferent administrator. His quick temper made enemies, he always thought too much of his own consequence, and brooded over fancied slights. As Franklin said, John Adams was "always honest, often great, but sometimes mad." His great quality was courage; his great talent, political construction. Adams's *Thoughts on Government* inspired the Constitution of Virginia, whilst that of Massachusetts, the only Revolutionary constitution that has endured to this day, was almost completely his work. If Jefferson showed less political courage than Adams, it was because he found that tact was a more valuable quality in political life than bluntness; but nothing could have been more morally courageous than his daring to govern according to pacifist principles when the rest of the world was at war. Jefferson was inferior to Adams as a drafter of constitutions, but the Yankee had none of the virtuosity which makes the Virginian one of the most significant figures of the eighteenth century.
>
> —SAMUEL ELIOT MORISON,
> "John Adams and Thomas Jefferson"

Morison presents Adams's qualities, then contrasts them with those of Jefferson—the comparison is not made point by point, as it is in this paragraph of R. H. Tawney:

> The difference between industry as it exists today and a profession is, then, simple and unmistakable. The essence of the former is that its only criterion is the financial return which it offers to its shareholders. The essence of the latter, is that, though men enter it for the sake of livelihood, the measure of their success is the service which they perform, not the gains which they amass. They may, as in the case of a successful doctor, grow rich; but the meaning of their profession, both for themselves and for the public, is not that they make money but that they make health, or safety, or knowledge, or good government or good law. They depend on it for their

income, but they do not consider that any conduct which in- creases their income is on that account good. And while a boot-manufacturer who retires with half a million is counted to have achieved success, whether the boots which he made were of leather or brown paper, a civil servant who did the same would be impeached. —*The Acquisitive Society*

A paragraph of comparison and contrast, on the other hand, may serve merely to illuminate qualities:

The realist at last loses patience with ideals altogether, and sees in them only something to blind us, something to numb us, something to murder self in us, something whereby, in- stead of resisting death, we can disarm it by committing sui- cide. The idealist, who has taken refuge with the ideals be- cause he hates himself and is ashamed of himself, thinks that all this is so much the better. The realist, who has come to have a deep respect for himself and faith in the validity of his own will, thinks it so much the worse. To the one, human nature, naturally corrupt, is held back from ruinous excesses only by self-denying conformity to the ideals. To the other these ideals are only swaddling clothes which man has out- grown, and which insufferably impede his movements. No wonder the two cannot agree. The idealist says, "Realism means egotism; and egotism means depravity." The realist declares that when a man abnegates the will to live and be free in a world of the living and free, seeking only to con- form to ideals for the sake of being, not himself, but "a good man," then he is morally dead and rotten, and must be left unheeded to abide his resurrection, if that by good luck arrive before his bodily death. Unfortunately, this is the sort of speech that nobody but a realist understands.

—G. B. SHAW, *The Quintessence of Ibsenism*

Shaw is not concerned here with arriving at a relative estimate: he is merely saying that the idealist and the realist cannot agree. Notice that he does not overload the paragraph with unnecessary transitions. The parallel construction of the sentences (*The realist . . . The ideal- ist . . . The realist . . . To the one . . . To the other . . . The idealist says . . . The realist declares . . .*) substitutes for words and phrases like *similarly, likewise, by contrast.*

ANALOGY

A simple comparison presents a number of likenesses and differences between two people, objects, or ideas; an analogy is a *systematic com- parison* of two dissimilar things—point by point at its most thorough

—for the purpose of illustration. If, for example, we wish to explain a complex operation of the mind that is difficult to imagine, we could compare it to a familiar object that has a number of points of resemblance:

It is, of course, part of the very genius of the human mind that it can, as it were, stand aside from life and reflect upon it, that it can be aware of its own existence, and that it can criticize its own processes. For the mind has something resembling a "feed-back" system. This is a term used in communications engineering for one of the basic principles of "automation," of enabling machines to control themselves. Feed-back enables a machine to be informed of the effects of its own action in such a way as to be able to correct its action. Perhaps the most familiar example is the electrical thermostat which regulates the heating of a house. By setting an upper and a lower limit of desired temperature, a thermometer is so connected that it will switch the furnace on when the lower limit is reached, and off when the upper limit is reached. The temperature of the house is thus kept within the desired limits. The thermostat provides the furnace with a kind of sensitive organ—an extremely rudimentary analogy of human self-consciousness.[1]

The proper adjustment of a feed-back system is always a complex mechanical problem. For the original machine, say, the furnace, is adjusted by the feed-back system, but this system in turn needs adjustment. Therefore to make a mechanical system more and more automatic will require the use of a series of feed-back systems—a second to correct the first, a third to correct the second, and so on. But there are obvious limits to such a series, for beyond a certain point the mechanism will be "frustrated" by its own complexity. For example, it might take so long for the information to pass through the series of control systems that it would arrive at the original machine too late to be useful. Similarly, when human beings think too carefully and minutely about an action to be taken, they cannot make up their minds in time to act. In other

[1] I do not wish to press the analogy between the human mind and servomechanisms to the point of saying that the mind-body is "nothing but" an extremely complicated mechanical automaton. I only want to go so far as to show that feed-back involves some problems which are similar to the problems of self-consciousness and self-control in man. Otherwise, mechanism and organism seem to me to be different in principle—that is, in their actual functioning—since the one is made and the other grown. The fact that one can translate some organic processes into mechanical terms no more implies that organism is mechanism than the translation of commerce into arithmetical terms implies that commerce *is* arithmetic.—A. W. W.

words, one cannot correct one's means of self-correction in-definitely. There must soon be a source of information at the end of the line which is the final authority. Failure to trust its authority will make it impossible to act, and the system will be paralyzed. —ALAN W. WATTS, *The Way of Zen*

Watts admits that his analogy is rudimentary, but he does much with it. In the first paragraph, he shows that the mind "can criticize its own processes," in the same way an electrical thermostat controls the temperature of a house by correcting its own action. In the second paragraph, he develops the analogy further. The original machine (the furnace) needs another system to adjust it (the thermostat). Watts then *enlarges* his analogy: the more automatic the system, the more feed-back systems it requires. But there is a limit to the series, a limit set by "frustration" caused by the complexity of its own operations: "There must soon be a source of information at the end of the line which is the final authority."

The advantage of the analogy is that it involves two dissimilar things. Watts points this out in his footnote which indicates the *limits* of his analogy: "feed-back involves some problems which are similar to the problems of self-consciousness and self-control in man." It is essential to indicate in some way, as Watts does, the differences and limits of the analogy; for the value of the analogy depends on how carefully it is limited and how precisely the differences are indicated.

EXAMPLE

E. B. White makes a point about the English language through an example:

The English language is always sticking a foot out to trip a man. Every week we get thrown, writing merrily along. Even Dr. Canby, a careful and experienced craftsman, got thrown in his own editorial. He spoke of "the makers of textbooks who are nearly always reactionary, and often unscholarly in denying the right to change to a language that has always been changing . . . ." In this case the word "change," quietly sandwiched in between a couple of "to's," unexpectedly ex-ploded the whole sentence. Even inverting the phrases wouldn't have helped. If he had started out "In denying to a language . . . the right to change," it would have come out this way: "In denying to a language that has always been changing the right to change . . . ." English usage is sometimes more than mere taste, judgment, and education—sometimes it's sheer luck, like getting across a street.

—*The Second Tree from the Corner*

The example *is* the point. Without it, the reader would not understand why English usage is "sheer luck."

The same point applies to the following discussion of "kitsch," which Gilbert Highet has tried to define ("it means vulgar showoff, and it is applied to anything that took a lot of trouble to make and is quite hideous"):

> In the decorative arts kitsch flourishes, and is particularly widespread in sculpture. One of my favorite pieces of bad art is a statue in Rockefeller Center, New York. It is supposed to represent Atlas, the Titan condemned to carry the sky on his shoulders. That is an ideal of somber, massive tragedy: greatness and suffering combined as in Hercules or Prometheus. But this version displays Atlas as a powerful moron, with a tiny little head, rather like the pan-fried young men who appear in the health magazines. Instead of supporting the heavens, he is lifting a spherical metal balloon: it is transparent, and quite empty; yet he is balancing insecurely on one foot like a furniture mover walking upstairs with a beach ball; and he is scowling like a mad baboon. If he ever gets the thing up, he will drop it; or else heave it onto a Fifth Avenue bus. It is a supremely ridiculous statue, and delights me every time I see it. —"Kitsch"

The detail, illustrating the vulgar and hideous as Highet perceives these qualities, is indispensable because each person will perceive "kitsch" in his own way. Remember that one good example is enough; too many examples will shift emphasis from your idea.

PROCESS

Anyone who has struggled with a confusing set of directions knows how important it is to be able to explain in simple, concrete language how to assemble a swing set or operate a power tool. Process writing is particularly important in college—in laboratory reports and notebook entries, for example.

There are different kinds of process. One is the mechanical (assembling a swing set); a second, the natural or organic (how fish breathe); a third, the historical (why the Norman invasion of England succeeded). The following letter of Benjamin Franklin, written in Philadelphia on October 19, 1752, illustrates both mechanical and natural process writing:

> Make a small cross of two light strips of cedar, the arms so long as to reach to the four corners of a large thin silk handkerchief when extended; tie the corners of the handkerchief

to the extremities of the cross, so you have the body of a kite; which being properly accommodated with a tail, loop, and string, will rise in the air, like those made of paper; but this being of silk, is fitter to bear the wet and wind of a thunder-gust without tearing. To the top of the upright stick of the cross is to be fixed a very sharp-pointed wire, rising a foot or more above the wood. To the end of the twine, next the hand, is to be tied a silk ribbon, and where the silk and twine join, a key may be fastened. This kite is to be raised when a thunder-gust appears to be coming on, and the person who holds the string must stand within a door or window, or under some cover, so that the silk ribbon may not be wet; and care must be taken that the twine does not touch the frame of the door or window. As soon as any of the thunderclouds come over the kite, the pointed wire will draw the electric fire from them, and the kite, with all the twine, will be electrified, and the loose filaments of the twine will stand out every way, and be attracted by an approaching finger. And when the rain has wet the kite and twine, so that it can conduct the electric fire freely, you will find it stream out plentifully from the key on the approach of your knuckle. At this key the phial may be charged; and from electric fire thus obtained, spirits may be kindled, and all the other electric experiments be performed, which are usually done by the help of a rubbed glass globe or tube, and thereby the sameness of the electric matter with that of lightning completely demonstrated.

Franklin's description of the simple mechanical process of making a kite and attaching objects to it is explicit and unambiguous. He describes the steps as they occur, and pauses to explain why a silk handkerchief is preferable and why the person holding the silk ribbon must stand in a sheltered place. In the second part of the letter, he describes a natural process: what happens when the wire attracts electricity from the thunderclouds. Notice how carefully he makes transitions from one step to the next without awkward statements like "The next step I shall describe is." He uses parallel prepositional phrases, "To the top of the upright stick" and "To the end of the twine," so that the steps are clearly distinguished. And he uses phrases like "At this key" to refer back to the preceding sentence. A simple "and" toward the end is more effective than "The next stage of the process is" would be.

If the process can be divided into a number of stages occurring at different times, the stages should be kept separate and distinct, and presented chronologically, unless there is a reason to present them in another order. Historical and natural processes are usually of this kind and present problems in organization different from those of mechanical processes, particularly when stages overlap. Frequently the writer wishes to comment on causes and effects in addition to describing the process.

CAUSE AND EFFECT

The exactness of cause and effect analysis depends on the subject and the purpose of the essay. In informal writing we may present causes and effects on the basis of our observation and reflection without attention to strict logical definition and tests. In writing of greater formality, the reasons will usually be stated with more precision:

> The hothouse character of American humor reflected a growing artificiality in American life. It was, perhaps, inevitable that as Americans moved from country to city and embraced a technological civilization they should lose touch with nature, and with its discipline, and come to live at second hand. The change was both physical and psychological. An ordinary snowstorm disrupted the communications, heating, and food supply of a whole city; a telephone strike created nationwide chaos. Labor-saving devices multiplied and largely defeated their own purpose: few Americans of the twentieth century found time to live as spaciously as had their ancestors a century earlier, and every time-saving machine required another to fill the time that had been saved. Automobiles did not in fact expand horizons but merely made it easier to reach them and thus to ignore them, and as Americans ceased to walk they lost familiarity even with their own countryside. Children who studied the geography of China could not name the trees that shaded their own streets, while their parents, who thought nothing of a transcontinental automobile junket, were ignorant of the most elementary facts about the climate and soil of the country they traversed. Workingmen lost much of their craftsmanship, and the nation which lived by cars and radios could not produce mechanics sufficiently skilled or sufficiently honest to repair either. The average woman no longer baked bread or indulged in what had once been called fancywork; men ceased making furniture and boys lost the knack of whittling or of improvising their own games. Dictation and the typewriter all but killed the art of letter writing, and no letters of a twentieth-century statesman yet published compared in literary finish with those written by busy men like Jefferson and Washington. Everyone was literate, but telegraph companies found it profitable to prepare canned mes-

sages of sympathy and congratulation. Businessmen, educators, and administrators, who used pieces of paper as counters for real things, came in time to believe that the counters were the real things, and a generation which kept the most elaborate records knew, perhaps, less about human nature than did those innocent of forms and questionnaires. Stockbrokers judged the economic health of the nation not so much by what was grown on farms or made in factories as by what was bet on the stock exchange. No businessman could be sure whether he was rich or poor until he had scanned the stock-market quotations of the day, and school systems that boasted a refined technique of intelligence and aptitude tests seemed unable to teach spelling or geography. Language, too, became artificial and derivative: under the tutelage of advertisers, government bureaucrats, and schools of education, people learned to say simple things in complicated ways, and Latin words crowded out Anglo-Saxon. Recreation came to be enjoyed vicariously. From playing games Americans took to watching them and then to listening to them on the radio. Even enthusiasm ceased to be spontaneous and was artificially organized and evoked by cheer leaders. Men who enjoyed artificial adventures in the pages of mysteries or westerns, and women who acquired artificial complexions, found little difficulty in adopting artificial emotions: they turned to the radio and the movies for excitement and sensation, laughter and tears, and learned about love from the magazines.

—HENRY STEELE COMMAGER, *The American Mind*

Commager is arguing that the artificiality of American humor arises from the increasing tendency of Americans to "live at second hand" and lose contact with nature, craft, and language among other experiences. Since the reasoning must be from particular experiences to a generalization about them and cannot demonstrate that the "progressive atrophy of the creative instinct of the average American" was an inevitable result, the analysis can achieve only a high degree of probability. The number of examples Commager provides increases the probability of his thesis, though there is an obvious limit to the amount and kind of detail needed.

The following paragraph on the boulevards of Paris is more complex in its organization because it seeks to distinguish main from subordinate causes:

The esthetic effect of the regular ranks and the straight line of soldiers is increased by the regularity of the avenue: the unswerving line of march greatly contributes to the display of power, and a regiment moving thus gives the impression that it would break through a solid wall without losing a beat.

That, of course, is exactly the belief that the soldier and the Prince desire to inculcate in the populace: it helps keep them in order without coming to an actual trial of strength, which always carries the bare possibility that the army might be worsted. Moreover, on irregular streets, poorly paved, with plenty of loose cobblestones and places of concealment, the spontaneous formations of untrained people have an advantage over a drilled soldiery: soldiers cannot fire around corners, nor can they protect themselves from bricks heaved from chimney tops immediately overhead: they need space to maneuver in. Were not the ancient medieval streets of Paris one of the last refuges of urban liberties? No wonder that Napoleon III sanctioned the breaking through of narrow streets and cul-de-sacs and the razing of whole quarters to provide wide boulevards: this was the best possible protection against assault from within. To rule merely by coercion, without affectionate consent, one must have the appropriate urban background. —LEWIS MUMFORD, *The City in History*

The effect is the wide regular avenues; the main cause, the "esthetic effect of the regular ranks and the straight line of soldiers." A subordinate cause is the danger of spontaneous uprisings, which were harder to control in narrow, loosely paved streets. The paragraph moves from the main cause to the subordinate causes and back briefly to the main, with appropriate emphasis on each.

Another kind of causal analysis depends on a distinction between mediate and immediate causes and effects. Again the purpose of the essay determines the nature of the analysis. In the following passage, the anthropologist A. L. Kroeber is concerned with Robert Fulton's contribution to the invention of the steamboat:

Fulton came at the critical moment when, after thirty years of experiment, pioneering, and outlay, success was at last around the corner for someone operating in favorable American waters. Fulton had the advantage of knowing nearly all previous inventors, ships, or their plans. He had personality and charm, utilized these to form good connections, as with Livingston; and this connection not only financed him but secured the monopoly of New York State waters. This gave him the straight, deep, well-populated Hudson River, its hundred and fifty miles flanked by hills instead of roads, as a proprietary right of way. His United States patent claims on his steamboats fell to pieces, as they deserved to, because as an inventor Fulton was belated and was more versatile than profound. The *Clermont's* Watt engine was imported bodily from England, and the main reason for her success was the engine. There was then no plant or shop in America that could produce a steamtight engine operating smoothly and reliably: that was Britain's contribution. Fulton had what was worth more to him than an invention—a virtual patent on a great river that nature had made as it were to order for steam transportation. So the *Clermont* finally made money, or convinced investors that steamboats would make money; and therewith the battle was definitely won for the now twenty-odd-year-old invention. By 1811 Fulton had a steamboat on the faraway Mississippi—while the whole of Europe was still in the phase of having given up the problem.—*Anthropology*

Kroeber begins with mediate, or indirect, causes (Fulton's knowledge of inventors, ships, and their plans, his personal qualities and good connections) and continues with more immediate ones (his access to a river that made experimentation possible and the *Clermont* a commercial success). If the purpose of the analysis was to examine the importance of character in shaping history, the mediate causes would be of chief concern. The writer, indeed, may find it necessary to point out which causes are mediate or immediate if the context of the analysis does not make the distinction clear.

COMBINED PARAGRAPH DEVELOPMENT

Many paragraphs combine different kinds of analysis—definition with division and comparison and contrast, for example. In the following paragraph, Aldous Huxley analyzes the difficulties of the modern advertiser:

The task of the commercial propagandist in a democracy is in some ways easier and in some ways more difficult than that of a political propagandist employed by an established dictator or a dictator in the making. It is easier inasmuch as almost everyone starts out with a prejudice in favor of beer, cigarettes and iceboxes, whereas almost nobody starts out with a prejudice in favor of tyrants. It is more difficult inasmuch as the commercial propagandist is not permitted, by the rules of his particular game, to appeal to the more-savage instincts of his public. The advertiser of dairy products would dearly love to tell his readers and listeners that all their troubles are caused by the machinations of a gang of godless international margarine manufacturers, and that it is their patriotic duty to march out and burn the oppressors' factories. This sort of thing, however, is ruled out, and he must be content with a milder approach. But the mild approach is less exciting than the approach through verbal or physical violence. In the long run, anger and hatred are self-defeating emotions. But in the short run they pay high dividends in the form of psychological and even (since they release large quantities of adrenalin and noradrenalin) physiological satisfaction. People may start out with an initial prejudice against tyrants; but when tyrants or would-be tyrants treat them to adrenalin-releasing propaganda about the wickedness of their enemies—particularly of enemies weak enough to be persecuted—they are ready to follow him with enthusiasm. In his speeches Hitler kept repeating such words as "hatred," "force," "ruthless," "crush," "smash"; and he would accompany these violent words with even more violent gestures. He would yell, he would scream, his veins would swell, his face would turn purple. Strong emotion (as every actor and dramatist knows) is in the highest degree contagious. Infected by the malignant frenzy of the orator, the audience would groan and sob and scream in an orgy of uninhibited passion. And these orgies were so enjoyable that most of those who had experienced them eagerly came back for more. Almost all of us long for peace and freedom; but very few of us have much enthusiasm for the thoughts, feelings and actions that make for peace and freedom. Conversely almost nobody wants war or tyranny; but a great many people find an intense pleasure in the thoughts, feelings and actions that make for war and tyranny. These thoughts, feelings and actions are too dangerous to be exploited for commercial purposes. Accepting this handicap, the advertising man must do the best he can with the less intoxicating emotions, the quieter forms of irrationality.

—*Brave New World Revisited*

Huxley begins by comparing and contrasting the advertiser and the political propagandist whose job it is to popularize a dictator. The chief point of contrast is their approach to those they wish to influence: the advertiser cannot appeal to the "savage instincts" of the public as the political propagandist can. Huxley then traces the effects of these two kinds of appeal—the kinds of psychological satisfaction each produces—with an appropriate illustration: Hitler. His focus, however, is on the "high dividends" of appealing to anger and hatred and the causes that make such appeals possible: ". . . almost nobody wants war or tyranny; but a great many people find an intense pleasure in the thoughts, feelings and actions that make for war and tyranny." The more immediate cause is the release of adrenalin and noradrenalin, but little is said about this.

The paragraph is really about the advertiser, even though most of it is devoted to the political propagandist; therefore, to achieve the appropriate emphasis, Huxley begins with the advertiser and discusses his problem briefly (he can start out with a prejudice in favor of a product, and he knows what he can and cannot do), and ends with the advertiser (he must do his best with "the less intoxicating emotions, the quieter forms of irrationality"). Thus, the arrangement of ideas—the use of the beginning and end of the paragraph to focus on the advertiser—provides just the right emphasis; and the various kinds of analysis—contrast, cause and effect, example, even process (in this case, the description of Hitler's speeches)—are kept distinct, without complicated or awkward transitions.

EXERCISES

1. Use one of the following statements to develop a paragraph. State the central idea in the first sentence and restate it at the conclusion in different words. Then rewrite the paragraph by building to the central idea instead of starting with it.

   a. The desire to take medicine is perhaps the greatest feature which distinguishes man from animals.—Sir William Osler

   b. Every one is more or less mad on one point.—Rudyard Kipling

   c. Each honest calling, each walk of life, has its own elite, its own aristocracy based on excellence of performance.—James B. Conant

   d. All our words from loose using have lost their edge.—Ernest Hemingway

2. Write a paragraph on one of the following statements. Build your ideas to a climax and indicate through transitions which ideas are main and which subordinate:

   a. There is really no such thing as bad weather, only different kinds of good weather.—John Ruskin

   b. Friendship is a common belief in the same fallacies, mountebanks and hobgoblins.—H. L. Mencken

   c. The value the world sets upon motives is often grossly unjust and inaccurate.—H. L. Mencken

   d. It is easier to stay out than get out.—Mark Twain

3. Write a description of a college campus or public building as a person would see it from one approach. Establish a dominant mood on the basis of the kind of activity prevailing at a certain time of day (for example, the campus at noon, as classes empty). Maintain a consistent point of view and mood throughout.

4. Write a paragraph discussing the etymology and the denotative and connotative meanings of one of the following words:

   a. ditch   c. crusade
   b. farce   d. fiddle

5. Write a paragraph defining and dividing one of the following. Specify the principle of division in the course of the paragraph:

   a. moochers   c. human leeches
   b. weepers   d. backseat drivers

6. Write a paragraph comparing and contrasting two courses in a particular field (for example, two courses in biology or English). Use the comparison and contrast to arrive at a relative estimate.

7. Develop one of the following statements by example:

a. The art of reading is to skip judiciously.—P. G. Hamerton

b. It is the folly of the world, constantly, which confounds its wisdom.—Oliver Wendell Holmes

c. We live under a government of men and morning newspapers.—Wendell Phillips

d. All professions are conspiracies against the laity.—G. B. Shaw

8. Write a paragraph describing in detail how to ride a bicycle or operate a manual gearshift or assemble a complex piece of machinery. Keep the stages of your analysis clear and distinct.

9. Write a paragraph tracing the causes of your ability (or lack of ability) in a school subject, or the effects of a useful course or book.

10. Analyze in writing the structure of the following paragraph:

> Like a nimble dialectician, the political novelist must be able to handle several ideas at once, to see them in their hostile yet interdependent relations and to grasp the way in which ideas *in the novel* are transformed into something other than the ideas of a political program. The ideas of actual life, which may have prompted the writer to compose his novel, must be left inviolate; the novelist has no business tampering with them in their own domain, nor does he generally have the qualifications for doing so. But once these ideas are set to work within the novel they cannot long remain mere lumps of abstraction. At its best, the political novel generates such intense heat that the ideas it appropriates are melted into its movement and fused with the emotions of its characters. George Eliot, in one of her letters, speaks of "the severe effort of trying to make certain ideas incarnate, as if they had revealed themselves to me first in the flesh." This is one of the great problems, but also one of the supreme challenges, for the political novelist: to make ideas or ideologies come to life, to endow them with the capacity for stirring characters into passionate gestures and sacrifices, and even more to create the illusion that they have a kind of independent motion, so that they themselves—those abstract weights of idea or ideology—seem to become active characters in the political novel.
>
> —IRVING HOWE, *Politics and the Novel*

THE
SENTENCE

SENTENCE SENSE

We will begin this discussion of the sentence with a question that arises whenever a sentence you have written is marked a "fragment" or a "run-on." If the sentence is one you speak routinely, why is it considered unacceptable in writing? In short, are written sentences basically different from spoken ones?

The answer is yes and no: No, because written sentences begin as spoken ones; yes, because they end by being something more. Your command over the possibilities of sentence structure begins with your recognition that written sentences are usually more tightly constructed and may be more carefully planned. There are sentences you will speak and seldom write—or write but almost never speak.

What is sometimes called the "run-on" sentence illustrates the difference. In speech the breaks or junctures between sentences are not always distinct, as they must be in writing, and therefore sentences can seem to run on. The recursive quality of English sentences—their capacity for infinite expansion—is another cause of the "run-on." The following noun phrase can be developed infinitely without becoming ungrammatical:

The boxes that stand on the table next to the chair near the door that opens into the hall . . .

The place at which we decide to close this noun phrase is determined by our sense of the intelligible, of the point at which the listener loses track of the idea; it is also determined by a way of thinking about experience, by a style of thought. For this reason the usual definition of the sentence as a complete statement or thought is not a dependable one.

Sentences, indeed, almost always reflect a style of thought, whatever their context. The Chicago journalist Studs Terkel recorded the following statements:

> Most that disturbs me today is when I talk to some of my neighbors, none of them, they don't like this Vietnam going on, but here's where they say: "What's the use? Who are we? We can't say nothing. We have no word. We got the President. We elected him. We got congressmen in there. They're responsible. Let them worry. Why should I worry about it?"
> [Eva Barnes]

> They took my fingerprints, my name, my address, where I work, how long I been working there. They put me in a room, second floor in the back, where all the bums from Clark Street, there was about seventy-five or a hundred bums there.
> [Carlos Alvarez]   —*Division Street—America*

Though the first passage contains ungrammatical constructions and the sentence runs on beyond the normal drop in pitch following "neighbors" (a drop in pitch that usually marks the end of the sentence), it is nonetheless expressive of Eva Barnes's feelings and certainly constitutes a complete utterance. A formal revision at best would bring the statement to the standard of a class of people for whom the *absence* of double negatives is a measure of social distinction; the statement, at worst, could be deprived of the rhythms that in speech and thought supply coherence and transition to ideas.

The break in the grammatical pattern in the second statement is certainly more apparent because the clause beginning "where all the bums from Clark Street" is completed by an imbedded sentence, "there was about seventy-five or a hundred bums there," instead of the usual verbal phrase (*were*). Those who would condemn the sentence would probably not notice that the same break occurs for emphasis in the statement of Governor George Romney of Michigan in 1964:

> I'd much rather have an approach in the field of education or these other areas of need where, if there are States that are not able to pay their way because of their backwardness or disadvantages, then to help them and have it recognized that we're treating them as States that are not able to meet their own needs.   —*U.S. News and World Report*, March 9, 1964

Indeed, they are probably little aware of how much their own speech "runs on" or fails to observe the grammatical signals considered important in writing. It is a curious commentary on popular superstitions about language that the statements of Eva Barnes and Carlos Alvarez would be perfectly intelligible to people who cannot distinguish grammaticality from considerations of decorum and taste and, incidentally, would not be amused by a transcription of their ordinary speech.

This point concerning grammaticality must be made because many of what people assume are the "rules" of good English are matters of convention—of general agreement on what comprises "intelligible" language. The same is true of the general notion of the sentence: for speakers of all classes and many writers a "sentence" ends at the limit of intelligibility. The noun phrase cited earlier ("The boxes that stand on the table") could be run on infinitely, but every speaker knows from experience at what point to close the phrase.

Whatever our aptitude for language and our intelligence, each of us shows a command of the grammar of English before we learn to read and write; as children we spoke complex grammatical sentences we had not heard before. Linguists differ on whether this ability is inborn or acquired. But there is no disagreement that the ability exists. The point is worth making because you may forget that you enter your class in composition not as a beginner but as a practiced user of the language; you build on what you know, learning to deal with words with greater facility, with an increasing awareness of the possibilities for expression offered by the written sentence. If you have had trouble with sentence "fragments," your problem may be that you rely on habits of speech entirely. Fragmentary sentences are common in speech, in part because the speaking situation provides a context lacking when you write; in a conversation, you may respond to other statements in a series of phrases that you can immediately clarify if your partner indicates he does not understand. There is no way for your reader to indicate his confusion if he cannot understand your written fragmentary sentences. The point to remember is that what is clear in speech is not always clear in writing, for reasons we have noted; conventions of writing come into existence and command our attention in composition because we cannot always depend in writing on the signals we depend on in speech.

One important difference between spoken and written sentences will clarify this point. It is unusual to hear many spoken sentences *begin* with dependent clauses, though they may stand alone.[1] The

---

[1]The functional positions indicated below are commonly distinguished by grammarians, though the classifications are not agreed upon by all linguists:

| | Indirect | Direct | Predicate | |
| Subject | Object | Object | Nominative | Appositive |

The tall man, who gave my son the car keys, is my brother, Jim.

Relative clause functioning as adjective
expanding *man*

| Predicate | Noun |
| Adjective | Adjunct |

I'm certain that he has the car keys.

Relative clause functioning as adjective complement

emphasis we desire is the chief determiner, as in the following transcription in which the opening phrase is a reduced clause and one dependent clause stands alone for special emphasis:

> Every time I get tenants in there, I rent to two people and twenty-seven people occupy it. I'd done everything I could for the house, but now I'm letting the city tear it down. I've given up, I can't cope. Because my own tenants will just knock out the windows with their own fists. They'll pay the rent, but then they'll say fix this, and knock it out. [Gladys Pennington]
> —STUDS TERKEL, *Division Street—America*

The tendency in spoken English to break up sentences in this way may be a result of a need to reduce the number of grammatical operations that come into play. In written sentences we can control emphasis by beginning with a dependent clause.

Emphasis is a more complex matter since it is always an achievement of intonation in speech and equivalents of intonation in writing. A consideration of emphasis, then, must begin with intonation.

I'll read the fine print carefully, when I find the time.

      Adverbial expanding Adverbial expanding
       the main clause   the main clause

       Verb   Direct
     Complement   Object

He called *his friends those who shared his political convictions.*

English sentences traditionally have been classified according to the kind and number of clauses they contain. A *simple sentence* contains one independent clause and no dependent clauses:

> We spoke to the candidate.

A *compound sentence* contains two or more independent clauses and no dependent clauses:

> He will run for office, but he will not announce his candidacy.

A *complex sentence* contains one independent clause and at least one dependent clause:

> He said he would run for office.
> [The dependent clause *completes* the independent clause.]

> He will run for office because he is concerned about the economy.
> [The dependent clause *expands* the independent clause.]

A *compound-complex sentence* contains two or more independent clauses and one or more dependent clauses:

> He will run for office but he will not announce his candidacy because he wants to avoid making public statements at this time.

INTONATION: A SIMPLE TEST OF
"SENTENCE SENSE"

The normal intonation pattern of the English sentence is the following:

$$^2\text{I'm going}/^3\text{home.}^1$$

The voice begins at medium pitch (2), moves to high on the syllable which receives the most stress (3), and falls before the conclusion of the last word (1): If the last word of the sentence is a pronoun, the pitch rises on the preceding word. This is the basic pattern from which innumerable patterns derive:

$$^2\text{His } ^3\text{books}^3 \; ^2\text{are } ^3\text{heavy.}^1$$
$$^2\text{My } ^3\text{brother,}^2 \; ^3\text{Jim,}^2 \text{ is a } ^3\text{teacher.}^1$$

These pitch indications are at best approximations that vary from speaker to speaker. Each establishes his own pattern of intonation and stresses which a listener intuits from the context of his statements.[2]

In speech we achieve emphasis through intonation as well as word order; in writing, mainly through word order. Thus, the following transcription of spoken English would vary in emphasis depending on how it was read:

> As far as I'm concerned, when States use States' rights as a shield for not granting elemental and inherent human rights and citizenship rights, then they're abusing the concept of States' rights.
> —GOVERNOR GEORGE ROMNEY, *U.S. News and World Report*,
> March 9, 1964

Most speakers would emphasize "States' rights," calling attention to the phrase as a concept and some would in addition express approval or sarcasm through intonation. It would be difficult to indicate this

---

[2]Four stresses are usually distinguished: acute ($\diagup$), marking first or heaviest stress; circumflex ($\wedge$), second; grave ($\diagdown$), third; breve ($\cup$), weak. The sentences labeled for pitch may be marked for stress as follows:

His books are heavy.

My brother, Jim, is a teacher.

The second sentence makes the presumption that the speaker has only one brother. Had he two brothers, the intonation and stress patterns would indicate this fact:

My brother Jim is a teacher.

difference in writing without stating the attitude exactly. Some writers would, if the context permitted, put the phrase in quotation marks, as if to say "so-called States' rights."

Another speaker would rely on another kind of sentence composed of shorter phrases, each with its particular emphasis and rhythm:

> We lived eight miles from the mine, and we had to ride it horseback. I was riding behind my dad. Many times I'd have to git off and hammer his feet out of the stirrups. They'd be froze in the stirrups. It was cold, you know. When you come out of the mines, your feet would be wet of sweat and wet where you're walking on the bottom. And get up on those steel stirrups, while you're riding by eight miles, your feet'd be frozen and you couldn't git 'em out of the stirrups. I'd have to hammer 'em out. His feet were numb, and they wouldn't hurt till they started to get warm, and then they would get to hurtin'. [Buddy Blankenship]
> —STUDS TERKEL, Hard Times

In all sentences, we rely on stress and intonation for precision—so much so that often what we say seems ungrammatical if written exactly as spoken:

Where you going?

Since "where're" is in many dialects sounded as a pitch slightly higher than "where" the listener thinks he has heard "where're" and will not misunderstand the question. Sometimes an entire spoken sentence depends on intonation for clarity. Here is a sentence quoted earlier:

> I'd much rather have an approach in the field of education or these other areas of need where, if there are States that are not able to pay their way because of their backwardness or disadvantages, then to help them and have it recognized that we're treating them as States that are not able to meet their own needs. [Governor George Romney]

As often happens in impromptu speech, there is a shift in the structure of the sentence halfway through; if the speaker had written the statement, he would have perhaps written "we would help them" instead of "then to help them." Because "then to help them and have it recognized" would be intonated for major emphasis and clarity, however, the listener has no difficulty following the speaker's thought.

Indeed, for emphasis we sometimes break the pattern in speech and loosen the sentence in ways that depend on intonation:

> The proper level of development to support defense efforts, or peaceful atomic energy, whether you want to have a space

program—these are decisions related to needs and can be understood by the policy makers.

—JEROME B. WIESNER, *U.S. News and World Report,*
February 3, 1964

At first glance the clause "whether you want to have a space program" may seem to qualify the phrases that precede it. A reading of the whole sentence, however, sets us right: the clause is an appositive of "these," so that "whether [or not] you want to have a space program" is one of the "decisions." We understand this immediately when we hear the statement, because the speaker will most likely give the same stress to "whether" that he gives to "proper level" instead of dropping his voice slightly to indicate qualification. Intonation indicates which of the two meanings the speaker intends.

These examples show that, though we can indicate intonation through punctuation to an extent (italics, exclamation points, for example), we must not depart too much, if at all, from the natural stresses of speech. Sentences that do are likely to be awkward and stilted. But the distinction between the spoken and written sentence is an important one. Habits that make writing ineffective—run-on sentences, indefinite pronoun references—are routine in speech. As a rule, the written sentence must be tighter and more carefully constructed than the spoken sentence. Clear, vigorous written sentences echo the rhythms and natural stresses of speech without carrying over the looseness and imprecisions that intonation can control.

EMPHASIS IN THE SIMPLE SENTENCE

Let us begin, then, with the simplest ways to improve the sentences you write. The beginning and end positions in the simple sentence are the emphatic positions—the end often more emphatic than the beginning:

> The word *ideology*—it has many ambiguous meanings and
> emotional colorations.   —DANIEL BELL, "Sociodicy"

The natural subject *ideology* appears in its normal position at the beginning of the sentence and gains emphasis through reinforcement. Where the subject appears may depend merely on idiom:

> There are no seats left.

Compare this sentence with

> No seats are left.

The difference is one of emphasis. The first sentence is more colloquial and less emphatic; the second, less colloquial and more emphatic.

In many sentences the subject is not the actor. Compare:

The facts of the accident were hard for *John* to recall.
It was hard for *John* to recall the facts of the accident.
John found it hard to recall the facts of the accident.

All three of these sentences are grammatically correct; the difference lies in the stress you give "John." Awkwardness may arise, however, if you bury the actor of the sentence:

It was because it was so dark that the driver did not see the bridge.

The writer of this sentence could use fewer words without a sacrifice in meaning and avoid the awkward repetition of *was:*

The driver did not see the bridge because of the darkness.

THE PASSIVE RIGHTLY USED

The passive voice can be used to keep the verb near the subject when the subject is modified by a lengthy clause:

ACTIVE	PASSIVE
The speaker, who had served in the first Roosevelt administration and had vigorously opposed some of the New Deal programs, attacked the policies of the present administration.	The policies of the present administration were attacked by the speaker, who had served in the first Roosevelt administration and had vigorously opposed some of the New Deal programs.

The passive voice is rightly used when the concern is not with the actor:

The car was destroyed in the accident.

Indeed, the sentence may seem awkward if the actor is mentioned:

The car was completely demolished by John in the accident.

In this sentence, "John" should be in the subject position. Frequently the passive voice is purposely used to minimize personal responsibility: "The order has been lost," not "I lost the order." Though the passive voice has important uses, you should avoid it when the person performing the action deserves emphasis.

OVEREXPANDED SUBJECTS

Let us return to that noun phrase we could have expanded infinitely, and consider the "run-on" sentence. A simple subject or subject complement can be obscured by expanding it with a series of modifiers, as in this English translation of a French sentence:

> This was the day immediately following that on which I had seen file past me against a background of sea the beautiful procession of young girls.
> —MARCEL PROUST, *Within a Budding Grove,*
> translated by C. K. Scott Moncrieff

It is hard to determine what part of this sentence contains the important idea; the string of modifiers may cause the reader to start the sentence again. The string of modifiers in the following sentence does not confuse the reader because their reference is immediately clear:

> I cannot remember the moment when I ceased to air my old royalist convictions and stuffed them away in an inner closet as you do a dress or an ornament that you perceive strikes the wrong note.   —MARY MCCARTHY, *On the Contrary*

As we indicated at the beginning of this section, the number of modifiers that may be added is a matter of style. But however a sentence is constructed, the main idea must stand out:

> Like a boil that can never be cured so long as it is covered up but must be opened with all its ugliness to the natural medicines of air and light, *injustice must be exposed,* with all the tension its exposure creates, *to the light of human conscience and the air of natural opinion before it can be cured.*
> —MARTIN LUTHER KING, JR., "Letter from Birmingham Jail"
> (italics added)

The inordinate length of the opening adjectival modifier here makes it desirable that the subject and predicate not be divided; the division of the verb ("must be exposed") from its complement does not obscure the sentence, in part because the modifying phrase (beginning "with all the tension") is relatively short. The number of elements in the verb phrase, including modifiers, may be increased without loss of clarity when these are presented in the order of their importance. The order of climax, as we shall see, focuses attention:

> The failure of the protest novel lies in its rejection of life, the human being, the denial of his beauty, dread, power, in its insistence that it is his categorization alone which is real and which cannot be transcended.
> —JAMES BALDWIN, *Notes of a Native Son*

AWKWARD SHIFTS IN SENTENCE STRUCTURE

Let us return to simpler matters of sentence construction. The following shifts in sentence structure are usually the result of carelessness:

TENSE: The cat ran when the dog barks.
VOICE: He smashed the fender and the door was dented.
PERSON: Let's all write your Congressman.

You will find shifts in mood more difficult to avoid, particularly when they involve a corresponding shift in person:

If you have trouble with grammar, English 120 provides a thorough review for anyone with writing problems.

We have seen that expanded noun phrases may lead the writer to lose track of the structure:

The fact that England won the war it did not solve her colonial problems.

Expanded noun phrases may also result in ambiguity:

The book you told me about a store downtown has for sale.

The following sentence appeared in an Ohio college newspaper:

Films and film strips may be borrowed by all faculty and students for a limited time period, while the faculty may borrow records at any time.

The trouble in this sentence arises through the shift in meaning of the word *time* from duration to a particular hour of the day or evening.

INEQUIVALENT SUBJECTS AND SUBJECT COMPLEMENTS

A more complex difficulty arises in sentences like

The one movie I saw was in August.

Was suggests that the title of the movie will follow. The confusion arises because forms of *be* can express both equivalence and time relationships. The subject and subject complement (or predicate nominative) are equivalent and interchangeable in this sentence:

The title of the movie is *2001*.
2001 is the title of the movie.

In the following, the subject and the subject complement are not equivalent or even close in meaning:

The only help I need is knowing how to trim the sail.

In learning will improve the sentence:

The only help I need is in learning how to trim the sail.

Many sentences based on forms of *be* can be effectively shortened:

The reason he is going to New York is because he is attending a conference.	His reason for going to New York is to attend a conference.
The fact that he must give a talk is the reason he is nervous.	The reason he is nervous is that he must give a talk. OR He is nervous because he must give a talk.

COORDINATION

The conjunctions *and, but, for, yet, or, nor* and the semicolon give equal emphasis to ideas:

> For happiness is individual, and to make happiness the object of society is to resolve society itself into the ambitions of numberless individuals, each directed towards the attainment of some personal purpose.
>
> —R. H. TAWNEY, *The Acquisitive Society*

In the sentence

> The law is neither a scientific instrument nor an adjunct to any absolute moral doctrine.
>
> —DAVID L. BAZELON, "The Awesome Decision"

the subject complements, *instrument* and *adjunct,* serve the same grammatical function and therefore receive equal emphasis. The sentence could be revised for single emphasis:

> The law, which is not a scientific instrument, is not an adjunct to any absolute moral doctrine.

But the revision is ineffective because the relationship of the dependent clause to the rest of the sentence is in doubt. Is the law *not* an adjunct because it is *not* a scientific instrument? The original sentence avoids this difficulty.

In the following sentence, John Steinbeck makes "sat" and "seemed to hear" equally important actions and gains additional emphasis by introducing "he" before "seemed":

> Jody sat quietly listening, and he seemed to hear Gitano's gentle voice and its unanswerable, "But I was born here."
>
> —*The Red Pony*

The following revision

> Jody, sitting and quietly listening, seemed to hear Gitano's gentle voice and its unanswerable, "But I was born here."

would perhaps sound awkward because of the intrusive repetition of the same or similar vowel sounds in at least six of the first nine words.

The sentence construction otherwise would be acceptable.

Grammatical coordination may be a source of irony:

> The uglification of Paris, the most famously beautiful city of
> Europe, goes on apace, and more is being carefully planned.
> —GENÊT, "Letter from Paris," *The New Yorker*, May 2, 1964

Here we expect the second independent clause to say the opposite—
something is being done to *stop* the "uglification" of Paris. Revised
for single emphasis, the sentence loses its bite:

> As the uglification of Paris goes on apace, more is being care-
> fully planned.

The subordination of the first clause and consequent omission of
"and" reduces the expectation built into the original sentence.

In many sentences, ideas are coordinated *merely* to show their
relationship:

> Manet was a great painter, combining a selective eye and a
> tactful hand with admirable honesty of purpose; but he
> lacked the consciousness of tragic humanity.
> —KENNETH CLARK, *Looking at Pictures*

And coordination is often necessary to avoid choppiness and incoherence:

> The smoke of burning cotton streaked the day, and the flare of it
> luridly starred the night; for even in his haste Mouton was determined
> that no fraction of the financial king should fall to the Yankees.
> —J. W. DE FOREST,
> *A Volunteer's Adventures*

In the original sentence the relationship of ideas is immediately clear;
the sentence comprises a single thought—hence the grammatical
coordination. In addition, the third independent clause (beginning
with *for*) is more emphatic than it would be standing alone.

EXCESSIVE COORDINATION

The following sentence runs on monotonously:

> Gitano jerked upright and he seized a piece of deerskin and
> he tried to throw it over the thing in his lap, but the skin
> slipped away.

When the sentence contains a series of clauses and all are coordinated,
no single one is likely to stand out. In the original sentence, the

emphasis falls on the second independent clause and on the last—which completes the sequence of actions:

> Gitano jerked upright and, seizing a piece of deerskin, he tried to throw it over the thing in his lap, but the skin slipped away. —STEINBECK, *The Red Pony*

Steinbeck might have made the final clause a separate sentence to give it special emphasis. Compare the following:

They snarl and swear at each other and curse the general for ordering such marching and curse the enemy for running away instead of fighting and they fling themselves down in the dust and refuse to move a step further.	They snarl and swear at each other; they curse the general for ordering such marching; they curse the enemy for running away instead of fighting; they fling themselves down in the dust, refusing to move a step further.

—J. W. DE FOREST,
A Volunteer's Adventures

The first sentence is so loaded with coordinating conjunctions that subjects and predicates do not stand out. In the original sentence DeForest achieves a staccato effect through semicolons. The sentences are not monotonous because the clauses vary in length.

CONJUNCTIVE ADVERBS

Thus, however, therefore, nevertheless, and so forth are commonly used as adverbs in single clauses:

> The newspapers, however, contained no report of the episode.

In compound sentences these adverbials can be obtrusive if the sentence is short and informal (*therefore* usually occurs in formal speech and writing):

> It's stopped raining; therefore, I'm going.

Therefore is not obtrusive in the following sentence:

> It had been snowing all day and the streets had become slick; we therefore decided not to go.

The length of the sentence and the position of "therefore" after "we" prevent awkwardness. Many writers avoid using conjunctive adverbs in short sentences and use them sparingly in longer ones—preferably after the subject, unless they want to emphasize the adverb.

FUSED SENTENCES

The following sentence makes two entirely different statements:

The book is lying on the floor someone must have dropped it.

The intonation patterns show this clearly:

[2]The [3]book [2]is [3]lying on the [3]floor.[1]
[3]Some[2]one [2]must [2]have [3]dropped [2]it.[1]

In revising the fused sentence, a semicolon may substitute for the period. Compare the following:

Conversation abounds in groups of words that do not form conventionally complete and logical sentences many verbs are omitted, clauses are uttered which are to be attached to the whole context of the conversation rather than to any particular word in a parsable sentence single words stand for complete ideas.

Conversation abounds in groups of words that do not form conventionally complete and logical sentences. Many verbs are omitted; clauses are uttered which are to be attached to the whole context of the conversation rather than to any particular word in a parsable sentence; single words stand for complete ideas.

—C. C. FRIES,
American English Grammar

COMMA FAULTS

The following sentence contains three ideas that can stand alone and are distinct enough so that commas, which usually indicate slight pauses, are misused:

The book was selling well in all but one of the stores, I wondered why, the explanation was simple.

The sentence is best punctuated thus:

The book was selling well in all but one of the stores; I wondered why. The explanation was simple.

Some writers—often in informal contexts—use a comma (instead of a colon) when a second clause completes the meaning of the first, or expands it:

The more highly public life is organized the lower does its morality sink; the nations of today behave to each other worse than they ever did in the past, they cheat, rob, bully and bluff, make war without notice, and kill as many women and children as possible; whereas primitive tribes were at all events restrained by taboos.

—E. M. FORSTER, "What I Believe"

This use of the comma is occasionally found in more formal contexts:

> The artist, always using his freedom, remains a rebel even when he is a stranger; his basic rebellion, in this time or any other, is directed at the universe itself, and the universe cannot be undone by history, it remains, and it provides the stuff which the artist, man of letters or man of paint or stone or the twelve-tone scale, at once rebukes and celebrates.
>
> —MARK SCHORER, *The World We Imagine*

SUBORDINATION

The position in the sentence of nominal and adjectival dependent clauses is rather fixed:

> *Whoever goes to the store* should mail this letter on the way.
> The man *who is at the door* wishes directions.

Adverbial clauses, on the other hand, are not so fixed and may be placed before or after the independent clauses, depending on the degree of emphasis desired:

> Wilson was a Southerner by birth and breeding, although he made his career in the North.
>
> —GERALD W. JOHNSON, "The Cream of the Jest"

Had the adverbial clause come at the beginning, the emphasis would fall on the idea that Wilson was a Southerner.

In simple sentences, the end is usually the more emphatic part because the predicate position expresses the action or goal; this characteristic carries over to complex sentences when the context permits. Thus, in Johnson's sentence the adverbial clause receives the emphasis because it comes at the end. Grammatical subordination, incidentally, does not mean that the main clause *necessarily* contains the most important idea.[3] In the following sentences the dependent elements contain ideas at least as important as that of the main clause:

> But from the first the cows worried him, coming up regularly twice a day to be milked, standing there reproaching him with their smug female faces.
>
> —KATHERINE ANNE PORTER, "Noon Wine"

> Frequenters of resorts, big July mosquitoes wet and gross with a summer's licentiousness, they bore down upon me on the shore breeze, whining with excitement and mooning ceaselessly about my ears.
>
> —WILLIAM STYRON, *Set This House on Fire*

[3]See James Sledd, *A Short Introduction to English Grammar* (Chicago: Scott, Foresman, 1959), pp. 275–76.

MISPLACED EMPHASIS

The arrangement of sentence elements obviously determines the distribution of emphasis. The following sentences have identical meaning; neither is awkward:

> Looking at pictures requires active participation, and a certain amount of discipline in the early stages.

> Looking at pictures requires active participation, and, in the early stages, a certain amount of discipline.
> —KENNETH CLARK, *Looking at Pictures*

But note the following:

> The conquest of his heart was complete when he entered the house.

> When he entered the house the conquest of his heart was complete.
> —WASHINGTON IRVING, *The Legend of Sleepy Hollow*

The first sentence drops in interest because the adverbial clause receives undue emphasis. In the second, the emphasis falls properly on the main clause, which in this instance contains the important idea.
Now compare the following:

> The peace of his mind was at an end, and his only study was how to gain the affections of the peerless daughter of Van Tassel, from the moment Ichabod laid his eyes upon these regions of delight.

> From the moment Ichabod laid his eyes upon these regions of delight, the peace of his mind was at an end, and his only study was how to gain the affections of the peerless daughter of Van Tassel. —*Ibid.*

In the second sentence, the second main clause is more emphatic, in part because it comes at the end of the sentence and in part because it is longer than the first main clause.

SUBORDINATION: EXPANDING THE MAIN CLAUSE

As we have seen, the number of possible modifiers in a sentence depends on keeping the noun and verb phrases relatively short and prominent. Each subordinate element added to the core idea must be immediately clear in its reference. In Irving's sentence

> From his Herculean frame and great powers of limb, he had received the nickname of BROM BONES, by which he was universally known. —*Ibid.*

the placement of the prepositional phrase at the beginning makes it possible to add the final clause. In the following revision of the sentence

> He had received the nickname BROM BONES, by which he was universally known, from his Herculean frame and great powers of limb.

the meaning is not immediately clear because the phrase beginning "from his Herculean frame" cannot complete "known." The placement of modifiers depends, then, on considerations of emphasis and clarity—clarity having priority:

> A fat brown goose lay at one end of the table and at the other end, on a bed of creased paper strewn with sprigs of parsley, lay a great ham, stripped of its outer skin and peppered over with crust crumbs, a neat paper frill round its shin and beside this was a round of spiced beef. —JAMES JOYCE, "The Dead"

A partial revision of this sentence suggests the incoherence that can result from misplaced modifiers:

> A fat brown goose lay at one end of the table and at the other end lay a great ham, on a bed of creased paper strewn with sprigs of parsley, *stripped of its outer skin and peppered over with crust crumbs* . . .

A second reading clears up the confusion, but a sentence should be immediately clear.

Even greater confusion can result when the sentence contains one main clause and a large number of modifiers. Though he uses three modifying clauses, the author of the following sentence avoids confusion:

> During the last waiting period, Luke had had a "hot" laboratory built, rather like a giant caricature of a school laboratory, *in which*, instead of dissolving bits of iron in beakers under their noses, they had a stainless steel pot surrounded by walls of concrete *into which* they dropped rods of metal *that* they never dared to see. —C. P. SNOW, *The New Men*

The first *which* clause modifies the first *laboratory*, not the second. Had the comparison that precedes "in which" been to something else, the sentence would be constructed differently to avoid confusion (two sentences would probably be necessary). A similar problem arises with the second *which* clause, which modifies "pot," not "walls of concrete." The context prevents confusion here; it is important however that the *which* clause appear as close as possible to its antecedent. The sentence probably could not take more modifiers without becoming incoherent. The following is an example of a sentence collapsing under the weight of its modifiers, even though the noun and verb phrases are not widely separated:

> Terms of amplitude, terms of atmosphere, those terms, and those terms only, in which images assert their fulness and roundness, their power to revolve, so that they have sides and backs, parts in the shade as true as parts in the sun—these were plainly to be my conditions, right and left, and I was so far from overrating the amount of expression the whole thing, as I saw and felt it, would require, that to retrace the way at present is, alas, more than anything else, but to mark the gaps and the lapses, to miss, one by one, the intentions that, with the best will in the world, were not to fructify.
>
> —HENRY JAMES, Preface to *The Wings of the Dove*

CONCISION THROUGH SUBORDINATION

Sentences may be wordy and unclear because single words and phrases are subordinated improperly or expanded unnecessarily. In the sentence of C. P. Snow quoted above, certain modifiers are reduced from longer constructions:

> . . . Luke had had a "hot" laboratory built, *which was* rather like a giant caricature of a school laboratory, in which . . . they had a stainless steel pot *that was* surrounded by walls of concrete into which they dropped rods of metal. . . .

The reduction of a very few words increases the number of modifiers that can be added and promotes clarity.

The meaning of a sentence can also be obscured by needless repetition or qualification and too many subject-verb combinations:

> Approaching thus the momentous spaces, and considering with reference to a new and greater personalism, the needs and possibilities of American imaginative literature, through the medium-light of what we have already broach'd, it will at once be appreciated that a vast gulf of difference separates the present accepted condition of these spaces, inclusive of what is floating in them, from any condition adjusted to, or fit for, the world, the America, there sought to be indicated, and the copious races of complete men and women, along these Vistas crudely outlined.
>
> —WALT WHITMAN, *Democratic Vistas*

Too little subordination can be just as ineffective. A series of main clauses, without any subordination, can be monotonous and blur the focus of the sentence. Compare:

A cross swell had set in from the direction of Formosa Channel about ten o'clock. It did not disturb these passengers much. The *Nan-Shan* had a flat bottom, rolling chocks on bilges. Her beam had great breadth. Thus she had the reputation of an exceptionally steady ship in a seaway.

A cross swell had set in from the direction of Formosa Channel about ten o'clock, without disturbing these passengers much, because the *Nan-Shan*, with her flat bottom, rolling chocks on bilges, and great breadth of beam, had the reputation of an exceptionally steady ship in a seaway. —JOSEPH CONRAD, *Typhoon*

WORD ORDER

In English sentences, an adverbial clause can precede or follow the main clause and phrases, and single-word modifiers can stand in several positions with different emphasis or meaning:

> I have *only* one thing to say. [emphasis on *one*]
> I have one thing to say *only*. [emphasis on *only*]
> *Only* I have the right to speak. [I—and no one else]

It is important, therefore, to distinguish between differences in emphasis and differences in meaning. The following sentences differ in meaning:

> The progress of civilization is not a *wholly* uniform drift towards better things.

> The progress of civilization is not *wholly* a uniform drift towards better things.
> —ALFRED NORTH WHITEHEAD, *Science and the Modern World*
> (italics added)

In the first sentence "wholly" modifies "uniform"; in the second, "wholly" modifies the entire phrase that follows.

The placement of the modifier in the following sentence introduces a more complex problem:

> John was not appointed because he was class president.

John may or may not have been appointed. Does the adverbial clause modify the negative verb ("was not appointed") or the entire independent clause? The following revision clears up the ambiguity:

> Because he was class president, John was not appointed.

So long as their reference is clear, the placement of modifiers can be a matter of emphasis:

Books are the best of things, well used; abused, among the worst. —R. W. EMERSON, *The American Scholar*

The first part of the sentence creates the expectation that the second part will say "among the worst of things, abused." The inversion gives emphasis to both "abused" and "among the worst."

UNUSUAL WORD ORDER

Emerson's sentence exhibits a somewhat unusual word order. You will do well to avoid extreme modifications of the normal subject-verb-object pattern, except in usual contexts. The sentence

Anger, Hanna could express without self-consciousness, but not much else. —C. P. SNOW, *The New Men*

is a rather common inversion used for emphasis. It is close enough to the spoken idiom not to sound strange. The following sentence is even more extreme in its departure from the spoken idiom:

Odd enough was it certainly that the question originally before him, the question placed there by Kate, should so of a sudden, find itself lodged by another.
—HENRY JAMES, *The Wings of the Dove*

The inversion at the beginning of the sentence from the idiomatic "It was certainly odd" is obviously intended to emphasize the oddity of the situation. The inversion is given even more emphasis by the uncommon use of the passive construction ("the question placed there by Kate"). The effectiveness of the sentence, or its ineffectiveness, depends on its context.[4] Where word order is altered in an unusual way, it is best altered without *other* prominent alterations in the sentence or paragraph. The success of the grammatical inversions that conclude the following sentence depends on the natural word order of the rest of it:

It is the middle and pure height and whole of summer and a summer night, the held breath, of a planet's year; high shored sleeps the crested tide: what day of the month I do not know, which day of the week I am not sure, far less what hour of the night. —JAMES AGEE, *Let Us Now Praise Famous Men*

[4]The sentence opens a paragraph that continues: "This other, it was easy to see, came straight up with the fact of her beautiful delusion and her wasted charity; the whole thing preparing for him as pretty a case of conscience as he could have desired, and one at the prospect of which he was really wincing."

DANGLING MODIFIERS

Words that hang in the sentence without specific reference produce incoherence. Absurdities like the following are easily spotted and corrected:

> Sprinting down the trail, a snake was seen.

The following sentence, when spoken, will not strike every reader as ungrammatical:

> Driving home, the car stalled.

Its equivalent occurs occasionally in written English when context clearly indicates the actor. Where awkwardness arises, a simple revision can be made, usually without having to specify the actor:

> AWKWARD: The performance began by singing the national anthem.

> REVISED: The performance began with the singing of the national anthem.

SPLIT CONSTRUCTION

It is often necessary to split a natural phrase like the infinitive to avoid ambiguity. In the sentence

> His aim is further to promote the growth of the arts in the area.

"further" may modify the whole sentence or merely "to promote." The sentence

> His aim is to further promote the growth of the arts in the area.

avoids this ambiguity. You will do best, however, not to split the infinitive with too many words:

> We asked to, thinking there would be room, ride with the others.

Few speakers and writers would think of splitting a subject from its predicate in the following way:

> We, wondering what had caused the explosion, talked in whispers.

The modifier is put before or after the main clause, depending on the kind of emphasis desired. The split does occur, however, when the subject of the sentence is not a pronoun:

The crowd of people, wondering about the explosion, talked in whispers.

REPETITION

The repetition of an auxiliary phrase is a common way to achieve emphasis:

> A man with more character would have protested vigorously— would have made himself heard regardless of the indifference he met.

Another way is to repeat a key word or derivatives of it:

> In 1900, a man could cross the nation and smell different smells, taste different foods, hear different accents and be cheated by different methods.
> —JOHN KEATS, *The Insolent Chariots*

> The murder of Banquo brings Macbeth a new experience of fear: it brings the ghost of Banquo to haunt him.
> —WILLARD FARNHAM, *Shakespeare's Tragic Frontier*

> The world dismisses curiosity by calling it idle, or mere idle, curiosity—even though curious persons are seldom idle.
> —E. S. MORGAN, "What Every Yale Freshman Should Know"

ELEGANT VARIATION

H. W. Fowler gave the name "elegant variation" to the practice of hunting for synonyms to avoid repeating a word or phrase. Awkwardness and unintentional confusion may result from this practice:

> He thought and thought about the problem, and later reflected upon it more.

The substitution of "reflected upon" implies a difference in thinking, but all that is meant is that the man later thought more about the problem. To avoid repeating a person's name in a sentence, you may write:

> Pierre Salinger was a close friend of John F. Kennedy; the press secretary gave the President valuable help in dealing with reporters.

Additional variations, however, could prove annoying:

> The former California newspaperman served the President efficiently.

The variation would be justified only if the additional information illuminated the previous statement.

Of course, you should try to use a more precise word when the context permits. In the sentence

> After peering down the mine shaft, he looked up at the sky.

"peering" is more precise than "looking" would be, because it suggests squinting slightly to see into a dark, narrow space. However, the repetition of "look" would not be awkward.

AWKWARD REPETITION

The repetition of a word with slightly different meanings may create awkwardness:

> It's a likely place to camp, and is likely to please the group.

The first "likely" means *satisfactory*; the second means *probably*. Some kinds of repetition occur for emphasis, as we have seen. A problem with such repetitions can arise when these seem to say more than a close analysis reveals:

> Democracy has been so retarded and jeopardized by powerful personalities, that its first instincts are fain to clip, conform, bring in stragglers, and reduce everything to a dead level.
> —WALT WHITMAN, *A Backward Glance O'er Travel'd Roads*

The differences between *clip, conform,* and *reduce everything* are too slight to warrant the concluding phrase. Repetitions of this sort occur frequently when the writer is trying to achieve special emphasis.

LOOSE AND PERIODIC SENTENCES

Moderately periodic sentences are often used in modern prose to express emphatic ideas. Instead of beginning with the main idea, the periodic sentence builds to it:

> With Dickens' mounting dislike and distrust of the top layers of that middle-class society with which he had begun by identifying himself, *his ideal of middle-class virtue was driven down to the lower layers.*
> —EDMUND WILSON, "Dickens: The Two Scrooges"

The degree of emphasis or dramatic intensity depends in part on the length of the sentence and the occurrence of the subject and verb at the end. But separating the subject from the verb with lengthy modifiers may also create suspense:

> *The hanging judge*, that evil old man in scarlet robe and horsehair wig, whom nothing short of dynamite will ever teach what century he is living in, but who will at any rate interpret the law according to the books and will in no circumstances take a money bribe, *is one of the symbolic figures of England.*
>
> —GEORGE ORWELL, *The Lion and the Unicorn*

In the following sentence, concerning the flight of airplanes, the writer creates less suspense, in part because the idea expressed is not itself suspenseful:

> And those disparate rhythms of flight that I found so delightful to watch, *Walt Disney*, in his film *Snow White*, where deer and rabbits and other animals are shown running together at different speeds and gaits, *has rendered them for the first time in plastic art.* —EDMUND WILSON, "Miami"

The sentence is looser in construction than Orwell's, with emphasis distributed throughout. The addition of a modifying phrase or clause at the end of a periodic sentence will loosen it even further:

> To lay before us the full character of this passion, to show us how it first comes into being and then comes to dominate the world about it and the life that follows upon it, Emily Brontë gives her material a broad scope in time, *lets it, in fact, cut across three generations.*
>
> —MARK SCHORER, "Technique as Discovery"

> With the exception of a camper's tent on the upper part of the beach, and a few isolated gray shacks perched on dune tops behind it, there was nothing ahead but the wide belt of sand curving around one unseen corner after another *with the flat easing and stretching sea beside me.*
>
> —JOHN HAY, "An Unimagined Frontier"

A loose sentence begins with the main idea; phrases and clauses that develop the main idea follow:

> The snow came down in large torn flakes, all over the buildings of Wayne University, grass, trees, and the pale radiance of a network of slow-motion super-highways beyond.
>
> —HERBERT GOLD, *The Age of Happy Problems*

In such sentences, phrases and clauses that explain and develop the main idea vary in the emphasis they receive; for if the phrases and clauses are less important than the main idea, this is not to say that they are unimportant. Indeed, they may increase in emphasis depending on how the sentence is constructed:

The Nile was rising, filling the air with the dank summer moisture of its yearly inundations, climbing the stone wall at the bottom of the Embassy garden inch by slimy inch.

—LAWRENCE DURRELL, *Mountolive*

Punishment as such, remember, is supposed to fit the crime, not the criminal. When the sentence has been served, the warden of the penitentiary signs a certificate to that effect, and the prisoner rejoins society—*even though it may be obvious that the punishment has worked no cure and indeed may have intensified the prisoner's criminal impulses.* On the other hand, an inmate of a mental hospital is released only when certified by the staff as cured, or at least not dangerous to himself or others. —DAVID L. BAZELON, "The Awesome Decision"

Coordinated elements may be added to the main ideas as afterthoughts:

As the automobile became more general, the various tumult of our native land subsided, and now that nearly everyone has at least one car, scarcely one American in fifteen lives anywhere near his birthplace, and Americans drift about their continent as easily as tumbleweeds, and with as much sense of direction or purpose.

—JOHN KEATS, *The Insolent Chariots*

Modern expository prose depends on a mixture of moderately periodic and loose sentences. How many or how few, and the degree of emphasis in each, depend on the writer and the context. The following sentences are periodic, but are varied in the degree of emphasis they achieve so that they avoid the ponderous:

The cozy liberal superstition about urbanization, the fatalistic optimism that the more citified we get the more civilized we become, the hypothesis that integration is a sort of hidden dividend of urbanization would not seem to be sustained by recent experience. The liberal urban middle class that was supposed to have such a leavening and liberating effect on racial prejudices has picked up and moved out to the suburbs—white middle class to all-white suburbs, and black middle class to all-Negro suburbs. They motor in from their respective segregated retreats occasionally to attend interracial meetings and hear speakers deplore problems of urban decay, but their personal response to those problems is withdrawal.

—C. VANN WOODWARD, "The North and the South of It"

The passage is an excellent model to follow in seeking a middle ground between excessive looseness and periodic construction.

EXPANDING THE SENTENCE

Like the sentences we speak, the sentences we write grow by the addition of details—presented in words, phrases, clauses so arranged that the focus of the sentence is maintained. The sentence of Lawrence Durrell quoted earlier moves from a general statement

> The Nile was rising

to specific detail that completes the impression:

> filling the air with the dank summer moisture of its yearly inundations, climbing the stone wall at the bottom of the Embassy garden inch by slimy inch.

When ideas are coordinated in the sentence, further expansion is possible; as we have seen, a large number of modifiers reach the limit of intelligibility rather quickly, without coordination. The following series of sentences begins with short ones, each containing a single idea; the final sentence presents one connected experience, controlled by a point of view, but depending on coordination:

> I trotted by the ball. Its trade name "Duke" was face up. The referee was waiting, astride it, a whistle at the end of a black cord dangling from his neck. The offensive team in their blue jerseys, about ten yards back, on their own twenty-yard line, moved and collected in the huddle formation as I came up, and I slowed, and walked toward them, trying to be calm about it, almost lazying up to them to see what could be done. —GEORGE PLIMPTON, Paper Lion

A shift to another point of view or another stage in the episode would require a new sentence. So long as the grammatical reference remains clear and the focus does not veer, the number of coordinate or subordinate elements will not seem excessive.

PARALLELISM

Coordinate structures in English are naturally parallel, and few speakers or writers misuse them. The sentence

> We are going to swim and play tennis.

contains parallel structures that we achieve without planning or thought. We are unlikely to speak or write

> We are going to swim and playing tennis.

Mistakes of this sort are easily corrected if we remember that words and phrases that serve the same grammatical function (for example, subjects or predicates of the same verb) ordinarily have the same grammatical form. Thus it is customary to make the sentence elements that follow correlatives (*either/or, not only/but also*) grammatically parallel:

> *Either we are going to swim or we are going to play tennis.*
>   [clauses]
> We are going *either to swim* or *to play tennis.* [phrases]
> INFORMAL: We are going either to swim or play tennis.

> America represents for Hawthorne *not only* the marginal settlement, set between corrupt civilization and unredeemed nature, *but also* the rule of moral law in the place of self-justifying passion or cynical gallantry [nominal phrases]
>   —LESLIE FIEDLER, *Love and Death in the American Novel*

You will discover that parallelism is one of the easiest kinds of sentence construction to master and, cultivated in moderation, is a highly effective means to concision and properly distributed emphasis. Compare the following sentences:

Dealing with men is as fine an art as it is to deal with ships.	To deal with men is as fine an art as it is to deal with ships.

—JOSEPH CONRAD,
The Mirror of the Sea

The absence of parallelism in the first sentence creates awkwardness; more seriously, the sentence obscures the parallelism of the ideas. Here is another example of parallel construction that underscores the parallelism in ideas:

> *To be able to be aware of fear,* then, without giving in to anxiety; *to train* our fear in the face of anxiety to remain an accurate measure and warning of that which man must fear— this is a necessary condition for a judicious frame of mind.
>   —ERIK H. ERIKSON, *Childhood and Society*

Indeed, whole clauses may be given special emphasis by making them parallel in structure:

> *Never before has* the intelligence of man placed so much material power at his disposal; *never before has* he employed the power at his disposal for the realization of purposes more diverse or more irreconcilable.

—CARL BECKER, *Modern Democracy*

In the previous paragraph we suggested that parallelism be cultivated in moderation. Strict parallelism carried through a paragraph or an essay will make your writing seem excessively formal and stiff; sentences that depart too far from the natural rhythms and stresses of the spoken idiom will probably seem strained and artificial to the modern reader. Here is how one writer varies a series of predicates slightly: The sentence conveys the thoughts of a young lady awakening in an old house:

> Too many people have been born here, and have wept too much here, and have laughed too much, and have been too angry and outrageous with each other here.
>   —KATHERINE ANNE PORTER, "Pale Horse, Pale Rider"

The word *here* gains its impact from its omission in the third predicate of the series. One final point should be made. A series of parallel elements may be varied in length and even in construction:

> Apart from ethnic differences, the very nature of migrancy makes it possible to isolate certain values and social characteristics commonly found among migrants: a spirit of resignation; a sense of being trapped; an astonishing lack of bitterness; a fierce family loyalty; a buoyant, often subtle wit; a tendency to spend money, when they have it, to meet not only immediate needs but immediate desires; a longing to be somebody, manifested sometimes as a blatant groping for status, more often as a craving for recognition as a human being; a longing for a better life for their children; a quick and generous sympathy for neighbors in trouble; a high incidence of stamina and courage.
>   —LOUISA R. SHOTWELL, *The Harvesters*

Were the parallel elements approximately the same length, this long sentence would be monotonous.

BALANCE

Parallel elements that contain similar or identical ideas are said to be in balance. Before the twentieth century, many writers like the English essayist and historian Macaulay favored a symmetrical and rhythmical balancing of phrases and clauses:

> To reverse the rod, to spell the charm backward, to break the ties which bound a stupefied people to the seat of enchantment, was the noble aim of Milton. To this all his public conduct was directed. For this he joined the Presbyterians; for this he forsook them. He fought their perilous battle; but he turned away with disdain from their insolent triumph.
>   —THOMAS BABINGTON MACAULAY, *Milton*

Today this kind of balance is reserved for intensely dramatic statements:

I cannot sit idly by in Atlanta and not be concerned about what happens in Birmingham. Injustice anywhere is a threat to justice everywhere. We are caught in an inescapable network of mutuality, tied in a single garment of destiny. Whatever affects one directly, affects all indirectly.
—MARTIN LUTHER KING, JR., "Letter from Birmingham Jail"

Most modern writers, in less highly charged contexts, balance their sentences with much less elaboration. In the following sentences, the opening nominal clauses are balanced; the remainder of the sentences are varied, however:

Grace strikes us when we are in great pain and restlessness. It strikes us when we walk through the dark valley of a meaningless and empty life. It strikes us when we feel that our separation is deeper than usual, because we have violated another life, a life which we loved, or from which we were estranged. It strikes us when our disgust for our own being, our indifference, our weakness, our hostility, and our lack of direction and composure have become intolerable to us.
—PAUL TILLICH, "You Are Accepted"

Sometimes phrases or independent clauses, containing almost the same number of words, are balanced for the purpose of contrast:

The hero exposes to all mankind unsuspected possibilities of conception, unimagined resources of strength.
—ARTHUR M. SCHLESINGER, JR., "The Decline of Heroes"

There are no barbarian hosts without the gates, but there are plenty of potential barbarians within them.
—CARL BECKER, Modern Democracy

Finally, balance is sometimes achieved by juxtaposing clauses containing the same, or almost the same, number of words without regard to exact grammatical parallelism:

War does one good—it teaches people geography.
—WILL DURANT, The Age of Faith

The advice given about periodic sentence construction—to cultivate it in moderation—applies also to balance.

ANTITHESIS

Contrasting ideas, parallel in construction and sometimes balanced, gain in impact:

Shallow understanding from people of good will is more frustrating than absolute misunderstanding from people of ill will. Lukewarm acceptance is much more bewildering than outright rejection.

—MARTIN LUTHER KING, JR., "Letter from Birmingham Jail"

The more exact the parallelism, the clearer the contrast will be.

LOOSE	EXACT
If a free society cannot help the numerous poor, it cannot save the few who are rich.	If a free society cannot help the many who are poor, it cannot save the few who are rich.
[The essential contrast does not immediately stand out.]	—JOHN F. KENNEDY, *Inaugural Address*
	[The first idea is subordinated to good effect. Not only the verbs but also the complements are parallel and stand out.]
Dante gives us a philosophical goal, and we have to recall and retrace the journey; Goethe provides us with a philosophic journey; we must divine the goal.	Dante gives us a philosophical goal, and we have to recall and retrace the journey; Goethe gives us a philosophic journey, and we have to divine the goal.
[The variations obscure the contrast of ideas.]	—GEORGE SANTAYANA, *Three Philosophical Poets*

LENGTH

There is no necessary relation between the length of a sentence and the action or thought it expresses. Sentence length is largely a matter of style—of characteristic ways of expressing ideas, shaped by a knowledge of effective communication in the past and sometimes by a desire to express experience and thought in a new way. George Plimpton, whose sentences were quoted earlier, characteristically unites several actions in a long sentence that could have been broken up:

> Watching his keys, the blockers form, he knew that the ball had been shoveled to Brown on an end sweep toward him, and moving desperately he got by the blockers and to him, and hauled him down, the first time he could remember ever doing it alone, and when he started to get up he discovered the force of the impact and Brown's momentum had knocked the face bar off his helmet and it was lying on his chest. —*Paper Lion*

Managing a sentence of this length, as we noted earlier, depends on keeping the reference of ideas clear.

In skilled writing, the length of the sentence varies according to the rhythm of thought. In the following passage the short sentences at the end suggest a quickening of thought, an intense response:

Then he looked wistfully out of the window. Already he was a prisoner of industrialism. Large sunflowers stared over the old red wall of the garden opposite, looking in their jolly way down on the women who were hurrying with something for dinner. The valley was full of corn, brightening in the sun. Two collieries, among the fields, waved their small white plumes of steam. Far off on the hills were the woods of Annesley, dark and fascinating. Already his heart went down. He was being taken into bondage. His freedom in the beloved home valley was going now.

—D. H. LAWRENCE, *Sons and Lovers*

The following passages show that a similar mood can be conveyed through different lengths of sentence and their construction. The first passage isolates the perceptions of the narrator; the second combines them in a single long sentence:

Paul went out to play with the rest. Down in the great trough of twilight, tiny clusters of lights burned where the pits were. A few last colliers straggled up the dim field path. The lamplighter came along. No more colliers came. Darkness shut down over the valley; work was done. It was night.

—*Ibid.*

Our shouts echoed in the silent street. The career of our play brought us through the dark muddy lanes behind the houses where we ran the gauntlet of the rough tribes from the cottages, to the back doors of the dark dripping gardens where odors arose from the ashpits, to the dark odorous stables where a coachman smoothed and combed the horse or shook music from the buckled harness.   —JAMES JOYCE, "Araby"

SHORT SENTENCES

Short sentences may be used in different ways for special emphasis. In the following passage very short sentences are used to describe the feelings of a doctor caught in a paralyzing fog, in particular, the disconnections of the total experience:

The case was an old man and he had died all of a sudden. Acute cardiac dilation. When we were ready, we started back. Then I began to feel sick. The fog was getting me. There was an awful tickle in my throat. I was coughing and ready to vomit. I called to my driver that I had to stop and get out. He was ready to stop, I guess. Already he had walked four or five miles. But I envied him. He was well and I was awful sick.

—BERTON ROUECHÉ, "The Fog"

A series of this many short sentences is exceptional. In ordinary exposition, short sentences usually follow or are mixed with long ones, sometimes to provide special emphasis:

He looked suddenly stricken, shrunken, immensely old, as though the frightful impact of the bullet had paralyzed him without knocking him down. At last, after what seemed a long time—it might have been five seconds, I dare say—he sagged flabbily to his knees. His mouth slobbered. An enormous senility seemed to have settled upon him.

—GEORGE ORWELL, "Shooting an Elephant"

A most effective kind of sentence arrangement employs a series of short sentences to build to a relatively long one:

The problems of a tortured, convulsive humanity stagger the nation. Unprecedented times demand of us unprecedented behavior. The task that confronts us will try our souls. It will exact a high price in discipline of mind and in austerity of spirit. It will determine whether we are worthy of our high place in the world, whether we are worthy of our forefathers who converted a wilderness into a country, fair and free, and left to us all the riches, material and spiritual, that they wrought in pain.

—ADLAI STEVENSON, Major Campaign Speeches

CLIMAX

As in the paragraph, arranging ideas in a sentence in the order of increasing importance, or ending with the most emphatic idea—even without the buildup we find in the passage just quoted—produces a sense of climax:

If the elephant charged and I missed him, I should have about as much chance as a toad under a steam-roller.

—GEORGE ORWELL, "Shooting an Elephant"

To those peoples in the huts and villages of half the globe struggling to break the bonds of mass misery, we pledge our best efforts to help them help themselves, for whatever period is required—not because the Communists may be doing it, not because we seek their votes, but because it is right.

—JOHN F. KENNEDY, Inaugural Address

When the ideas are less dramatic the sense of climax is less pronounced, as in the following sentences—each of which builds to a climax. Note that the concluding sentence of the paragraph restates the opening one:

> The essence of the corporate state is that it is relentlessly single-minded; it has just one value, the value of technology as represented by organization, efficiency, growth, progress. No other value is allowed to interfere with this one—not amenity, not beauty, not community, not even the supreme value of life itself. Thus, the state is essentially mindless; it has only one idea, and it merely rolls along, never stopping to think, consider, balance, judge. Only such single-valued mindlessness would cut the last redwoods, pollute the most beautiful beaches, invent devices to injure and destroy plant and human life. To have just one value is to be a machine.
> —CHARLES A. REICH, *The Greening of America*

ANTICLIMAX

Anticlimax results when the natural rise in importance is interrupted:

CLIMAX

In all the brouhaha about teenagers we are inclined to forget, it seems to me, that they are primarily reflections of us, of our foibles and fumblings and aspirations, our fears and frustrations, our hopes and our beliefs. —RUSSELL LYNES, "Teenagers in the Looking Glass"

ANTICLIMAX

In all the brouhaha about teenagers we are inclined to forget that they are primarily reflections of us, our hopes and beliefs, our fears and frustrations, our aspirations and foibles and fumblings, it seems to me.

It should be noted that anticlimax can be used to achieve a particular kind of irony:

> The Chief Justice was rich, quiet, and infamous.
> —THOMAS BABINGTON MACAULAY, *Warren Hastings*

INCOMPLETE SENTENCES

Dependent clauses are set apart from the main clause they modify or complete, only for special emphasis. The following example is perhaps the one most commonly found:

In the case of any person whose judgment is really deserving of confidence, how has it become so? Because he has kept his mind open to criticism of his opinions and conduct.

—JOHN STUART MILL, *On Liberty*

Setting off single phrases is less common and tends to suggest the informality of conversation:

I believe in aristocracy, though—if that is the right word, and if a democrat may use it. Not an aristocracy of power, based upon rank and influence, but an aristocracy of the sensitive, the considerate and the plucky.

—E. M. FORSTER, "What I Believe"

One must be fond of people and trust them if one is not to make a mess of life, and it is therefore essential that they should not let one down. They often do. The moral of which is that I must, myself, be as reliable as possible, and this I try to be.   —*Ibid.*

The road. Ah, the road. Let us think of *this* together, you and I.   —JOHN KEATS, *The Insolent Chariots*

AWKWARD OMISSION OF WORDS

Omitting words that are redundant or needless is important in achieving concision. Careless omission may obscure or confuse your meaning. The following sentences are awkward or confusing:

He asked [that] his parents be told.

The rumor going around is [that] his business is failing.

The sun was out and the clouds [were] drifting east.

He's interested [in] and gentle with animals.

He has [been] and will continue to be president.

He wants to go if she is [going].

An Olds engine is larger than a Volkswagen [engine].

We usually hear what is wrong when we speak sentences like these. Writing them, we need to imagine how the sentences will sound to another reader. It is preferable to repeat a word rather than risk misunderstanding, even if the repetition *sounds* awkward.

SENTENCE RHYTHM

In poetry the meter of a line registers forcibly when it is in tension with the rhythm of natural phrases. The meter of these words of Juliet, awaiting Romeo after their wedding, is iambic (an unstressed syllable, or lightly stressed syllable, is followed by a stressed):

> Gallop apace, you fiery-footed steeds,
>
> Towards Phoebus' lodging; || such a waggoner
>
> As Phaethon would whip you to the west,
>
> And bring in cloudy night immediately.

It is impossible to read these lines in strict iambic rhythm or scan them easily, in part because not all of the feet are iambic (Gallop) and because the relative stresses of certain phrases break the regular pattern:

> Gallop apace | you fiery-footed steeds |
> Towards Phoebus' lodging | such a waggoner
> As Phaethon | would whip you | to the west
> And bring in cloudy night | immediately.

These variations suggest the inflections of the voice and modulations of feeling—so skillfully that the rhythm does not call attention to itself.

All effective sentences, whether they occur in prose or poetry, have their distinctive rhythm. How marked and regular the rhythm is depends on the content and mood. The following lines, arranged as poetry by John S. Barnes, occur in a prose novel of Thomas Wolfe:

> The river is a tide of moving waters:
>
> By night it floods the pockets of the earth.
>
> By night it drinks strange time, dark time.

Wolfe's prose is highly charged with feeling; the markedly regular rhythm is thus appropriate. The following sentences show that similar rhythmic patterns intensify the statements considerably:

[The American Dream] Not just an idea, but a condition: a living human condition designed to be coeval with the birth of America itself, engendered created and simultaneous with the very air and word America, which at that one stroke, one instant, should cover the whole earth with one simultaneous suspiration like air or light.

—WILLIAM FAULKNER, "On Privacy"

The house and all that was in it had now descended deep be-
neath the gradual spiral it had sunk through; it lay formal
under the order of entire silence.

> —JAMES AGEE, *Let Us Now Praise Famous Men*

The dominant rhythm of both sentences is iambic; but the pattern is
broken by varied phrasal rhythms. As Faulkner's sentence builds to a
climax, the iambic rhythm becomes increasingly regular; Agee's sentence seeks the reverse effect through the same means.

Even when the content calls for intensification, highly rhythmic
patterns should be used sparingly. A constant rhythmic prose, without variation, will produce monotony and obscure the meaning. The
following sentence shows how *occasional* balancing of phrases can
heighten feeling and at the same time avoid monotony or undue
intensification:

> Weeping willows are great amber fountains beside the ponds,
> and along the watercourses at least a dozen varieties of lesser
> willows glow red and russet as though some secret incandes-
> cent fluid coursed their stems.
>
> —HAL BORLAND, "The Vital Willows"

Prose that lacks natural rhythm or alliterates or falls into marked patterns, without concern for meaning, will grate the ear or distract the
reader from the content. The following sentences fall down on one
or more of these counts:

> The dynamic force of habit taken in *con*nection with the *con*-
> tinuity of habits with one another explains the unity of *char*-
> acter and *con*duct, or speaking more *concr*etely of motive and
> act, will and deed.
>
> —JOHN DEWEY, *Human Nature and Conduct*
> [excessive alliteration]

> Habit means *s*pecial *s*en*s*itivene*ss* or ac*c*e*ss*ibility to *c*ertain
> cla*ss*es of *s*timuli, *s*tanding predilection*s* and aver*s*ion*s*, *r*ather
> than ba*r*e *r*ecu*rr*ence of *s*pecific act*s*.
>
> —*Ibid.* [excessive alliteration and consonance—*s* and *r*]

H. W. Fowler's advice on rhythmic speech and writing is worth quoting. Fowler states:

> The prose writer's best guide to rhythm is not his own experi-
> ments in, or other people's rules for, particular cadences and
> stress-schemes, but an instinct for the difference between what
> sounds right and what sounds wrong. It is an instinct culti-
> vable by those on whom nature has not bestowed it, but on
> one condition only—that they will make a practice of reading
> aloud. That test soon divides matter, even for a far from sen-

sitive ear, into what reads well and what reads tamely, haltingly, jerkily, lopsidedly, top-heavily, or otherwise badly. . . .
In all this, reading aloud need not be taken quite literally; there is an art of tacit reading aloud . . . reading with the eye and not the mouth, that is, but being as fully aware of the unuttered sound as of the sense.

—*Modern English Usage* (London: Oxford University Press, 1937), pp. 504–05

EXERCISES

1. Analyze the style of thought in a recorded transcription of the speech of your classmates. Compare this style with specimens of their writing and comment on significant similarities and differences.

2. Correct or improve the following sentences. Indicate the basis of the fault.

a. He said a suit my size had come in and would I try it on.

b. There are rotten cherries in the carton picked by you.

c. Her reputation was her chocolate cake, not to mention her cherry pie.

d. The beginning writer can learn something from reading closely for style, but don't imitate apishly.

e. Hanson was not reelected because of his speeches on restrictive tariffs.

f. John helped Bill with the loading, despite his hostility.

g. Interesting are the books I read during vacation.

h. To keep alive during the winter, you should water these shrubs heavily in the fall.

i. The manager wants to, after school starts and he knows what his needs are, hire boys to bag groceries.

j. She explained yesterday her car had broken down.

k. The children on the swings ignored the calls of their mothers, pushing one another gleefully.

l. He entered the library by the back entrance.

m. I think his idea the most original of the concepts presented.

n. Plato and Aristotle walked through the garden discussing politics. The author of the *Apology* spoke to the future teacher of Alexander, who tried to conquer the world, not as a teacher but as a friend.

o. In Idaho I paid more for electricity than Ohio.

p. We always have and always will be supporters of his policies.

3. Determine the extent to which each of the following sentences is periodic. Rewrite two of them as loose sentences and comment on the relative effectiveness of the revisions.

a. The ancient Greeks thought that the fundamental forms of matter—

out of which all other forms could be produced—were air, earth, fire and water. In the nineteenth century all matter was found to be composed of atoms of what were termed the chemical elements—hydrogen, helium, carbon, neon, gold, uranium, to name a few.—William Alfred Fowler, "The Origin of the Elements"

b. When it became evident that Jews were escaping to Sweden by boat, Germans used police dogs to try to sniff out the human cargo aboard the ships. To overcome this hazard, a Danish scientist concocted a powder made of dried human blood and cocaine which, when dusted on the decks of the ships, completely deadened the dogs' sense of smell—Nora Levin, *The Holocaust*.

c. When the Germans came aboard with their dogs, the seamen, pretending to blow their noses, would let the gray powder fall to the decks near the dogs.—*Ibid.*

4. Recast the following sentences with changes of emphasis but without changes of meaning. Comment on the relative effectiveness of the revision.

a. There was once a great painter of water dragons who worked only from hearsay. Taking pity on his blindness, a real dragon swam up out of the pond and appeared to the artist—who died of fright.—Alexander Eliot, "The Sense of Truth"

b. Life as we live it is tragic because it is unreal. Born to reality, living to penetrate reality, we refuse even to believe in it.—*Ibid.*

c. Art, because it imagines the individual within a given situation, reaffirms the "I" in each one of us and opens up the possibility of a life where people do not merely live in better conditions, but where they really might be themselves—their better selves.—Stephen Spender, "The Connecting Imagination"

5. Combine the following series of sentences into larger sentences. Aim for parallelism where possible but vary the pattern to avoid stiffness and excessive formality; change words and phrases to conform to modern usage. The original sentences are by Samuel Johnson.

> Thus they rose in the morning. They lay down at night. They were pleased with each other. They were pleased with themselves. All but Rasselas was pleased. In the twenty-sixth year of his life, Rasselas began to withdraw himself from their pastimes. He withdrew from their assemblies. He began delighting in solitary walks. He delighted in silent meditation. He often sat before tables covered with luxury. He forgot to taste the dainties that were placed before him. He rose abruptly in the midst of the song. He retired hastily beyond the sound of music. His attendants observed the change. They endeavored to renew his love of pleasure. He neglected their officiousness. He repulsed their invitations. He spent day after day on the banks of rivulets. Trees sheltered these rivulets. Here he sometimes listened to the birds in the branches. He sometimes observed the fish playing in the

stream. Anon he cast his eyes upon the pastures. He observed the mountains filled with animals. Some of these were biting the herbage. Some were sleeping among the bushes.

6. Rewrite the following passage so that it conforms to modern usage. Then comment on the important differences between your revision and the original.

> The Puritans were men whose minds had derived a peculiar character from the daily contemplation of superior beings and eternal interests. Not content with acknowledging, in general terms, an overruling Providence, they habitually ascribed every event to the will of the Great Being, for whose power nothing was too vast, for whose inspection nothing was too minute. To know him, to serve him, to enjoy him, was with them the great end of existence. They rejected with contempt the ceremonious homage which other sects substituted for the pure worship of the soul. Instead of catching occasional glimpses of the Deity through an obscuring veil, they aspired to gaze full on his intolerable brightness, and to commune with him face to face. Hence originated their contempt for terrestrial distinctions. The difference between the greatest and the meanest of mankind seemed to vanish, when compared with the boundless interval which separated the whole race from him on whom their own eyes were constantly fixed. They recognized no title to superiority but his favor; and, confident of that favor, they despised all the accomplishments and all the dignities of the world. If they were unacquainted with the works of philosophers and poets, they were deeply read in the oracles of God. If their names were not found in the registers of heralds, they were recorded in the Book of Life. If their steps were not accompanied by a splendid train of menials, legions of ministering angels had charge over them.—Thomas Babington Macaulay, *Milton*

7. The following sentence is built through an addition of modifiers;

> The trees now were taller, much taller, and farther apart, with now too a greater feeling of distance beyond them; and at the ends of the aisles of vision thus opened into blue light were tremendous and extraordinarily beautiful buildings, of an unimaginable intricacy, which teased the eye, and sent a sensation as of *tracing* something into the fingertips.—Conrad Aiken, "Prologue to an Autobiography"

Use the following core sentences to build longer ones through similar additions.

a. The character of the university had changed.

b. The students were less easy to please than they had been.

c. The mood of the country altered as the war progressed.

8. Dorothy L. Sayers, in an essay on plain English, quotes the following sentence of what she terms the "telegraphic style":

He found Parliament boring, the work futile, except in its more stormy moments to which he contributed twice by threatening the House to keep them sitting all night, including the Thursday before one Easter recess when legislators were anxious to get their trains out of London, holiday bound.

She comments that "the telegraphist revels in involved syntax." What is wrong with the sentence she quotes?

PUNC-
TUATION

Many sentences break an accustomed pattern to express a way of thought or action more effectively. But, as we have seen, the break must not be too great; it must not depart too far from familiar patterns. This same aspect of style applies to punctuation. A departure from accustomed use registers more forcibly when it is infrequent; an occasional dash is more apt to catch the attention than a string of dashes within a single paragraph or page. It is important, then, that you be aware of the ordinary uses of punctuation and also of special uses and their effects. The following examples may be helpful.

THE COMMA WITH INDEPENDENT CLAUSES

The comma normally marks a minor pause and is occasionally omitted in a short sentence:

> The unhappy Captain had no one to hate and for the past months he had been miserable.
> —CARSON MCCULLERS, *Reflections in a Golden Eye*

The comma usually occurs where the clauses are long or the subject of the second clause is different from the first:

> The Captain used Seconal, and his habit was of such long standing that one capsule had no effect on him.   —*Ibid.*

If the coordinating conjunction is omitted, a semicolon normally is used:

The human race seems doomed to run, intellectually, on its
lowest gear. Sound ideas, when by chance they become articulate, annoy it and terrify it; it prefers the sempiternal slobber.
—H. L. MENCKEN, "Forgotten Men"

Complementary independent clauses usually are punctuated by a
comma or a colon (see p. 59) and not a semicolon:

Man proposes, God disposes.

The comma is also used by some writers in informal sentences where
the pitch of the voice would normally remain unchanged:

But actual life is not like that, it doesn't have a total meaning,
it is simply a wild confusion of events from which we have to
select what we think significant for ourselves.
—JOYCE CARY, Art and Reality

The correct use of the comma in these sentences should not be confused with the comma fault (see p. 59)—the incorrect use of a
comma between independent clauses not connected by a conjunction
but separated by a noticeable drop in pitch:

I'm going to the movie at school, I don't know what time it
will end, but I should be home before eleven.

THE COMMA WITH NONRESTRICTIVE MODIFIERS

A nonrestrictive element is a word, phrase, or clause considered unessential to the meaning of the sentence:

First, write your name on the cover of the booklet.
The children, who had been swimming, ran to their mothers.

If the modifiers were omitted these sentences would have the same
meaning. In the second sentence we know who the children are; the
dependent clause provides important but not essential information. It
would be essential only if it identified the children:

The children who had been swimming ran to their mothers;
the children who had been playing on the swings ran to the
sandpile.

Restrictive elements are essential to the meaning of the sentence:

A philosopher has always been thought of as someone who
tries to achieve a complete view of the universe as a whole,
and of man's place in the universe; he has traditionally been
expected to answer those questions about the design and purpose of the universe, and of human life, which the various

special sciences do not claim to answer; philosophers have generally been conceived as unusually wise or all-comprehending men whose systems are answers to those large, vague questions about the purpose of human existence *which present themselves to most people at some period of their lives.*

—STUART HAMPSHIRE, *Spinoza*

The two *which* clauses are restrictive because they identify "those questions" and the "large, vague questions"; the *who* clause toward the beginning of the sentence is restrictive because it identifies the "someone." In the following sentences the dependent clauses limit or qualify the independent clauses and consequently are not set off:

Helium is common in stars compared with other elements because it is produced in appreciable quantities inside them. The abundances of the rest of the elements are so small that it is natural to ask whether all the material in the Universe started its life as hydrogen.

—FRED HOYLE, *The Nature of the Universe*

If the dependent clause introduces the sentence, it may be set off regardless of how it restricts or qualifies the independent clause:

When a star like the Sun shrinks to about the size of the Earth a new form of pressure begins to develop inside. This new pressure is important because it operates without a high temperature's being necessary. When it comes into action, it will allow a star like the Sun to cool off without any further collapse occurring. —*Ibid.*

It should be stressed that the clause is restrictive if it is considered essential. The dependent clause is considered to be restrictive:

Beyond the drawing room is a commodious library that contains few books. —MARK SCHORER, *The World We Imagine*

The sentence could be rewritten:

Beyond the drawing room is a commodious library, which contains few books.

COMMAS WITH SERIES

Commas are used to separate members of a series, the day and year in dates, and parts of an address:

Albert Einstein, born on March 14, 1879, at Ulm, Germany, came to the United States in 1932, and lived and died in Princeton, New Jersey.

The omission of commas in series depends on the function of the modifiers. In the sentence

> They were the daughters of a spry, hardworking little washer-woman, who went about from house to house by the day.
> —KATHERINE MANSFIELD, "The Doll's House"

the noun phrase "little washerwoman" is modified by two coordinate adjectives. "Hardworking" and "little" could be separated by a comma if they were reversed ("spry, little, hardworking washerwoman"). In the following sentence the modifying words are not all coordinate:

> They all turned in natural curiosity and saw indeed a very beautiful slender girl, her head shining like a silver yellow peony above her rather skimpy black dress.
> —KATHERINE ANNE PORTER, "The Leaning Tower"

In the phrase "a very beautiful slender girl," "very" modifies "beautiful"; the phrase "very beautiful" modifies the noun phrase "slender girl." A comma might have been introduced, however, because "beautiful" and "slender" can be reversed ("beautiful, slender girl"). In the second phrase "a silver yellow peony," "silver" modifies "yellow" and not "peony": a comma is not optional.

THE COMMA TO AVOID AMBIGUITY

Compare the following:

AMBIGUOUS	CLEAR
Outside the house looked shabby.	Outside, the house looked shabby.
The rooms above all looked clean.	The rooms, above all, looked clean.
After milking the farmer watered the stock.	After milking, the farmer watered the stock.

THE SEMICOLON

The semicolon joins independent clauses where the conjunction is omitted. It also joins ideas that the writer wishes to indicate are coordinate:

> She was the only person in the world who knew of a certain woeful shortcoming in his nature; Captain Penderton was inclined to be a thief.
> —CARSON MCCULLERS, *Reflections in a Golden Eye*

> What appears to the organization man as an almost criminal insubordination is to the trained professional a vital necessity;

unless he is allowed to follow his own judgment in matters pertaining to his specialty, he becomes a hack.

—HYMAN RICKOVER, *Education and Freedom*

Everywhere Mozart went he made for himself bitter enemies. Every mediocrity who met him immediately hated him; only those who loved music more than themselves admired and loved him; the egoists and careerists immediately recognized him as not one of their kidney and detested his superiority, which they called arrogance.   —W. J. TURNER, *Mozart*

The semicolon always occurs before adverbials that serve as conjunctions—*thus, however, therefore, furthermore, on the other hand, on the contrary, indeed,* etc.—if a period is not used:

There are three or four reasons why we should go; indeed, there are more reasons than these.

In addition, the semicolon is often used to suggest an afterthought or, as in the following sentence, a strong pause:

We shall have occasion to discuss the nature of metaphor more exactly; and perhaps it will suffice for the moment to declare my conviction that true metaphor, so far from being an ornament, has very little to do even with an act of comparison.   —JOHN MIDDLETON MURRY, *The Problem of Style*

Infrequently it introduces abbreviated clauses:

I regarded myself as a wallflower; I did not like my face, and not many of my "best" clothes; was an introvert.

—MARIANNE MOORE, "If I Were Sixteen Today"

THE SEMICOLON WITH SERIES

The semicolon is used to separate large sentence elements, some of which may contain commas:

In his sacred role, as prophet, scholar, or artist, the intellectual is hedged about by certain sanctions—imperfectly observed and respected of course, but still effective: he has his privacy, perhaps his anonymity, in the interstices of modern urban civilization; he commands a certain respect for what seem to be his self-denying qualities; he benefits, if he is an academic, from the imperfectly established but operative principle of academic freedom; he has foundations, libraries, publishing houses, museums, as well as universities, at his service.

—RICHARD HOFSTADTER, *Anti-Intellectualism in American Life*

And it may punctuate an abbreviated series:

> But the peculiar evil of silencing the expression of an opinion
> is, that it is robbing the human race; posterity as well as the
> existing generation; those who dissent from the opinion, still
> more than those who hold it.
> —JOHN STUART MILL, On Liberty

THE COLON

The colon separates independent clauses when the second explains
or develops the first:

> This fact seems to emerge from our investigation: we are not
> omnipotent in the field of musical creation.
> —PAUL HINDEMITH, A Composer's World

> Not merely does technology claim priority in human affairs:
> it places the demand for constant technological change above
> any considerations of its own efficiency, its own continuity, or
> even, ironically enough, its own capacity to survive.
> —LEWIS MUMFORD, The Pentagon of Power

We look to the second clause to complete the first; the two clauses
are like those sentences in which a comma is used to indicate this
relationship:

> Man proposes, God disposes.

The colon is a more formal way to show this; however, it is less frequent in very short sentences like the above.

The colon may substitute for a dash to indicate a final appositive:

> The physics of the twentieth century bears one signature writ
> very large: Albert Einstein.
> —PHILIP MORRISON, "Cause, Chance, and Creation"

The first word following a colon is capitalized if it introduces a direct
quotation or a series of parallel or complementary statements:

> The thing about him was the extraordinary sense he gave to
> being alive: This makes his death so grotesque and unbeliev-
> able. No one had such vitality of personality—a vitality so
> superbly disciplined that it sometimes left the impression of
> cool detachment, but imbuing everything he thought or did
> with an intense concentration and power.
> —ARTHUR M. SCHLESINGER, JR.,
> "A Eulogy: John Fitzgerald Kennedy"

THE DASH

The dash is commonly used to set off a final appositive or to make an abrupt interruption of thought:

> For the American of the nineteenth century equality became, above all, equality of opportunity—an equal start in a competitive struggle.
> —JAMES B. CONANT, *The American High School Today*

In the sentence

> To fill the hour—that is happiness.
> —RALPH WALDO EMERSON, "Experience"

the dash makes the pause abrupt: "that" receives full emphasis. A colon, again, is usually more formal.

Dashes are the usual way of setting off a parenthetical question or exclamation:

> What made this emotion so overpowering was—how shall I define it?—the moral shock I received, as if something altogether monstrous, intolerable to thought and odious to the soul, had been thrust upon me unexpectedly.
> —JOSEPH CONRAD, *Heart of Darkness*

> When he spoke to women—how easily and insolently he spoke now!—they listened and laughed and looked at him sideways and dropped their eyelids over the admission, the invitation of their glance.   —ALDOUS HUXLEY, *Antic Hay*

An appositive coming in the middle of a sentence is set off with dashes unless it is being introduced parenthetically (in which case parentheses are needed):

> Pericles finds the foundations of these freedoms—political freedom, civil freedom, freedom from toil and want, and freedom from fear—in the spirit of the Athenians.
> —RICHARD MCKEON, *Thought, Action, and Passion*

Dashes can also be used to indicate an interruption of thought:

> "There hasn't been a drop of medicine or a mouthful of invalid food for months here. He was shamefully abandoned. A man like this, with such ideas. Shamefully! Shamefully! I—I—haven't slept for the last ten nights. . . ."
> —JOSEPH CONRAD, *Heart of Darkness*

DIRECT AND INDIRECT QUOTATIONS

Direct quotations appear inside double quotation marks. If the quotation itself contains another, single quotation marks are used. The following passage from an American edition of Conrad's *Lord Jim* is in quotation marks because Marlow, one of the narrators, is reporting the statement of Mr. Jones, the chief officer of Captain Brierly, who leaps from his ship following Jim's trial for desertion:

> " 'This was the last time I heard his voice, Captain Marlow. These are the last words he spoke in the hearing of any living human being, sir.' At this point the old chap's voice got quite unsteady. 'He was afraid the poor brute would jump after him, don't you see?' he pursued with a quaver. 'Yes, Captain Marlow. He set the log for me; he—would you believe it?—he put a drop of oil in it too. There was the oil-feeder where he left it near by. The boatswain's mate got the hose along aft to wash down at half-past five; by-and-by he knocks off and runs up on the bridge—"Will you please come aft, Mr. Jones," he says. "There's a funny thing. I don't like to touch it." It was Captain Brierly's gold chronometer watch carefully hung under the rail by its chain.' "

Notice that the words of the boatswain's mate appear inside double quotation marks.[1] In some sentences, indirect quotation may be used to avoid quoting one statement within another:

> He told the registrar, "The Dean told me I would have to get permission to take the course."

Periods and commas occur inside the final quotation marks, colons and semicolons outside. Question marks and exclamation points appear inside the quotation marks if they punctuate only the quoted material, and outside if they punctuate the complete sentence.

QUOTATION MARKS AND ITALICS

The chapter "The Reformation" in Crane Brinton's *A History of Western Morals*, or the article "When Art Becomes Propaganda," in the *Saturday Review*, or the poem "Sunday Morning" in *The Collected Poems of Wallace Stevens* appear within quotation marks to distinguish the chapter or article from the complete book or magazine. Short stories, essays, and short poems also appear within quotation marks. A long work like John Hersey's *Hiroshima* is italicized though it originally appeared in a magazine (*The New Yorker*). Italics are used for all long works, including newspapers (the *Akron Beacon-Journal*). Quotation marks are often used to call attention to a special word or phrase:

[1] In English editions today, this system of punctuation is reversed: direct quotations appear between single quotation marks; quotations within quotations appear between double quotation marks, and so on.

The medieval idea of "curteisye" is exemplified in "The Knight's Tale."

They should not, however, be used to call attention to an inappropriate phrase or to slang. If the word or phrase is inappropriate, punctuation will not improve it.

BRACKETS

Brackets are used to introduce a clarification or comment into a quotation, or a parenthesis within a parenthesis:

The newspaper editorial stated: "We despute [sic] his opinion." [Sic means that there has not been an error in quotation.]

The dispatch said: "The crowd greeted him [Senator Fulbright] with banners."

(The statement may be found in the British edition [London, 1922], the only edition in which it appears.)

THE APOSTROPHE

The apostrophe indicates contraction and possession.

The boy's hat isn't on the table. [possessive singular and contraction]

The boys' hats are on the table. [possessive plural]

The department's executive committee recommends the proposal. [a collective noun taking the possessive singular]

Jones's hat is on the table. Joan's hat is on the chair. [The 's in Jones's is necessary to avoid confusion with Joan's.]

The possessive 's may be omitted if its addition would make the word or phrase hard to pronounce and its omission would not create ambiguity in a particular context, as in the examples just cited. But the practice of writers varies here. Some prefer to include the final 's in all circumstances, ignoring difficulties of pronunciation, possibly on the assumption that, in writing, the 's is seen and not heard:

The most striking instance of Aristophanes's confidence and boldness is that he represents Cleon on the stage as a rascally Paphlagonian leather-seller.

—MATTHEW HODGART, *Satire*

This first theoretical argument by a poet on behalf of his own art was, of course, preceded by numerous discussions of other people's works, such as Aristophanes' biting criticism of Euripidean tragedy, Plato's reflections on the value of poetry, the *Poetics* of Aristotle, and many other examples which are now mostly lost to us.

—BRUNO SNELL, *Discovery of the Mind*

Compound words and phrases have the apostrophe on the final word:

> I am the executor of my father-in-law's will.
> He is the editor of William Byrd of Virginia's diaries.
> Bunthorne appears in Gilbert and Sullivan's *Patience*.

The apostrophe also indicates omissions and plurals: *the election of '72; the 1860's; and's, if's, and but's.*
The apostrophe is used with *of* in phrases like "a play of Shakespeare's" to indicate one of many of a kind:

> *Othello* is a play of Shakespeare's.

Finally, the use of the possessive with inanimate objects can be awkward:

> WEAK: The car's engine is making noises.
> BETTER: The engine of the car is making noises.

THE HYPHEN

There is no dependable rule to indicate what phrases are hyphenated; the dictionary must be consulted. A few practices are standard: Phrases used as adjectives, prefixes to proper names, and compound numbers are hyphenated:

> He was ticketed in a low-speed zone.
> He is the ex-Mayor Locher of Cleveland.
> COMPARE: He is the ex-mayor of Chicago.
> The city is twenty-five million dollars in the red.

Though we write *painless* and *antilabor*, we also write *hill-less* and *anti-imperialist* to make these words easier to read.

EXERCISES

1. Punctuate the following sentences without adding periods:

a. E. M. Forsters novel A Passage to India was published in 1924 fourteen years after his previous novel Howards End it was thought to be his last until the recent discovery of a manuscript.

b. There can be only one explanation for what happened he underestimated the speaking power of his opponent.

c. The issue of Newsweek that you requested is not in the library the May 2 issue of Time which contains the same information is available.

d. On the floor were a number of articles a box of old clothes books photographs of the family a stack of old magazines that reached nearly to the ceiling parts of a camera assorted dishes.

e. The articles on the floor the box of old clothes the stack of five year old magazines parts of a camera assorted dishes must have been there a long time since there was a thin layer of dust on them.

f. I am astonished no appalled that the damage should have been so great.

g. I fell to the floor can you understand the predicament I was in and waited for someone to open the door.

h. I thought there was nothing I could do but wait for help.

i. Put the box on the floor gently he asked it contains stereo equipment.

j. According to a recent book the track of the wolf Hitler was fascinated by the word wolf perhaps because his first name means fortunate wolf.

k. Sir Isaac Newton was born at woolsthorpe near grantham in lincolnshire england on December 25 1642 the son of a farmer who had died before his birth.

2. Punctuate the following passage, using not more than six periods.

> My father's tone of thought and feeling I now felt myself at a great distance from greater indeed than a full and calm explanation and reconsideration on both sides might have shown to exist in reality but my father was not one with whom calm and full explanations on fundamental points of doctrine could be expected at least with one whom he might consider as in some sort a deserter from his standard fortunately we were almost always in strong agreement on the political questions of the day which engrossed a large part of his interest and of his conversation on those matters of opinion on which we differed we talked little he knew that the habit of thinking for myself which his mode of education had fostered sometimes led me to opinions different from his and he perceived from time to time that I did not always tell him how different I expected no good but only pain to both of us from discussing our differences and I never expressed them but when he gave utterance to some opinion or feeling repugnant to mine in a manner which would have made it disingenuousness on my part to remain silent.
>
> —John Stuart Mill, *Autobiography*

3. In Joseph Conrad's *Chance*, the chief narrator Marlow reports the statements of another narrator Fyne concerning the heroine of the novel, Flora de Barral, who appears to have eloped with Fyne's brother-in-law, Captain Anthony. Punctuate the following words of Fyne. The double quotation marks enclose Marlow's account; the single, Fyne's:

> " 'I don't blame the girl he was saying he is infatuated with her anybody can see that why she got such a hold on him I cant

understand she said yes to him only for the sake of that fatuous swindling father of hers its perfectly plain if one thinks it over a moment one neednt even think of it we have it under her own hand in that letter to my wife she says she has acted unscrupulously she has owned up then for what else can it mean I should like to know and so they are to be married before that old idiot comes out he will be surprised commented Fyne suddenly in a strangely malignant tone he will be met at the jail door by a Mrs. Anthony a Mrs. Captain Anthony

DICTION

THE MORALITY OF WORDS

Our choice of words, more often than we realize, is a matter of morality, and not mere aptness. "In our time," George Orwell says, "political speech and writing are largely the defense of the indefensible." The language of politics consists mostly of

> . . . euphemism, question-begging and sheer cloudy vagueness. Defenseless villages are bombarded from the air, the inhabitants driven out into the countryside, the cattle machine-gunned, the huts set on fire with incendiary bullets: this is called *pacification*. Millions of peasants are robbed of their farms and sent trudging along the roads with no more than they can carry: this is called *transfer of population* or *rectification of frontiers*.
> —"Politics and the English Language" in *The Orwell Reader* (New York: Harcourt Brace Jovanovich, 1956), p. 363.[1]

[1]The Nazis spoke of the murder of six million Jews as the "final solution." Hermann Goering wrote to Heydrich in 1941: "I herewith commission you . . . to carry out all preparations with regard to . . . a *total solution* of the Jewish question in those territories of Europe which are under German influence . . . I furthermore charge you to submit to me as soon as possible a draft showing the . . . measures already taken for the execution of the intended *final solution* of the Jewish question." At Nuremberg Goering had reason to drop the euphemism: "The first time I learned of these terrible exterminations was right here in Nuremberg."—W. L. Shirer, *The Rise and Fall of the Third Reich* (New York: Simon and Schuster, 1960), p. 964.

No person is exempt from this indictment. In everyday situations we depend on euphemism and the like. In the area of "social maladjustment," the poor are the "culturally deprived"; slums are "depressed" or (somewhat more accurately) "blighted" neighborhoods; juvenile criminals are sometimes the "exceptional" or "unusual" (as are the "mentally retarded" or crippled—a tragic confusion). Euphemisms are dangerous because they disguise the causes and confuse the issue of responsibility, even when they are meant to soothe feelings or soften painful facts. Some euphemisms are no doubt needed for this purpose: the phrase "culturally deprived" at least looks in the direction of a solution, and perhaps causes the least pain.

Sensitivity to euphemism is only one aspect of that total sensitivity to language that marks the literate man. Through language we come to understand ourselves and the world; by putting an experience into words we discover its quality and meaning. Our capacity for rational thought and action exists in proportion to our command over words. Choosing the right word, then, is not merely a matter of having a vocabulary and knowing how to use it. The words we choose reveal our thoughts and the quality of our experience. The early nineteenth-century British writer William Hazlitt said: "The proper force of words lies not in the words themselves, but in their application." Their application is ultimately a moral consideration.

In the sections that follow, you will be concerned with matters that, properly understood and applied, can increase your sensitivity to the meaning of words. It is hard enough to know when others are writing nonsense; it is doubly hard to know when we ourselves are doing so. We quoted earlier H. W. Fowler's statement that the careful writer *listens* to his own sentences. We must add here that he listens also to his words—revises them as he discovers a more precise word for one he has used, a word with exactly the right connotation, conveying an attitude or implication absent in another. Your attention to these matters, incidentally, should help you to make the best use of your dictionary—for example, of its invaluable synonym listings which indicate exact connotations. We will begin our discussion of diction with connotation, since it is one of the basic qualities of words, and proceed to the more complex qualities of figurative language.

CONNOTATION

We indicated in our discussion of definition that words have a denotation and a connotation: they point to and name objects, ideas, feelings; they may also suggest auras of meaning, associated feelings, attitudes. "There are no epiphanies to be had on television," Jonathan Miller once commented, in a review of television programs. He might have chosen "revelations" or "insights" or "discoveries," words that would have given an approximate indication of his meaning. "Epiphanies" suggests something more than these: insight as momentous as a supernatural revelation. The word not only *denotes* a special kind of insight; it *connotes* associated ideas and auras of meaning.

An important qualification needs to be made at this point. Language may be used chiefly to express a feeling: expletives are chosen always for the feelings they convey, and sometimes for their descriptive power. Some words are almost purely connotative; the people who use them may identify a feeling associated with the word but not an idea. A novel is described by a reviewer as "delicious": the word suggests at best a range of feelings; it points to nothing specific. Norman Mailer depends on an almost purely connotative word in the following sentence:

> Like children, hipsters are fighting for the sweet, and their language is a set of subtle indications of their success or failure in the competition for pleasure.   —"The White Negro"

"Sweet" and "pleasure" are not exact synonyms; Mailer explains that the "sweet" has the connotation for the hipster of the scarce: "And so the sweet goes only to the victor, the best, the most, the man who knows the most about how to find his energy and how not to lose it." The dictionary will not provide even an approximate meaning for the word. In his description of Hip talk, Mailer provides the context of meaning:

> What makes Hip a special language is that it cannot really be taught—if one shares none of the experiences of elation and exhaustion which it is equipped to describe, then it seems merely arch or vulgar or irritating. It is a pictorial language, but pictorial like nonobjective art, imbued with the dialectic of small but intense change, a language for the microcosm, in this case, man, for it takes the immediate experiences of any passing man and magnifies the dynamic of his movements, not specifically but abstractly so that he is seen more as a vector in a network of forces than as a static character in a crystallized field. . . . For example, there is real difficulty in trying to find a Hip substitute for "stubborn." The best possibility I can come up with is: "That cat will never come off his groove, dad." But groove implies movement, narrow movement but motion nonetheless. There is really no way to describe someone who does not move at all.   —*Ibid.*

This qualification noted, let us return to words whose connotations can be easily indicated. Here, again, is Orwell's description of a mortally wounded elephant:

He looked suddenly stricken, shrunken, immensely old, as though the frightful impact of the bullet had paralyzed him without knocking him down. At last, after what seemed a long time—it might have been five seconds, I dare say—he sagged flabbily to his knees. His mouth slobbered. An enormous senility seemed to have settled upon him.

—"Shooting an Elephant"

Orwell might have written that the elephant *sank* or *drooped*. Neither would be the right word because the elephant does not immediately fall (*droop* connotes a gradual sinking). *Sag* connotes a loss of vigor as well as firmness—exactly the impression the wounded animal creates. *Slobber* suggests a somewhat heavier flow of saliva than *drool*—one reason for the association of *slobber* with sentimental gushing. "The elephant drooled" would be an imprecise sentence.

In deciding which words to use, you would have to examine the dictionary definitions to be certain of their connotations. The synonym listings will often provide the information you need. For example, one synonym listing distinguishes a smile from a grin, a simper, and a smirk. The denotation and connotation is given for each word: a smirk is a self-satisfied smile, suggesting conceit or complacence.

VARIETIES OF USAGE

We made the point in our earlier discussion of the speech of Eva Barnes and Carlos Alvarez (see pp. 47–48) that uncultivated speech is not necessarily unclear or "inexpressive." Cultivated speech and writing, indeed, are susceptible to faults almost never encountered in the language of the little educated—jargon, for example. In distinguishing varieties of usage, we must keep in mind that the sociologist, the sports-announcer, the diplomat, Eva Barnes, and Carlos Alvarez each has his own informal and formal styles of speaking and writing, determined by his sense of appropriateness to the occasion. Throughout this book we have been considering one standard of English—the general standard of most educated people, of those who run the important affairs of the country, teach its children, govern its commerce, publish its newspapers. In the discussion that follows we will be using the words *informal* and *formal* in a restricted sense, to refer to varieties of cultivated English.

The difference between *sore* and *angry* ("I'm sore about what happened") and *raw* and *unfair* ("a raw deal") lies not in their denotation but in their conventional informality and formality. The word *conventional* has to be stressed, because occasions and not words are informal or formal, and people's ideas change on such matters; indeed, at any single moment it is difficult to state what is appropriate to the satisfaction of everyone, though few would consider white tie and jacket appropriate at the beach or Bermuda shorts at a funeral. Most situations fall between these extremes. The same qualification can be made about formal and informal uses of language.

At one extreme is the formal language of legal documents; at the other extreme is the informal language of sports columns. Much formal writing is characterized by careful parallelism and balance as well as by moderately periodic construction and climax in sentences; much informal writing, by rather looser sentences, abundant colloquialisms and slang (vigorous, hybrid expressions created for special uses), and contractions. The general English of cultivated writers draws upon both of these styles: sentences more tightly constructed than informal ones but less tight than formal (less obvious parallelism, balance, and periodic construction); a vocabulary using colloquialisms and contractions, and less abstract and specialized than that of formal writing.

In the following passage the diction consists of words familiar to educated people; the sentences are more carefully constructed than informal ones, though not so long and tightly constructed as many formal sentences:

> Ever since Hiroshima (Nagasaki, for some reason, gets very little sympathy) it has been fashionable to say that another war would destroy civilization. Even Mr. Malenkov fell into that phrasing once, though usually he makes it clear to his flock that only capitalist civilization would be destroyed. But both the expressions of concern and the sometimes fantastic remedies that have been proposed to avert the danger have usually had a materialistic emphasis—as if civilization consisted of improved real estate, which would be flattened by hydrogen or atomic bombs. But civilization is not buildings, however beautiful or historic or whatever they contain. Civilization is something inside the people, or some of the people, who live and work in those buildings—the way they feel, the way they think, their capacity for thinking. Certainly it needs some economic foundation—more now than it used to, since now there must be some technological foundation too. But all that is only the background, not the thing itself.
>
> —ELMER DAVIS, "Can Civilization Survive?"

If in the passage "destroy" were changed to "decimate" or "extirpate," "remedies" to "panaceas," and "the way they feel" to "their manner of feeling," the changes would increase the formality of the passage, aside from any changes in meaning. The following passage, by contrast, is highly informal:

> He had played tackle himself because he was big and slow on his feet but he threw a beautiful soft pass. He would set my

fingers on the laces for me, cock my arm, and tell me just how hard to pitch it but I couldn't learn. My passes were straight enough and by the time I was fourteen they had a nice spiral but they were always too hard. They shot through his fingers if he was catching them over his shoulder or they bounced off his chest. He was very patient with me, taking an end's crouch with four fingers on the ground, galloping heavily over the grass beside the bed of late zinnias, then cutting in toward the back porch over and over again until his shirt was soaked and the lawn was black with his toe-prints—even at thirty-six or seven, he ran on his toes. It took about half an hour to poop him out and then he was through.

—ALLAN SEAGER, Amos Berry

The words "beautiful" and "nice" are not used in the precise way they would have to be used if the passage were more formal. But they satisfy the context; other words—"graceful," for example—would be out of place. The description, incidentally, in this instance need not be more precise than it would be in ordinary conversation. The expressive "cutting in" and "poop him out" are, however, both precise and suited to the subject—just as the numerous abstract words and phrases are suited to their subject in the following passage of formal writing:

The Medium mediates between us and raw reality, and the mediation more and more replaces reality for us. Many radio-stations have a news-broadcast every hour, and many people like and need to hear it. In many houses either the television set or the radio is turned on during most of the hours the family is awake. It is as if they longed to be established in reality, to be reminded continually of the "real," objective world—the created world of the Medium—rather than to be left at the mercy of actuality, of the helpless contingency of the world in which the radio-receiver or television set is sitting. And surely we can sympathize: which of us hasn't found a similar refuge in the "real," created world of Cézanne or Goethe or Verdi? Yet Dostoievsky's world is too different from Wordsworth's, Piero della Francesca's from Goya's, Bach's from Wolf's, for us to be able to substitute one homogeneous mediated reality for everyday reality in the belief that it is everyday reality. For many watchers, listeners, readers, the world of events and celebrities and performers—the Great World—has become the world of primary reality: how many times they have sighed at the colorless unreality of their own lives and families, and sighed for the bright reality of, say, Elizabeth Taylor's. The watchers call the celebrities by their first names, approve or disapprove of "who they're dating," handle them with a mixture of love, identification, envy, and contempt. But however they handle them, they handle them: the Medium has given everyone so terrible a familiarity with everyone that it takes great magnanimity of spirit not to be affected by it. These celebrities are not heroes to us, their valets.   —RANDALL JARRELL, A Sad Heart at the Supermarket

The sentence construction as well as the vocabulary suggest formal usage. The passage is typical of formal writing occurring in the editorial columns of The New York Times, the articles of The Atlantic and Harper's Magazine, written statements of government officials, and the like. The highly formal language of the following passage also depends on an abstract vocabulary but makes a wholly different impression:

> The visual sense when extended by phonetic literacy fosters the analytic habit of perceiving the single facet in the life of forms. The visual power enables us to isolate the single incident in time and space, as in representational art. In visual representation of a person or an object, a single phase or moment or aspect is separated from the multitude of known and felt phases, moments and aspects of the person or object. By contrast, iconographic art uses the eye as we use our hand in seeking to create an inclusive image, made up of many moments, phases, and aspects of the person or thing. Thus the iconic mode is not visual representation, nor the specialization of visual stress as defined by viewing from a single position. The tactual mode of perceiving is sudden but not specialist. It is total, synesthetic, involving all the senses. Pervaded by the mosaic TV image, the TV child encounters the world in a spirit antithetic to literacy.
> —MARSHALL MCLUHAN, Understanding Media

Spread over many pages, this kind of formal writing becomes monotonous and difficult to follow. It derives, incidentally, from what used to be called "curt style"—a writing style dominated by short phrases consisting of nominal and adjectival modifiers ("visual power," "representational art," "iconic mode"). Many writers who favor this style loosen their sentences through contrasts between formal sentence construction and concrete words or the reverse. In regard to a choice of words, the following advice of H. W. Fowler is worth quoting:

> . . . there is nothing to be ashamed of in buy or jam or say that they should need translating into purchase and preserve and remark; where they give the sense equally well, they are fit for any company and need not be shut up at home. Few things contribute more to vigor of style than a practical re-

alization that the *kuria onomata*, the sovereign or dominant or proper or vernacular or current names, are better than the formal words. —*Modern English Usage*, p. 190.

One additional distinction needs to be made. Words and phrases peculiar to a professional or occupational class are called *jargon* or *lingo*. In the following passage, many of the words are jargon words (or *argot*) peculiar to professional criminals, and are identified and explained by the author. These words would, of course, be inappropriate in other contexts:

Not only does one thief warn another thief of danger but also he avoids doing things which will put other thieves in danger. If a thief were going through a store and saw a booster working, he would not stop to watch the booster because this might cause someone else to look in the same direction and might result in the booster getting pinched. A great deal of trouble is caused by the curiosity of nonprofessional thieves or, in very rare instances, even of professional thieves. Two heels (sneak thieves) had got into the stockroom of a high-class jewelry house, had secured a tray of platinum watches, and were leaving the store. As they got to the center of the main floor a snatch-and-grab (unskilled) booster whom they knew and who knew them spoke to them. They chilled for him (pretended not to recognize him) and kept on going, but he turned around and stared after them. He should have known enough not to recognize and speak to them anywhere that they might be grifting, even if he was not a real professional, and besides he should never have stared after them when they chilled, which in itself was enough to let him know they were hot (in danger). This booster was known in the store and was being watched. When it was noticed that he spoke to the two who were going out and stared at them, the attention of the store copper was transferred to the other two, and he immediately started to cut them off at the door. The heels sensed this at once and reversed and maneuvered back to the stockroom, where they got a chance to clean themselves (get rid of the stolen goods). They were stopped and searched on the way out and warned to stay out of that store. Thus a good score (stolen object) and the opportunity of future success in that store were knocked out by someone who did not know his business.
—EDWIN H. SUTHERLAND, *The Professional Thief*

Words of this sort have a place in writing when the context clarifies their use. Misused or overused, they rob sentences of their vitality by enriching the prose to the point of surfeit. We will consider this second kind of jargon later in this chapter, with other kinds of faulty diction.

TONE

When we talk, we indicate our attitude toward the subject and the listener through vocal inflection. The difference between

What a book!

meant in admiration, and the same statement meant in sarcasm, is immediately clear in speech. In writing, not even the punctuation will make the meaning clear. The writer must depend, then, on other ways to establish his tone. He may have to indicate explicitly that he is being ironic; or exaggerate his praise or condemnation; or understate in such a way that his reader immediately understands the difference between what is being shown and what is being said about it; or simply state his attitude:

> . . . it is my indignant opinion that ninety percent of the moving pictures exhibited in America are so vulgar, witless, and dull that it is preposterous to write about them in any publication not intended to be read while chewing gum.
> —WOLCOTT GIBBS, More in Sorrow

> Go back, now, to the old days. Penmanship was then taught, not mechanically and ineffectively, by unsound and shifting formulae, but by passionate penmen with curly patent-leather hair and far-away eyes—in brief, by the unforgettable professors of our youth, with their flourishes, their heavy downstrokes and their lovely birds-with-letters-in-their-bills. You remember them, of course. Asses all! Preposterous popinjays and numskulls! Pathetic imbeciles! But they loved penmanship, they believed in the glory and beauty of penmanship, they were fanatics, devotees, almost martyrs of penmanship— and so they got some touch of that passion into their pupils.
> —H. L. MENCKEN, "The Educational Process"

Mencken is not engaging in hyperbole (deliberate exaggeration) or irony: he means exactly what he says, as does Gibbs. The following writer, by contrast, does resort to irony:

> This preoccupation of George Apley, not indeed unusual to one who is embarking on a new and untried stage of existence, that the friends of his own incarnation might be leaving him, should have been very quickly dissipated by the loyalty of these same friends at numerous small dinners which they

gave him in the interval between his engagement and his marriage in early June. Nevertheless, though Apley was fully aware, as he often said himself, that he was the happiest man in the world, he often gave way on such occasions to a strain of sentimental sadness. This was particularly true at his own bachelor's dinner, attended of course by the ushers, among whom the present writer, his old friends, Chickering, Walker, and Vassal, and several of his contemporary cousins were numbered. The writer remembers this occasion very well indeed. Though not unlike many others which he has attended, the group around the table was of the best. With such people around the board, all from very much the same section of life and each known so well to the other, there was no need for anyone to display the care or reticence which his caution and sense of fitness might have demanded of him at another time and place. The atmosphere in the private dining-room of the Parker House was one of a complete and un-alloyed friendship as course followed course. Thomas Apley, sensing the importance of this dinner, had sent over a half-dozen Madeira which had been to Charleston and back in ballast fifty years before, and had instructed the management to serve unlimited champagne. Vassal told several of his in-imitable stories and Walker sang songs in his fine baritone until everyone in the room, including the waiters, joined the chorus. Then there followed a round of toasts, one given by the writer himself. It was noticed at the time that Apley seemed distrait, but no more so than might be expected, until the company, each placing a foot upon the table, sang "Should auld acquaintance be forgot . . . ?"—at which point Apley actually gave way to tears. This sign of emotion was received with hearty applause, marred only by a display of carelessness on the part of one of the guests, who stepped out of a window. The dining-room, fortunately, was on the second story, so that a broken arm and two shattered front teeth were the only results of an accident that might have cast a gloom on the whole company.

—JOHN P. MARQUAND, *The Late George Apley*

Marquand is describing a very proper Bostonian's bachelor's dinner. The tone of the passage is complicated by the fact that the speaker shares the point of view of all the guests as well as of George Apley: we must see through this point of view to that of the author who understates ("marred only by a display of carelessness on the part of one of the guests, who stepped out of a window"). The author leads us in this way to make a judgment about Apley and his guests. His ordinary "care" and "reticence"—as well as his "preoccupation" over losing his friends and his "sentimental sadness"—will seem to most readers a little too much, and so too the singing of the company, "each placing a foot upon the table." The effect of the passage arises from the obvious disparity between what is shown and what is said: Marquand perhaps is implying that something is missing in Apley, possibly a warmth of feeling for which his "sentimental sadness" and the sentimentality of his company (the ludicrousness heightened by the "careless" behavior of one of the guests) cannot substitute.

There are other important ways of indicating irony—among them a careful selection of detail that speaks for itself:

> These trivia did not distract her [Queen Victoria] from the claims of the weak and defenseless. Third class passengers must be saved from railway accidents by making a director ride on every train—"we should soon see a different state of things!" The hazards of life in India distressed her: widows burnt alive and tigers addicted to human flesh, "women as well as men . . ."
>
> —ELIZABETH LONGFORD, Queen Victoria: Born to Succeed

There is a discernible voice in this passage, as there is in this introduction to a report on packaged discothèques:

> What else that's happening, Baby, these frenzied days, is the appearance of an instant, or do-it-yourself, or packaged, discothèque, which is the invention, or promotion, of the Seeburg Corporation, a Chicago-based outfit that is the world's largest manufacturer of coin-operated vending machines, and last week was New York's turn to watch a bunch of energetic Seeburg salesmen on the national demonstration circuit deliver the package to the people.   —LILLIAN ROSS, "Package"

Most of our examples have been of irony in various forms. It should be obvious that consistency of tone is especially important if irony in any form is to be effective. Thus it would not do for Marquand to interrupt the paragraph with a caustic remark. Shifts in tone are frequently necessary, however, and must be managed with care, even in passages where the tone is not ironic.

> Radio commentators provide an excellent lesson showing how much of language depends on inflection, how delicate is the line between fact and opinion. How quickly one learns to trust the dry, succinct Indiana speech of Elmer Davis; how promptly to note the quiet distinction he makes between his opinion and the facts he is reporting, sometimes by the faintest modulation, or by the parenthesis of half a sentence. How quickly revolted one becomes by those who use a war and

men dying in it for their own political hobbies of hate or for their own bland patrioteering—verbal warriors safe in the quiet and security of a radio studio.

—IRWIN EDMAN, Under Whatever Sky

This passage is rather formal in its construction: the two parts of the second sentence are parallel to the third sentence ("How quickly one learns . . . how promptly to note. . . . How quickly revolted one becomes"), and each sentence contains other parallel elements. The third sentence, in addition, builds to a climax. These formal characteristics intensify the earnest tone yet at the same time hold the indignation in check. The tone is thus, in this instance at least, qualified by the formal construction. There is no disparity between what is said and how it is said to suggest irony.

This analysis of tone suggests several conclusions. Tone is perhaps the most difficult element of composition to master, in part because you will not be able to fix your tone precisely before the actual writing. Usually you will discover it in the course of writing, as you discover your precise attitude in trying to state ideas for a particular audience. You may decide to examine a situation or an idea ironically; but the *point* of your irony (the implication you wish to convey, the meaning or discrepancy you wish to expose) probably will not be fully apparent until you have thought through your detail.

Your estimate of the interests and disposition of your audience determines the tone you will adopt. High school freshmen will respond in one way to an analysis of their attitudes; high school principals will most likely respond in another way. But the content of your remarks will not alone shape their response; both audiences will be influenced by the attitude you reveal toward them. They will know whether you are talking down to them or over their heads and whether you mean to do this. When speaking to an audience, you are easily able to gauge their response to your remarks and modify your presentation of details and your tone accordingly. When your audience is the invisible reader whose responses you must estimate, you may assume you have established a clear tone and prepared the reader for shifts in tone and thought. The solution is one we have cited before: you must listen to your writing as a second and third self. You must try to imagine what another person will think and feel as your words engage his attention.

CONCRETENESS

To choose the concrete is to choose the specific rather than the general: Buicks and Fords instead of merely automobiles, apples and peaches instead of merely fruit. There are times when specific detail is unnecessary and a general statement is sufficient. But an account of one's feelings would be meaningless without a landscape, a backdrop rendered in enough detail to make particular feelings understandable. The writer of the following passage provides this landscape in suggesting how it feels to change a tire in eight inches of mud:

> I lay on my stomach and edged my way, swam my way under the truck, holding my nostrils clear of the surface of the water. The jack handle was slippery with greasy mud. Mud balls formed in my beard. I lay panting like a wounded duck, quietly cursing as I inched the jack forward under an axle that I had to find by feel, since it was under water. Then, with superhuman gruntings and bubblings, my eyes starting from their sockets, I levered the great weight. I could feel my muscles tearing apart and separating from their anchoring bones. In actual time, not over an hour elapsed before I had the spare tire on. I was unrecognizable under many layers of yellow mud. My hands were cut and bleeding. I rolled the bad tire to a high place and inspected it. The whole side wall had blown out. Then I looked at the left rear tire, and to my horror saw a great rubber bubble on its side and, farther along, another. It was obvious that the other tire might go at any moment, and it was Sunday and it was raining and it was Oregon. If the other tire blew, there we were, on a wet and lonesome road, having no recourse except to burst into tears and wait for death. And perhaps some kind birds might cover us with leaves.
>
> —JOHN STEINBECK, *Travels with Charley in Search of America*

Steinbeck carefully builds his detail, and to an extent exaggerates it for the purpose of humor. He does not merely climb under the vehicle: he edges and swims his way under and holds his nostrils clear of the water. And he does not merely lie under it: he pants "like a wounded duck" and curses and grunts and bubbles, as mud balls form in his beard and his eyes start from their sockets. The rest of the passage is just as precise: Steinbeck does not comment vaguely that he felt miserable: he wonders whether "some kind birds might cover [them] with leaves."

In good descriptive writing, the experience is so totally realized through concrete detail that the reader can participate in it. The writer of the following description of rail passengers finding their way out of a tunnel, following an accident, succeeds in this aim:

> More passengers were crawling out onto the ledge from the forward cars. Others were still smashing glass. For some reason there was a sound of whimpering that I guessed came from the glass smashers. Is that the sound of terror? Had

anyone of the glass-smashers unfixed from his panic, he could have looked around by that time to see plenty of open empty windows. Yet, the sound of breaking glass continued, conjuring ugly images of what might happen to anyone who tried to crawl through the jagged edges. These were glimpses again, flashes of sensation and of thought within the continuum of the line in plodding motion. At the front of the train, the gagging motorman had his door open, and was helping gagging passengers onto the catwalk. I passed him, and now there was no wall on my left, but only what I guessed was at least a seven-foot drop to the tracks. With the train no longer there to close us into a narrow corridor, the sound of the coughing seemed to change, to come from everywhere in the tunnel at once, some of it from what seemed to be a good distance ahead, though distance itself seemed to have disappeared, whirled up in one present time and place inside the monstrous acrid choke and stink into which the train's headlight poured not a beam but a ghastly diffusion.

—JOHN CIARDI, "Out of the Rathole"

The detail here is as precise as the experience permits. Ciardi concentrates on sounds that effectively convey the sense of enclosure and changing spaces. The selection of a few sharp details accomplishes more than a crowded description would have (the headlight cannot penetrate the air of the tunnel, through which the passengers plod and would fall through instantly to the tracks if they lost their step).

IMAGERY

Attention to imagery will make it possible for you to convey your feelings with some exactness. Though we usually think of images as visual impressions, images may appeal to any of the senses—hearing (auditory), touch (tactile), smell (olfactory), taste (gustatory). The following sentences of Rachel Carson appeal to several senses:

Now I hear the sea sounds about me; the night high tide is rising, swirling with a confused rush of waters against the rocks below my study window. Fog has come into the bay from the open sea, and it lies over water and over the land's edge, seeping back into the spruces and stealing softly among the juniper and the bayberry. The restive waters, the cold wet breath of the fog, are of a world in which man is an uneasy trespasser; he punctuates the night with the complaining groan and grunt of a foghorn, sensing the power and menace of the sea.   —The Edge of the Sea

The appeal to the senses is a more restricted one in the following passage, in which a complex series of images is used to characterize a man of precise habits and an unexpected streak of sentimentality:

> The lofty walls of his uncarpeted room were free from pictures. He had himself bought every article of furniture in the room: a black iron bedstead, an iron washstand, four cane chairs, a clothes-rack, a coal-scuttle, a fender and irons and a square table on which lay a double desk. A bookcase had been made in an alcove by means of shelves of white wood. The bed was clothed with white bedclothes and a black and scarlet rug covered the foot. A little hand-mirror hung above the washstand and during the day a white-shaded lamp stood as the sole ornament of the mantelpiece. The books on the white wooden shelves were arranged from below upwards according to bulk. A complete Wordsworth stood at one end of the lowest shelf and a copy of the *Maynooth Catechism*, sewn into the cloth cover of a notebook, stood at one end of the top shelf. Writing materials were always on the desk. In the desk lay a manuscript translation of Hauptmann's *Michael Kramer*, the stage directions of which were written in purple ink, and a little sheaf of papers held together by a brass pin. In these sheets a sentence was inscribed from time to time and, in an ironical moment, the headline of an advertisement for *Bile Beans* had been pasted on to the first sheet. On lifting the lid of the desk a faint fragrance escaped—the fragrance of new cedarwood pencils or of a bottle of gum or of an overripe apple which might have been left there and forgotten.   —JAMES JOYCE, "A Painful Case"

Joyce does not immediately tell us what kind of man Mr. Duffy is: he prefers to *show* us. The walls of his room are bare; each piece of furniture has its prescribed place. Even the books are carefully arranged; the volume of Wordsworth—ironically, the great Romantic poet—is placed on the lowest shelf because of its bulk, not because Mr. Duffy wants the poems near him. There is no place in Mr. Duffy's life for disorder, and even the manuscript—his one venture into the world of imagination (significantly as a translator and not as a creator)—has its precisions: the stage directions are written in purple ink. His own papers are neatly fastened by a brass pin. The headline pasted to the first sheet, as well as the pencils, suggests something of the esthetic needs Mr. Duffy seeks to satisfy. Only after Joyce has shown us does he *tell* us about the character of the man (in the paragraph that follows the passage): "Mr. Duffy abhorred anything which betokened physical or mental disorder."

The detail, remember, is selected for the reader. By the end of the passage he must know how you have *imagined* a scene or character.

Generalizations like that about Mr. Duffy are exactly that: abstractions drawn from experience and observation. Generalizations will mean nothing to your reader until you allow him to see with your eyes and understand the basis of your judgments.

FIGURATIVE LANGUAGE

We come now to figurative language—another way to express feelings with exactness. In a review of television programs Jonathan Miller describes television as a "vast, phosphorescent Mississippi of the senses, on the banks of which one can soon lose one's judgment and eventually lose one's mind." This is *metaphor*. A metaphor, in its most general sense, is an extension of meaning, the use of a word in an unusual, unexpected context. More specifically, it is the identification of one object with another (television *is* "a vast, phosphorescent Mississippi"). Since television is like the Mississippi in its vastness and phosphorescence (and also because it goes on and on?), Miller writes about television as if it *were* the Mississippi. Thus, it has its banks on which one can lose his judgment and his mind.

Simile, on the other hand, is an explicit comparison using *like* or *as*: Miller says that television commercials "inhabit the crevices of the programs *like* vile, raucous parasites." If he had said that they "inhabit the crevices of the programs" without explicitly comparing them to parasites, the reader, if he were sensitive to the figurative language, might think of the commercials as being insects. Miller, incidentally, shifts from one figure to another in the same sentence: for these parasites not only "nip" and "tweak" but also "chatter" (like birds?). If the figure *obstrusively* contradicted other figures in the passage, it would be "mixed." Many figures, however, are mixed without being obtrusive because they fall into the same pattern of meaning, or there is a deliberate shift in the use made of the metaphor:

> If you try to nail anything down, in the novel, either it kills
> the novel, or the novel gets up and walks away with the nail.
> —D. H. LAWRENCE, "Morality and the Novel"

Many expressions were originally recognized as metaphors, but are no longer. Words and phrases of this sort (the *spur* of the moment, *struck* by the statement) are sometimes called *dead* metaphors. A gifted writer can bring these to life for striking effects:

> Film-making, like bird-watching, creeps up on the truth.
> —PENELOPE HOUSTON, "Towards a New Cinema"

> Spoofing has become the safety net for those who are unsure
> of their footing.   —PAULINE KAEL, *Kiss Kiss, Bang Bang*

The kind and amount of metaphor we use depend on the purpose and subject of our writing. Jonathan Miller's lively metaphorical sentences are colorful and give a startling sense of immediacy; Miller uses *hyperbole* (exaggeration) for the sake of humor, and so his startling, colorful metaphors have a purpose.

By contrast, John Updike uses figurative language much less colorfully, yet the passage has some surprises for the reader:

> After exams, in the heart of the Cambridge winter, there is a grateful pause. New courses are selected, and even the full-year courses, heading into their second half, sometimes put on, like a new hat, a fresh professor. The days delicately lengthen; there is a snowstorm or two; the swimming and squash teams lend the sports pages of the *Crimson* an unaccustomed note of victory. A kind of foreshadow of spring falls bluely on the snow. The elms are seen to be shaped like fountains. The discs of snow pressed by boots into the sidewalk by Albiani's seem large precious coins; the brick buildings, the arched gates, the archaic lecterns, and the barny mansions along Brattle Street dawn upon the freshman as a heritage he temporarily possesses. The thumb-worn spines of his now familiar textbooks seem proof of a certain knowingness, and the strap of the green book bag tugs at his wrist like a living and lightly fierce thing. The letters from home dwindle in importance. The hours open up. There is more time. Experiments are made. Courtships begin. Conversations go on and on; and an almost rapacious desire for mutual discovery possesses acquaintances.   —"The Christian Roommates"

The similes—the elms "shaped like fountains," the strap which tugs at the wrist "like a living and lightly fierce thing"—and the metaphors —the "discs of snow," the courses "heading into their second half," the teams that " lend the sports pages of the *Crimson* an unaccustomed note of victory," all of the sights that "dawn upon the freshman as a heritage he temporarily possesses," the letters that "dwindle in importance," the "experiments" students find they have time to make—vary in their immediacy. Some, indeed, call *no* picture to mind. Others do. The figurative reference to year-long courses which "sometimes put on, like a new hat, a fresh professor" comes as a surprise. We are surprised also by "the kind of foreshadow of spring" which "falls *bluely* on the snow"; used in this way, the adverbial stands out strikingly in the sentence. The passage is low-keyed, almost casual.

Appropriateness is determined not only by the audience but also by the subject and the situation being depicted. The figure in the following passage is startling yet completely appropriate in its highly dramatic context:

I thought of all this, standing quietly in the water, feeling the sand shifting away under my toes. Then I lay back in the floating position that left my face to the sky, and shoved off. The sky wheeled over me. For an instant, as I bobbed into the main channel, I had the sensation of sliding down the vast tilted face of the continent. It was then that I felt the cold needles of the alpine springs at my fingertips, and the warmth of the Gulf pulling me southward. Moving with me, leaving its taste upon my mouth and spouting under me in dancing springs of sand, was the immense body of the continent itself, flowing like the river was flowing, grain by grain, mountain by mountain, down to the sea. I was streaming over ancient sea beds thrust aloft where giant reptiles had once sported; I was wearing down the face of time and trundling cloud-wreathed ranges into oblivion. I touched my margins with the delicacy of a crayfish's antennae, and felt great fishes glide about their work.   —LOREN EISELEY, *The Immense Journey*

The passage is an *extended metaphor*. The man floating in the water *becomes* the water. He *streams* over ancient sea beds, *wears down* "the face of time" as water erodes the shore, *touches his margins* as water touches the shore, drifts, slides, and streams. The passage is doubly remarkable for its concreteness. The sky does not merely pass overhead: it *wheels*. The "immense body of the continent" does not merely move under him: it *spouts* under him (the metaphorical development is entirely consistent) in "dancing springs of sand" (the sand is made liquid). Here is a briefer example of extended metaphor in a discussion of modern technology:

> If science and technics have not been officially married, they have long lived together in a loose, common-law relationship that it is easier to ignore than to dissolve.
> —LEWIS MUMFORD, *The Pentagon of Power*

Metaphor is less common in exposition than in descriptive writing. The following passage shows how metaphors can be employed in exposition without dominating the discussion or obscuring the chief idea:

> In some societies and at some times the feeling, the style, has been set by the lions; in others, by the foxes. The Spartans were lions, the Athenians foxes, though these were contemporaneous societies. The medieval aristocracy of the West were lions; the American plutocracy of the Gilded Age were foxes. Both these latter groups were addicted to violence, and neither conducted life along the best standards of our Western thought. But their moral styles were different. The lions at their best are reliable and unprogressive; the foxes at their

best are unreliable and progressive, are at least agents of all sorts of change, some of which may be morally desirable. Most human societies in the West have been mixtures of the two, with neither so predominating as to produce all change or no change; moreover, lions and foxes alike have been minorities, leaders—the majority, perhaps fortunately, remaining mere men. The lions tend to be corrupted by the material prosperity, which good lion-led armies, helped by a few foxes in government and even in military affairs, bring to a society; the foxes, in the long run of their descendants, turn into lions, but rather stale ones, lacking the fine fresh confidence of the original lions—turn, in fact, into die-hard conservatives, full of radically archaic ideas.

—CRANE BRINTON, *A History of Western Morals*

Other kinds of figurative language are worth noting, among them personification—the attribution of human qualities to inanimate objects. In the following passage, the harbor walls and the ship are personified for the purpose of dramatic contrast:

The stony shores ran away right and left in straight lines, enclosing a somber and rectangular pool. Brick walls rose high above the water—soulless walls, staring through hundreds of windows as troubled and dull as the eyes of overfed brutes. At their base monstrous iron cranes crouched, with chains hanging from their long necks, balancing cruel-looking hooks over the decks of lifeless ships. A noise of wheels rolling over stones, the thump of heavy things falling, the racket of feverish winches, the grinding of strained chains, floated on the air. Between high buildings the dust of all the continents soared in short flights; and a penetrating smell of perfumes and dirt, of spices and hides, of things costly and of things filthy, pervaded the space, made for it an atmosphere precious and disgusting. The *Narcissus* came gently into her berth; the shadows of soulless walls fell upon her, the dust of all the continents leaped upon her deck, and a swarm of strange men, clambering up her sides, took possession of her in the name of the sordid earth. She had ceased to live.

—JOSEPH CONRAD, *The Nigger of the Narcissus*

The walls are like soulless people; the windows are the eyes through which they stare at the ship like "overfed brutes." The cranes crouch like brutes; chains hang from their long necks. The ship is a woman whom the "swarm of strange men" take possession of. Again, the startling figure is justified by the dramatic context. Like other figures of speech, personification is found occasionally in ordinary expository writing but is best used sparingly.

FAULTY DICTION

In the preceding sections we have been concerned with ways of expressing feeling and helping the reader to see life as we do. We have suggested that these ways can be used to bad effect; excessive dependence on metaphor and other figures of speech can obscure ideas and give the impression of over-richness. We shall consider now more ordinary faults of diction that are sometimes hard to avoid. We will review several points made earlier about sentence construction—awkward repetition, overloading, faulty reference—and make additional suggestions about how to avoid awkwardness and obscurity. In the glossary of usage that follows, we will consider some common errors in the use of words and expressions.

1. Certain repetitions in the same sentence can jar the ear. On the other hand, substitution merely to avoid repetition can produce sentences like the following:

> We have enough glasses but an insufficient number of knives and forks.
>
> COMPARE: We have enough glasses but not enough knives and forks.

Some writers do make substitutions to provide information economically; however, too many substitutions may seem affected:

> John Keats wrote his greatest poems in the space of a few years during which the young poet fell in love with Fanny Brawne. The author of *Endymion* wrote letters to the inhabitant of Hampstead that reflect the romantic idealism of his poems.
>
> COMPARE: John Keats wrote his greatest poems in the space of a few years, during which he fell in love with Fanny Brawne. He wrote letters to her that reflect the romantic idealism of poems like *Endymion*.

Endymion reminds us of Keats's romantic idealism; the information that Fanny Brawne lived at Hampstead is irrelevant and leads us from the main idea. Compare the following:

AWKWARD	IMPROVED
He cited a few examples of government waste and pointed to instances of economies that could be made.	He cited a few examples of government waste and of economies that could be made.
I'm convinced I should vote for the school levy but I'm not persuaded I should cast my ballot for the incumbent members of the board.	I'm convinced I should vote for the school levy but not convinced I should vote for the incumbent board.

2. *Of* phrases and *which* clauses strung together make sentences hard to speak and read:

AWKWARD	IMPROVED
Someone dented the fender of the car of the manager of the office.	Someone dented the fender of the office manager's car.
We discussed which questions we had answered right and which wrong on the exam which we took.	We discussed the questions we had answered right and answered wrong on the exam.

3. Certain phrases, often added to sentences to achieve euphony, can weaken emphasis or obscure the main thought:

> A deadened screaming went on steadily at his elbow, *as it were:* and from above the louder tumult of the storm descended upon these near sounds. —JOSEPH CONRAD, *Typhoon*

A phrase best avoided is *in terms of* because it is easily misused. The phrase means "in the language of":

> He explained the proposal in the terms of the signed accords.

In the following sentence the phrase has no precise meaning:

> In terms of the support available, there is no warrant for the proposal.

The writer perhaps means:

> The proposal is without support.

Thinking them elegant, people misuse *concept, evaluate, essential, motive, factor,* and the like. These words have synonyms that should be used if a more specific meaning is not intended: *idea* for *concept* (a more specific word, meaning generalization from particular instances); *judge* for *evaluate* (another more specific word, meaning appraise or judge according to a precise standard); *necessary* for *essential* (suggesting absolute need); *impulse* or *intention* for *motive* or *motivation; main* for *primary* (if the distinction is between main and subordinate rather than between first and second); *first* for *initial; perceptive* for *sensitive; important* for *crucial* (suggesting critical or decisive); *practice* for *tendency; part* or *element* for *factor* (suggesting a component of a process). The synonym listings of the dictionary, as we said earlier, indicate the precise differences among words with related meanings.

4. When words are used as circumlocution or euphemism, the writer may seem to be saying something unintended. If the teacher warns against "cooperative activities" when he means cheating, or asks for "independent thought" when he wants to discourage the class from reading "study notes" and "guides" to *Hamlet*, he will probably confuse his students.

5. Intensifiers like *very* should not substitute for strong adjectives that can stand alone (compare *very tired* and *exhausted*). Redundant modifiers (*wholly clear*, *perfectly correct*, *entirely wrong*, *fully informed*, *truly magnificent*) detract attention from the chief word and rob the sentence of vitality.

6. Words like *both* may give an unintended emphasis to a sentence. Compare:

> Both musicians performed their solos well.
> Both musicians share a common love of chamber music.

The first *both* is essential to the meaning of the sentence; the second is redundant (as is *common*) and possibly misleading (does the sentence refer to a third or fourth musician?).

7. Certain verbs derived from nouns—*enthuse* and *emote*, for example—occur in spoken English; they are best avoided in written English, in part because they are easily confused with their noun equivalents or roots.

> The disintegration of a family, where the family still has meaning, emotes tragedy in every one.
> —JAMES JONES, *From Here to Eternity*

8. Excessive or needless qualification will rob a sentence of vitality: Hitler perhaps had a twisted idea of German racial history, it seems. The words *perhaps*, *maybe*, *it seems*, and the like, are properly used when the writer wishes to indicate a degree of probability.

9. The following sentence is obscure:

> Men differ in respect of transmitted aptitudes, or in respect of the relative facility with which they unfold their life activity in particular directions; and the habits which coincide with or proceed upon a relatively strong specific aptitude or a relatively great specific facility of expression become of great consequence to the man's well-being.
> —THORSTEIN VEBLEN, *Theory of the Leisure Class*

A number of things are wrong here. First, the sentence departs so markedly from colloquial patterns that we *listen* for the end of the sentence. Second, the excessive parallelism and balance bury the main thought, particularly in the second part of the sentence. In the first part, the phrase *in respect of* (used twice) is needless. Here is a revision:

> Men differ in transmitted aptitudes or the relative facility with which they unfold their lives in different directions; and

the habits which coincide with or proceed from a relatively strong specific aptitude or facility are important to well-being.

The idea can be stated even more simply. The passage, in short, is full of the kind of "jargon" distinguished by Fowler: "talk that is considered both ugly-sounding and hard to understand: applied especially to (1) the sectional vocabulary of a science, art, class, sect, trade, or profession, full of technical terms . . . (2) hybrid speech of different languages; (3) the use of long words, circumlocution and other clumsiness."—*Modern English Usage*, p. 307.

GLOSSARY OF USAGE

a, an   Use *a* before a stressed consonant (book, half, hamlet); use *an* before a stressed vowel or before a syllable beginning with a silent *h* (honor, herb, hour, evening, orange).

accept, except   *Accept* means *to receive willingly* (I accept your offer); *except* means *to omit* or *exclude* when used as a verb (We excepted the book from those sent), and *with the exclusion* or *omission of* when used as a preposition (We sent all the books except one).

affect, effect   *Affect* means *to qualify, change,* or *arouse emotionally* (His illness affected his grades; I was deeply affected by the music). *Effect* means *to bring about* (The series of accidents effected a change in the law).

allusion, illusion   An *allusion* is an explicit or implicit reference to an event or character in real life or mythology or to a passage in a literary work (I alluded to the accident; he alluded to Macbeth's meditation on time); an *illusion* is a *misconception* or *fantasy* (The ghost you think you see is an illusion; he has all the illusions of the young).

along the lines of   WEAK: He is studying along the lines of medicine. IMPROVED: He is studying medicine.

already, all ready   *Already* means *previously* (He has already gone); *all ready* means *completely prepared* (We are all ready to go).

altogether, all together   *Altogether* means *completely* (The book is altogether credible); *all together* means *collected* (The books and papers are all together).

among   See *between*.

anywheres   The word is *anywhere*.

apparent, evident   *Apparent* is sometimes used to mean *evident*, but there is a difference in meaning. *Apparent* means *obvious, clearly seen* (the apparent influence of the wind on the water); *evident* means *clearly shown by the facts* (His guilt was evident in his statement to the police).

appear   See *seem*.

as far as   The phrase is incomplete in the sentence, "As far as football, I think we'll have a good season." IMPROVED: As far as football is concerned, I think we'll have a good season. OR As for football, I think we'll have a good season. Sometimes a sentence can be effectively shortened by omitting the phrase: I think we'll have a good season in football.

as to whether   Omit *as to* when it follows the verb (I asked whether he was coming, NOT I asked as to whether he was coming). The phrase is correct at the beginning of a sentence: As to whether a state of war exists, we cannot say at this time.

at   Omit in sentences like "Where are the girls (at)?"

basis   See *on the basis that.*

being as   The phrase is below standard: Being as it's Wednesday, we can't go. STANDARD: Because it's Wednesday, we can't go.

between, among   *Between* refers to *two* (between you and me), except when it connotes reciprocity (An agreement can be arranged between the several parties to the dispute); *among* means *more than two* (among the students).

can, may   In formal usage, *can* means *to be able* and *may* means *to be permitted* to do or not do something.

can't hardly   The expression is *can hardly.*

compare to, compare with   *Compare to* suggests similarity (The speaker compared the late President to Lincoln); *compare with* suggests both similarity and difference (The speaker compared Yale with Oxford).

(in) connection with   WEAK: He discussed my grades in connection with the scholarship. IMPROVED: He told me that my grades would hurt my chances for a scholarship.

continual, continuous   *Continual* means *at regular intervals* (I ask questions continually); *continuous* means *without interruption* (The fire alarm rang continuously for two minutes).

different from   In formal usage write *different from* instead of *different than.*

due to   In formal writing use as an adjectival only (His success was due to his perseverance); in adverbial positions substitute *owing to* (Owing to his grades, he was promoted, NOT Due to his grades, he was promoted).

enthuse   In formal usage avoid as a substitute for *be enthusiastic.*

factor   *Factor* means one of a number of conditions that bring about something. Don't confuse it with *reasons.*

farther, further   Though sometimes used interchangeably, the words can be distinguished as expressions of distance (We drove farther on Monday) and time or amount (He spoke further about the plans OR There were further discussions).

if, whether   In formal usage many writers avoid *if* in the sense of *whether* (I would like to know whether you have an opening in your firm).

imply, infer   *Imply* means to *hint* or *suggest* (I implied that I was bored). *Infer* means to *conclude from evidence* (I inferred from your remarks that the play bored you).

irregardless   The formal expression is either *regardless of* or *irrespective of. Irregardless* is a blend of the two.

its, it's   *Its* is the possessive of *it; it's*, the contraction of *it is.*

lay, lie   All forms of *lay* (lay, laid, have laid, am laying) take an object (I laid the book on the table; I now lay the book on the table). The forms of *lie* (lie, lay, have lain, am lying) do not take an object (I am lying down).

leave, let In standard usage *leave* means *to go from*, NOT *to permit* (Let him go; let that alone). "Leave him alone" is a colloquial expression.

less, fewer *Fewer* refers to number and to things countable (There are fewer people waiting than there were yesterday); *less* refers to a smaller amount of something not countable (There is less grass to mow). In informal usage *less* frequently substitutes for *fewer*. *Less* also refers to size or value (less tall, less expensive) or degree (less happy).

like, as if In formal usage *like* should not substitute for *as if* (He talks as if he knows his subject).

manner (in the manner of) The expression can be deadwood. WEAK: He is acting in the manner of his brother. IMPROVED: He is acting like his brother.

most Do not confuse with *almost*.

not so Avoid as an intensive in formal contexts (He is not so intelligent).

of, have The two words sound alike in many contexts. Spell them correctly. *Would've* is a contraction of *would have*, not *would of*.

on the basis that The expression can be awkward. WEAK: I didn't go on the basis that you'd call. IMPROVED: I didn't go because I thought you might call.

on the part of The phrase can be deadwood. WEAK: There was some objection on the part of John. IMPROVED: John objected.

presently, at present *Presently* means *in the near future* (I am coming presently); *at present* means *now* (I am busy at present).

seem, appear *Appear* usually means *to come into view*. (The actor appeared on the stage); *seem* means *to give the impression of* (He seems to be ill).

that, which Used as a relative pronoun, *which* refers to animals and objects; *that*, to persons as well as to objects (the Roosevelt that won the Nobel Peace Prize). Many cultivated writers use *that* to introduce restrictive adjectival clauses (The book that I was assigned to report on) and *which* to introduce nonrestrictive adjectival clauses (*Middlemarch*, which I was assigned to report on), except where the antecedent of the relative pronoun is a person (Theodore Roosevelt, who won the Nobel Peace Prize, became president in 1901).

then, than *Then* refers to time (I'm going then), *than* to comparison (I'm smarter than my brother).,

there, their, they're *There* is an adverb indicating place (The book there is mine), or an expletive (There are several books on the table); *their* is the possessive form of *they*; *they're* is the contraction of *they are*.

to, too *To* is a preposition indicating direction or ownership; *too* means *also* or *more than necessary* (much too hot). Neither should be confused with the number *two*.

unique The word means *one and only*. Don't use it with the comparative (more unique).

whom In informal as well as formal usage, *whom* is the correct form when it immediately follows a preposition governing it (for, to), unless the form of the word serves as the subject of a clause introduced by a preposition (Give the dollar to whoever comes to the door).

who's, whose *Whose* is the possessive form of *who*; *who's* is the contraction of *who is.*

your, you're *Your* denotes possession (your book); *you're* is the contraction of *you are.*

EXERCISES

1. Analyze a paragraph in a letter to the editor of your local newspaper, commenting on the connotations and denotations of particular words and phrases.

2. Classify the varieties of usage you find on the editorial page of your local newspaper or in the editorials of *The New York Times* and in those of another newspaper. Discuss the conclusions that you think can be drawn concerning the audience of the newspaper.

3. Analyze the tone of the following passages, distinguishing the means through which tone is achieved and comparing and contrasting them:

> A vital and restless breed of men, given to tapping our toes and drumming with our fingers, infatuated with every new crazy rhythm that rears its ugly beat, we have never truly loved harmony, the graceful structure of shapes and tones, and for this blindness and deafness we pay the awful price of continuous cacophony. It gets into language as well as music; we mug melody for the sake of sound effects, and the louder and more dissonant they are, the better we seem to like them. Our national veins have taken in the singing blood of Italy, Wales, Ireland and Germany, but the transfusion has had no beneficial effect. Great big blocky words and phrases bumble off our tongues and presses every day. In four weeks of purposeful listening to the radio and reading the newspapers I have come up with a staggering list, full of sound and fury, dignifying nothing: "automation," "roadability," "humature," "motivational cognition" (this baby turned up in a series of travel lectures and was never defined), "fractionalization," "varietism," "redesegregation," "additive," "concertization" (this means giving a concert in a hall, and is not to be confused with cinematization or televisionization). The colloquial deformity "knowledgeable," which should have been clubbed to death years ago, when it first began crawling about like the late Lon Chaney, has gained new life in recent months. It is a dented derby of a word, often found in the scrawny company of such battered straw hats as "do-gooder," "know-how," "update," "uptake" (I recently uptook the iodine uptake test for thyroidism), and others so ugly and strange I can't decipher them in my notes. One of them looks like "de-egghead," which would mean to disintellectualize or mentally emasculate—a crippling operation approved of by an alarming number of squashheads, in Washington and elsewhere.—James Thurber, "The Psychosemanticist Will See You Now, Mr. Thurber"

We are all familiar with the basic difference between English and French parliamentary institutions; copied respectively by such other assemblies as derive from each. We all realize that this main difference has nothing to do with national temperament, but stems from their seating plans. The British, being brought up on team games, enter their House of Commons in the spirit of those who would rather be doing something else. If they cannot be playing golf or tennis, they can at least pretend that politics is a game with very similar rules. But for this device, Parliament would arouse even less interest than it does. So the British instinct is to form two opposing teams, with referee and linesmen, and let them debate until they exhaust themselves. The House of Commons is so arranged that the individual Member is practically compelled to take one side or the other before he knows what the arguments are, or even (in some cases) before he knows the subject of the dispute. His training from birth has been to play for his side, and this saves him from any undue mental effort. Sliding into a seat toward the end of a speech, he knows exactly how to take up the argument from the point it has reached. If the speaker is on his own side of the House, he will say "Hear, hear!" If he is on the opposite, he can safely say "Shame!" or merely "Oh!" At some later stage he may have time to ask his neighbor what the debate is supposed to be about. Strictly speaking, however, there is no need for him to do this. He knows enough in any case not to kick into his own goal. The men who sit opposite are entirely wrong and all their arguments are so much drivel. The men on his own side are statesmanlike, by contrast, and their speeches a singular blend of wisdom, eloquence, and moderation. Nor does it make the slightest difference whether he learned his politics at Harrow or in following the fortunes of Aston Villa. In either school he will have learned when to cheer and when to groan. But the British system depends entirely on its seating plan. If the benches did not face each other, no one could tell truth from falsehood—wisdom from folly—unless indeed by listening to it all. But to listen to it all would be ridiculous, for half the speeches must of necessity be nonsense.—C. Northcote Parkinson, *Parkinson's Law*

4. Write a description of one of the following, using imagery and figurative language to develop your impression. Be careful not to make the imagery or metaphors obtrusive:

a. a city street after a heavy rain

b. a downtown street during a snowfall

c. a view from a window in your apartment or house

d. a body of water as a storm rises

e. the school cafeteria at noon

5. Use the synonym listings in your dictionary to distinguish the meanings of the following words. Then use one of the words in each group in a sentence that draws upon the precise meaning:

a. decrease, dwindle, diminish
b. respect, esteem, admire
c. proportional, commensurable, commensurate
d. honesty, integrity, veracity
e. brittle, crisp, friable
f. impromptu, extemporaneous, improvised
g. open, frank, candid
h. numerous, innumerable, manifold
i. petty, trivial, trifling, paltry
j. fresh, novel, original
k. import, purport, significance, meaning, sense
l. interpose, interfere, intervene, meditate
m. depart, withdraw, retire
n. empty, vacant, void, vacuous
o. insurrection, revolt, mutiny, uprising
p. loiter, dawdle, dally
q. suggest, hint, imply, infer, insinuate

THE
RHETORIC
OF THE
ESSAY

THE NATURE OF RHETORIC

The study of rhetoric is the study of effective communication, not merely of "correct" sentence construction, diction, and the like. Even if you observe the "rules" of grammar and usage your writing may not be convincing to anyone, perhaps not even to yourself if you approach writing as a routine exercise. To write effectively you must consider the nature of your audience, the arguments that audience will find most convincing, and your tone and point of view. To quote the phrase of Wayne Booth, you assume the "rhetorical stance." Of course you must do more than this to produce a satisfactory piece of writing. You will write about your own experiences, you will report honestly. You will not say anything you do not believe, or write less than the whole truth as you understand it. But the "rhetorical stance" is the necessary beginning.

In the previous chapters we have considered these matters individually. In this chapter we shall see how they come together in the composition of the whole essay—in the expository, the argumentative, and the autobiographical essay in particular. We will also discuss personal style again. We have seen the different choices different writers make. We have seen examples of the way they vary traditional methods to arrive at a sentence and paragraph construction, punctuation and diction suited to their individual purpose and reflecting their own style of thought. In the three essays reprinted and analyzed in this chapter we will look carefully at how a style of thought is reflected in the sum of choices of the whole essay.

A NOTE ON THE THEORY OF RHETORIC

In this chapter and the following chapter on logic, we will occasionally refer to traditional ideas about rhetoric useful today because of the help they give in defining three variables: audience, occasion, and the kind of truth a particular essay or argument embodies.

The art of rhetoric, as the Greek philosopher Aristotle and his Roman successors Cicero and Quintilian formulated it, consisted of the application of principles derived from the practice of skilled speakers. These principles were adapted to new situations and enlarged as rhetoric later embraced many new kinds of discourse other than argument—for example, the informal essay. For Aristotle, rhetoric was chiefly concerned with persuasion in orations. The three kinds of oratory he distinguished—that of the law court, the political arena, and the ceremonial occasion during which a great man or an institution was eulogized or censured—each has its own characteristics and special arguments and proofs (called special topics), fitted to particular purposes.[1] All three draw on common methods of development and proofs (called common topics). Each speaking situation calls for decisions based on the purpose of the discourse and the nature of the audience.

One of these decisions has to do with the kind of truth the essay or argument embodies. Though Aristotle's teacher Plato had sug-

[1]*Forensic* or *judicial* oratory includes any kind of defense or effort to pass judgment on an individual's past behavior. The form of the judicial oration depends on the specific issue as the lawyer or pleader sees it (the preliminary discussion might be devoted to a definition of this issue and the grounds on which the defendant is being tried); the procedures that follow—an account of what happened, the presentation of witnesses and documents, and the like—are routine though they vary in importance depending on the circumstances. *Deliberative* or *political oratory* is concerned with future action, government policy, and the like; *ceremonial* or *demonstrative oratory* with praise or censure of an individual or institution (the Gettysburg Address, for example). Each kind of oratory has its special arguments or topics: judicial oratory, justice and injustice; political oratory, the advantageous and disadvantageous; ceremonial oratory, honor and dishonor. The orator centers on these topics, subordinating all other considerations to them. Thus Mark Antony, in his funeral oration for Caesar (a ceremonial oration), argues that Caesar should be honored for his concern over the people of Rome and implies that Brutus and his fellow-conspirators are dishonorable men.

gested that an ideal rhetoric would be concerned with certain and necessary truths, like those of mathematics, Aristotle recognized that such practical sciences as politics, based on "opinions that are generally accepted," might arrive only at probable truth. Granted an essay might begin with statements resembling the axioms of geometry ("We hold these truths to be self-evident") and proceed to show that a number of conclusions follow from these necessarily (as in a declaration of rights such as the Declaration of Independence); an essay might also begin with highly probable assumptions from which highly probable conclusions are shown to follow. Aristotle devoted his rhetoric to the second kind of truth—probable truth. He promoted the view that rhetoric, more than being a concern with ways of pleasing an audience or persuading it, is a method of looking into truth, possessing its own procedures and differing from logic though closely allied with it (as we shall see), particularly in the methods that govern inductive reasoning.

Aristotle and his successors divided rhetoric into five considerations. The first of these—*Invention*—deals with the special and common topics that we mentioned above. The chapter on the paragraph dealt in part with such common topics as definition, division, comparison and contrast, cause and effect—methods of argument common to all kinds of discourse. To "invent" an argument means to find the most suitable procedures or methods of developing it. The second consideration of rhetoric, *Disposition*, deals with the parts of a discourse (the beginning, middle, and end and their parts) and their organization; the third consideration, *Style*, with choices in diction, the subject of the previous chapter. The fourth and fifth considerations, *Memory* and *Pronunciation*, lie outside the province of this book. We will begin our discussion of the elements of rhetoric with Invention—specifically with the common topics—and proceed to Disposition and Style.

THE COMMON TOPICS

We have examined such common topics as definition, division, and comparison and contrast as methods of development in the paragraph. In this section we shall consider these additional topics: in relation to comparison—*similarity, difference, degree;* in relation to *relationship,* in addition to *cause and effect—antecedent and consequent, contraries, contradictions;* in relation to *circumstance—the possible and impossible, past fact and future fact;* in relation to *testimony—authority, testimonial, statistics, maxims, law and precedent.*

1. Similarity. We saw that analysis through comparison and contrast seeks a relative estimate. Analysis through similarity develops comparisons for the purpose of increasing the probability of an argument, not to establish it conclusively: If you admit that people should be licensed to own automobiles, you will agree that they should be licensed to own firearms. The ground of the comparison is that both are lethal objects. The writer of the following passage is defending the proposition that men "are mysteriously ends in themselves" and resistant to definitions in terms of some other thing:

> I hear people deny this, but when they do they always argue for their position by claiming marvelous feats of super-machine calculation that machines can now do or will someday be able to do. But that is not the point; of course machines can outcalculate us. The question to ask is entirely a different one: Will they ever outlove us, outlive us, outvalue us? Do we build machines because machines are good things in themselves? Do we nurture them for their own good, as we nurture our children? An obvious way to test our sense of worth in men and machines is to ask ourselves whether we would ever campaign to liberate the poor downtrodden machines who have been enslaved. Shall we form a National Association for the Advancement of Machinery? Will anyone ever feel a smidgeon of moral indignation because this or that piece of machinery is not given equal rights before the law? Or put it another way: Does anyone value Gemini more than the twins? There may be men now alive who would rather "destruct," as we say, the pilot than the experimental rocket, but most of us still believe that the human being in the space ship is more important than the space ship.
> —WAYNE C. BOOTH, *The Knowledge Most Worth Having*

The argument, in brief, is this: If you do not value the space ship more than you value the pilot, then you *probably* do not value machines more than you do men. The analysis increases the probability of the conclusion: it does not establish it as a certain and necessary truth.

2. Difference. The topic of *difference* is the counterpart of contrast and is used for the same purpose as that of similarity—to strengthen the probability of the argument. In the paragraph just quoted, Booth suggests that we would not ask the same question about machines that we ask about men: we would probably not campaign to liberate downtrodden machines or to give them equal rights before the law. The argument, in brief, is this: If there is a difference in the kinds of questions we ask about men and machines, then we probably think about men and machines in different ways.

3. Degree. Basically, the topic of degree works from the less probable to the more probable or from a lesser to a greater good. Since people differ on the nature of goodness, the writer who depends on degree must take opinion into consideration. An audience of Congressmen will respond one way to an argument based on what public officials think is a relatively greater good; an audience of Weathermen is likely to respond differently. Here is a brief example of the use of degree in a court opinion—Chief Justice Earl Warren's argument, in his dissent in *Times Film Corporation v. Chicago* (1961), that censorship is the "most effective" means for restricting ideas and that the "censor's sword pierces deeply into the heart of free expression":

> It is axiomatic that the stroke of the censor's pen or the cut of his scissors will be a less contemplated decision than will be the prosecutor's determination to prepare a criminal indictment. The standards of proof, the judicial safeguards afforded a criminal defendant and the consequences of bringing such charges will all provoke the mature deliberation of the prosecutor. None of these hinder the quick judgment of the censor, the speedy determination to suppress.

The argument, in brief, is this: If the judicial controls in criminal prosecutions are admitted to be necessary, they are equally necessary over the censor whose decision is less contemplated than that of the prosecutor, for whom the law establishes standards of proof.

The following passage illustrates a different use of degree. The author wishes to establish that "it is reasonable to assume that any law, no matter how limited in scope, that prevents or makes it more difficult for dangerous or potentially dangerous persons to acquire firearms must have at least some effect":

> Every reliable study indicates that where gun control laws are most stringent, the murder rate, as well as the percentage of murders involving firearms, is lower than in areas where gun laws are weak or non-existent and which, hence, have a greater number of guns per capita. Contrary to popular belief, New York City, despite its rising incidence of crime, actually ranked only tenth among the nation's fifteen largest metropolitan areas in 1969 in number of homicides per 100,000 population, according to FBI data. Philadelphia, also with a strict gun law, ranked eleventh, and Chicago seventh. Even the District of Columbia ranked as far down as sixth. At a rate of 9.4 violent deaths per 100,000 inhabitants, New York stood far behind Houston's 16.8, St. Louis's 14.3, Cleveland's 13.8, Baltimore's 13.4, and the 13.0 rate for Detroit—all cities with weak, if any, gun laws.
>
> —CARL BAKAL, "The Failure of Federal Gun Control,"
> *Saturday Review*, July 3, 1971

Here the statistical evidence indicates a lower degree of crime of a particular sort in cities with stringent gun control laws than in those with weak gun laws or none. In his article Bakal offers other evidence in making his case. We will consider the implications of statistical arguments, including their limitations, in the next chapter.

4. Antecedent and consequent. An analysis through antecedent and consequent takes this form: If a particular situation existed, what would be its result? In the course of his majority opinion relating to reapportionment in Alabama (*Reynolds v. Sims*, 1964), Justice Warren stated:

> Legislators represent people, not trees or acres. Legislators are elected by voters, not farms or cities or economic interests. As long as ours is a representative form of government, and our legislatures are those instruments of government elected directly by and directly representative of the people, the right to elect legislators in a free and unimpaired fashion is a bedrock of our political system. It could hardly be gainsaid that a constitutional claim had been asserted by an allegation that certain otherwise qualified voters had been entirely prohibited from voting for members of their state legislature. And, if a State should provide that the votes of citizens in one part of the State should be given two times, or five times, or ten times the weight of votes of citizens in another part of the State, it could hardly be contended that the right to vote of those residing in the disfavored areas had not been effectively diluted. It would appear extraordinary to suggest that a State could be constitutionally permitted to enact a law providing that certain of the State's voters could vote two, five, or ten times for their legislative representatives, while voters living elsewhere could vote only once. And is it inconceivable that a state law to the effect that in counting votes for legislators, the votes of citizens in one part of the State would be multiplied by two, five or ten, while the votes of persons in another area would be counted only at face value, could be constitutionally sustainable.

The second part of this statement sets up a hypothetical case and indicates a highly probable consequence: the right to vote would be diluted if some votes were assigned greater weight than others. Arguments of this type usually contain unstated assumptions that need to be examined. Warren states his assumption that representative democracy implies the representation of individual—not group—opinion; but note that his statement of it is an elucidation and not a defense. If the assumption were directly challenged or a challenge were anticipated, it would have to be defended.

5. Contraries. Contrary terms are opposite terms belonging to the same genus—for example, tolerance and bigotry (two kinds of attitude toward those holding different or opposite opinions). The topic of contraries allows the writer to show that if one of two contrary statements is true, the other must be false, and that if one is demonstrably false, the other may be true. In his analysis of individualism in modern life, David Riesman criticizes the popular attitude that work should not be "impersonal" and that workers should share the emotions of their work experiences, much as older guild workers were thought to do. Riesman explores the implications of the contrary attitude:

> A contrary attitude would assume that we should be grateful to find, in our work, areas of freedom from people, where the necessary minimum of productive activity could be accomplished without the strain and waste of time involved in continuous concern for the morale of the working group. If men were not compelled to be sociable at work, they could enjoy sociability in their leisure much more than they often do now. In fact, while men in the nineteenth century may have underestimated their satisfactions from solitary occupations, hobbies and other pursuits, we tend today to reverse these extremes and to forget that men can enjoy, let us say, the physical rhythms of work or the private fantasies of leisure even when they are for long periods deprived of social comradeship at work and play. What is necessary is some sort of balance which will find room for quite idiosyncratic individual desires to be, variously, alone and with others.
>
> —*Individualism Reconsidered*

Riesman goes on to argue that the increasing flexibility of working conditions and the growing understanding of the psychological and physical problems engendered challenge and stimulate the worker. Riesman's argument is more or less probable, depending on the evidence he can muster; the contrast of attitudes adds force to the argument by exposing a common but somewhat mistaken view concerning the "impersonality" of modern life.

6. Contradictions. Patience and impatience, tolerance and intolerance are contradictory terms. The use of the topic of contradiction is apparent in the following passage from Justice Hugo Black's dissent in *Adler v. Board of Education* (1952):

> This is another of those rapidly multiplying legislative enactments which make it dangerous—this time for school teachers—to think or say anything except what a transient majority happen to approve at the moment. Basically these laws rest on the belief that government should supervise and limit the flow of ideas into the minds of men. The tendency of such

governmental policy is to mold people into a common intellectual pattern. Quite a different governmental policy rests on the belief that government should leave the mind and spirit of man absolutely free. Such a governmental policy encourages varied intellectual outlooks in the belief that the best views will prevail. This policy of freedom is in my judgment embodied in the First Amendment and made applicable to the States by the Fourteenth. Because of this policy public officials cannot be constitutionally vested with powers to select the ideas people can think about, censor the public views they can express, or choose the persons or groups people can associate with. Public officials with such powers are not public servants; they are public masters.

Black interprets the disputed legislation of New York State governing the political beliefs of school teachers as a "tendency . . . to mold people into a common intellectual pattern" and restates the opposite, and in his view desirable, policy in somewhat contradictory terms: "Such a governmental policy encourages varied intellectual outlooks in the belief that the best views will prevail." Formal logic demands that the contradictory terms be exactly opposite in wording; in much writing employing contradiction the wording approaches exactness.

7. Possible and impossible. This topic can take many forms, depending on the nature of the argument. It may be argued that a particular policy or action is feasible because a similar or even a seemingly less feasible one has proved to be so—as in Edith Hamilton's argument that ancient Greece in the fourth century achieved individual freedom consistent with public spirit and enterprise:

Is not that a challenge to us? Is it not true that into our education have come a slackness and softness? Is hard effort prominent? The world of thought can be entered in no other way. Are we not growing slack and soft in our political life? When the Athenians finally wanted not to give to the state, but the state to give to them, when the freedom they wished most for was freedom from responsibility, then Athens ceased to be free and was never free again. Is not that a challenge?
—"The Lessons of the Past"

A common form of this topic is working from part to whole: showing that a policy is feasible because conditions necessary to its success exist—that the will to responsible action and government exists in the country.

8. Past fact and future fact. Judicial oratory depended on showing that an action did actually occur (past fact); political oratory depended on showing that an action would occur (future fact). The uses of past and future fact are many, as are its forms, which resemble those of the possible and impossible. One form shows that the basis for a particular action or policy exists in the past and is possible because of the strength of past experience or contemporary facts or circumstances. In the following passage the writer asks whether Americans are likely to vest the power of public opinion in one man:

> To put this power absolutely in the hands of one man would be suicidal. We have had a grisly demonstration of that in the case of the German people, when the potent majority of them committed their minds and consciences to Hitler and blindly followed him to destruction.
>
> That the American people will go to any such extreme seems highly improbable. Our historical experience, our educational methods, even to some extent our prejudices and superstitions militate against it. Artemus Ward's complacent proclamation, "I am not a politician, and my other habits are good," was something more than a jape. It reflects a skepticism of Whitman's "elected persons" that is deeply embedded in the American character—a prejudice perhaps touched with superstition, but one that operates against any attempt at the deification of Caesar.
>
> It would be unrealistic, however, to deny that there are forces in the modern world that operate in the other direction; nor are they confined to the ideologies of Marx, Lenin or Mao. We seem, indeed, relatively immune to ideologies; in no large country has the Communist Party had less success in recruiting the masses, and even the Socialists have never polled as many as 1,000,000 votes. But there are conditions, not theories, that are subjecting the traditional American system to a considerable strain.
>
> —GERALD W. JOHNSON, "The U.S. Presidency"

Johnson is concerned both with what has happened and what will happen. The amount of evidence needed to persuade an audience depends on its knowledge: political scientists may need less than junior high school students. As we shall see, statistical arguments such as Johnson employs can be dangerous when the basis of the sample is left obscure or unexamined.

9. Law and precedent. Though these topics are distinct ones, we shall consider them together. Justice Warren's opinion in *Quinn v. United States* (1955), relating to the privilege of the Fifth Amendment, argues in part on the basis of historical precedent and prior interpretations of it by the Supreme Court:

> The privilege against self-incrimination is a right that was hard-earned by our forefathers. The reasons for its inclusion

in the Constitution—and the necessities for its preservations—are to be found in the lessons of history. As early as 1650, remembrance of the horror of Star Chamber proceedings a decade before had firmly established the privilege in the common law of England. Transplanted to this country as part of our legal heritage, it soon made its way into various state constitutions and ultimately in 1791 into the federal Bill of Rights. The privilege, this Court has stated, "was generally regarded then, as now, as a privilege of great value, a protection to the innocent, though a shelter to the guilty, and a safeguard against heedless, unfounded or tyrannical prosecutions." Co-equally with our other constitutional guarantees, the Self-Incrimination Clause "must be accorded liberal construction in favor of the right it was intended to secure." Such liberal construction is particularly warranted in a prosecution of a witness for refusal to answer, since the respect normally accorded the privilege is then buttressed by the presumption of innocence accorded a defendant in a criminal trial. To apply the privilege narrowly or begrudgingly—to treat it as an historical relic, at most merely to be tolerated—is to ignore its development and purpose.

Warren is careful to indicate the pertinence of the precedent he cites; the historical facts make a "liberal construction" of the amendment necessary. All such appeals to law and precedent, of course, are open to criticism and dissent. A writer may, in addition to citing law and precedent, cite maxims of the law, that is, concise statements of principle (Justice Holmes' "Great cases like hard cases make bad law") as well as the testimony of reliable eyewitnesses and commentators (Clarence Darrow's court experiences).

10. Authority. The appeal to authority in testimonials and arguments is one way to ground opinions as well as presumptions of fact. The force of the testimonial or argument depends on establishing the special authority of the person cited or quoted. Both John Ruskin, the nineteenth-century art and social critic, and Lewis Mumford, the twentieth-century critic of city planning and technology, are authorities on architecture, but each has a special authority, pertinent to the situation under discussion and perhaps limited to it.

THE PARTS OF THE ESSAY

The classical oration was organized according to a plan created, adapted, and modified by gifted orators. The value of this plan for the modern writer and speaker is that it offers a frame—a skeleton—which allows him to dispose his thoughts to the best advantage. In the course of organizing his presentation, he may choose to rearrange the parts or dispense with some of them. Here is an outline of the plan:

I. Introduction
    A. *Leading* the reader into the subject
    B. *Statement* or narration of the facts in the case or the background
    C. *Division of the arguments* to be used
II. Body of Argument
    A. *Proof* or arguments in support of the proposition
    B. *Refutation* of opposing arguments
III. Conclusion
    A. *Summary* of arguments
    B. Final *appeal* to the audience for support

The nature of each part differs according to whether the oration is judicial, deliberative, or demonstrative. Thus the deliberative oration, concerned with future events or policy, may dispense with the statement of facts or use it to suggest the background of the policy or circumstances that shape the problem. Each of these elements has found its way into the modern essay in modified form as we shall see.

INTRODUCTION

Whatever else the introduction does, it must indicate the subject of the essay and do so in a way that compels attention and engages interest. Building to the thesis statement at the end of the first or second paragraph accomplishes these purposes economically. Usually the reader needs introduction to the thesis; he needs some indication of why it is worth developing. If, for example, the thesis is that students are highly sensitive to criticism of their ideas, the paragraph might begin with the idea that most people prize their thoughts, regardless of how they derive them. A good introductory paragraph begins where the reader is and leads him to the thoughts of the writer.

In a long introductory paragraph to an article on the 1964 World Series, Roger Angell builds to his thesis in an instructive way:[1]

> As we all know, when the typical American business executive turns out his bedside light he devotes his next-to-last thought of the day to his corporate image—that elusive and essential ideal vision of his company which shimmers, or *should* shimmer, in the minds of consumers. Do they like us, he wonders. Do we look respectable? Honest? Lovable? Hmm. He sighs, stretches out, and tries to find sleep by once again striking out the entire batting order of the New York

[1] Reprinted by permission; © 1964 The New Yorker Magazine, Inc.

Yankees. As he works the count to three and two on Tom Tresh, it may suddenly occur to this well-paid insomniac that baseball itself has the most enviable corporate image in the world. Its evocations, overtones, and loyalties, firmly planted in the mind of every American male during childhood and nurtured thereafter by millions of words of free newspaper publicity, appear to be unassailable. It is the national pastime. It is youth, springtime, a trip to the country, part of our past. It is the roaring excitement of huge urban crowds and the sleepy green afternoon silences of midsummer. Without effort, it engenders and thrives on heroes, legends, self-identification, and home-town pride. For six months of the year, it intrudes cheerfully into every American home, then frequently rises to a point of nearly insupportable tension and absorption, and concludes in the happy explosion of the country's favorite sporting spectacle, the World Series. Given these ancient and self-sustaining attributes, it would seem impossible that the executives of such a business could injure it to any profound degree through their own carelessness and greed, yet this is exactly what has happened to baseball in the past ten years. The season that just ended in two improbably close pennant races and in the victory of the Cardinals over the Yankees in a memorable seven-game World Series was also the most shameful and destructive year the game has experienced since the Black Sox scandal of 1919.

—"The Series," *The New Yorker*, October 24, 1964

Instead of beginning with baseball, Angell begins with the business executive who, before trying to go to sleep, thinks about his "corporate image." But this executive is an insomniac who, instead of counting sheep, strikes out the New York Yankees in their batting order. Soon his thoughts shift to the "corporate image" of American baseball, which has the most enviable image of any institution in the world. It is so enviable, in fact, that it seems impossible that the executives of that business could injure it through "carelessness and greed." With considerable skill Angell has sprung his thesis—and he concludes the paragraph with a strong indictment: the season culminating in the 1964 World Series was "the most shameful and destructive year the game has experienced since the Black Sox scandal of 1919."

In this way Angell arouses the interest of his reader before he introduces his thesis. And the reader knows why the thesis is important. Baseball is the national pastime; the World Series is the major sporting event; something of value is being destroyed. Few introductory paragraphs are this elaborate, however.

In many essays, of course, the thesis is stated fully at the beginning of the first paragraph because nothing is gained by building to it; the practice is common in newspaper and magazine editorials which seldom can afford expansive beginnings. In other essays, it may be necessary to build to a statement of the thesis occurring at the end of the essay: the thesis will not be understood without considerable discussion. We saw that the topic sentence is often put at the end of a paragraph for the same reason.

Here are a number of alternate introductions, each serving a different purpose. President Kennedy opened his third State of the Union message in the following words:

> I congratulate you all, not merely on your electoral victory, but on your selected role in history. For you and I are privileged to serve the great Republic in what could be the most decisive decade in its long history. The choices we make, for good or ill, will affect the welfare of generations yet unborn. (January 14, 1963)

Kennedy not only reminds the new Congress that its choices will be important ones: he disposes his audience to consider his ideas favorably. By contrast his introduction to a television address concerning nuclear testing and disarmament immediately stresses the importance of the issue; the simple facts of the case are given attention:

> Seventeen years ago man unleashed the power of the atom. He thereby took into his mortal hands the power of self-extinction. Throughout the years that have followed, under three successive Presidents, the United States has sought to banish this weapon from the arsenals of individual nations. For of all the awesome responsibilities entrusted to this office, none is more somber to contemplate than the special statutory authority to employ nuclear arms in the defense of our people and freedom. (March 2, 1962)

But in his famous address at American University, Kennedy builds to a statement of his subject (not his thesis) through a quotation from an English poet that both provides a transition and takes notice of the place and audience:

> "There are few earthly things more beautiful than a University," wrote John Masefield, in his tribute to the English universities, and his words are equally true here. He did not refer to spires and towers, to campus greens and ivied walls. He admired the splendid beauty of the university, he said, because it was "a place where those who hate ignorance may strive to know, where those who perceive truth may strive to make others see."
>
> I have therefore chosen this time and place to discuss a

topic on which ignorance too often abounds and the truth is too rarely perceived, yet it is the most important topic on earth: world peace. (June 10, 1963)

In some essays, you must immediately disclose your personal character and interests. A formal statement of purpose would be out of place in the following introduction to an exploration of racial attitudes:

Two ideas puzzled me deeply as a child growing up in Brooklyn during the 1930's in what today would be called an integrated neighborhood. One of them was that all Jews were rich; the other was that all Negroes were persecuted. These ideas had appeared in print; therefore they must be true. My own experience and the evidence of my senses told me they were not true, but that only confirmed what a day-dreaming boy in the provinces—for the lower-class neighborhoods of New York belong as surely to the provinces as any rural town in North Dakota—discovers very early: *his* experience is unreal and the evidence of his senses is not to be trusted. Yet even a boy with a head full of fantasies incongruously synthesized out of Hollywood movies and English novels cannot altogether deny the reality of his own experience—especially when there is so much deprivation in that experience. Nor can he altogether gainsay the evidence of his own senses—especially such evidence of the senses as comes from being repeatedly beaten up, robbed, and in general hated, terrorized, and humiliated.

—NORMAN PODHORETZ, "My Negro Problem—and Ours"

Podhoretz stresses the paradoxical—a particularly effective way of engaging attention. Another way is to begin with an anecdote. The following introductory paragraph is dramatic and shocking:

Shortly before the war of 1914, an assassin whose crime was particularly repulsive (he had slaughtered a family of farmers, including the children) was condemned to death in Algiers. He was a farm worker who had killed in a sort of bloodthirsty frenzy but had aggravated his case by robbing his victims. The affair created a great stir. It was generally thought that decapitation was too mild a punishment for such a monster. This was the opinion, I have been told, of my father, who was especially aroused by the murder of the children. One of the few things I know about him, in any case, is that he wanted to witness the execution, for the first time in his life. He got up in the dark to go to the place of execution at the other end of town amid a great crowd of people. What he saw that morning he never told anyone. My mother relates merely that he came rushing home, his face distorted, refused to talk, lay down for a moment on the bed, and suddenly began to vomit. He had just discovered the reality hidden under the noble phrases with which it was masked. Instead of thinking of the slaughtered children, he could think of nothing but that quivering body that had just been dropped onto a board to have its head cut off.

        —ALBERT CAMUS, "Reflections on the Guillotine"

Unlike Podhoretz, Camus does not identify himself or comment on his character or interests. In some essays it may be necessary for you to outline the organization or the difficulties in the argument or exposition, or summarize the opinions of others on the subject. Scholarly articles often begin with an extensive review of criticism that is used incidentally to justify a new approach to the subject.

STATEMENT OF FACTS

The length of the statement of facts or narration will vary according to your purpose. As a rule the narration should be as brief and clear as possible without omitting important information. That of a book review may be extremely long if it is necessary to summarize the content in order to make a judgment about it; by contrast, too extended a summary can blur the focus and lose the attention of the audience. In his "Letter from Birmingham Jail," Martin L. King, Jr., explains his reasons for coming to the city—an explanation indispensable in light of the statement of the Birmingham clergymen that his activities were "unwise and untimely":

> I think I should indicate why I am here in Birmingham, since you have been influenced by the view which argues against "outsiders coming in." I have the honor of serving as president of the Southern Christian Leadership Conference, an organization operating in every southern state, with headquarters in Atlanta, Georgia. We have some eighty-five affiliated organizations across the South, and one of them is the Alabama Christian Movement for Human Rights. Frequently we share staff, educational and financial resources with our affiliates. Several months ago the affiliate here in Birmingham asked us to be on call to engage in a nonviolent direct-action program if such were deemed necessary. We readily consented, and when the hour came we lived up to our promise. So I, along with several members of my staff, am here because I was invited here. I am here because I have organizational ties here.
>
> But more basically, I am in Birmingham because injustice

is here. Just as the prophets of the eighth century B.C. left their villages and carried their "thus saith the Lord" far beyond the boundaries of their home towns, and just as the Apostle Paul left his village of Tarsus and carried the gospel of Jesus Christ to the far corners of the Greco-Roman world, so am I compelled to carry the gospel of freedom beyond my own home town. Like Paul, I must constantly respond to the Macedonian call for aid.

This passage is the beginning of a long account of the civil rights movement in Birmingham. King concludes the narration with a transition to his confirming arguments.

DIVISION OF THE ARGUMENTS

In a complex essay or oration in which the kinds of argument to be marshalled are not alike, a preliminary statement and perhaps a short analysis of these can be useful in helping your reader or listener keep track of them. Such a division of the argument is often a part of the formal discourse.

CONFIRMATION

King in his letter (a less formal discourse) proceeds directly to his confirmation. Here is a part of it:

You may well ask: "Why direct action? Why sit-ins, marches and so forth? Isn't negotiation a better path?" You are quite right in calling for negotiation. Indeed, this is the very purpose of direct action. Nonviolent direct action seeks to create such a crisis and foster such a tension that a community which has constantly refused to negotiate is forced to confront the issue. It seeks so to dramatize the issue that it can no longer be ignored. My citing the creation of tension as part of the work of the nonviolent-resister may sound rather shocking. But I must confess that I am not afraid of the word "tension." I have earnestly opposed violent tension, but there is a type of constructive, nonviolent tension which is necessary for growth. Just as Socrates felt that it was necessary to create a tension in the mind so that individuals could rise from the bondage of myths and half-truths to the unfettered realm of creative analysis and objective appraisal, so must we see the necd for nonviolent gadflies to create the kind of tension in society that will help men rise from the dark depths of prejudice and racism to the majestic heights of understanding and brotherhood.

This paragraph is a model of ordering of ideas. King begins by examining a chief criticism of the civil rights movement—its alleged dependence on "direct action" rather than on negotiation. His own argument is that negotiation itself depends on "constructive, nonviolent tension." He develops his argument through a series of topics:

1. **Definition.** He clarifies the meaning of "tension" ("Nonviolent direct action seeks to create such a crisis . . .").

2. **Division.** He distinguishes two kinds of tension—violent and nonviolent.

3. **Similarity** and **Authority.** His reference to Socrates illuminates the particular conception of nonviolent tension he is advocating and shows that a respectable intellectual tradition stands behind it.

4. **Antecedent and consequent.** King is arguing that if negotiation takes place under the conditions he urges, the South will cease living "in monologue." This particular argument is based on unstated but obvious assumptions.

The order of arguments in the confirmation is determined by the rhetorical situation. As a rule, it is best to build to the argument that the particular audience is likely to find most cogent or forceful; this procedure is usually the most effective when the audience is a general one. If a special audience is thought or known to be hostile, a good procedure is to begin with the most convincing argument and end with a restatement of it. Where a series of arguments varies in probability or cogency, it is usually best to begin and end with a relatively stronger argument.

No ordering of ideas should risk anti-climax, whatever the circumstances, nor should the principle of order be obscure. This does not mean you have to specify it. As in the paragraph, simple transitions will clarify the organization if the order of ideas is unclear; the transitions should be as unobtrusive as possible.

REFUTATION

The refutation of opposing arguments occurs to an extent in the confirmation, as in King's letter. But a direct and thorough one may be reserved for later, when the audience is perhaps disposed to examine ideas that previously were held uncritically. The nature of the refutation and the appeal the writer makes depends, as always, on the rhetorical situation. An appeal to emotion, if suited to the occasion (as in President Kennedy's inaugural address), is not to be scorned if it is based on a strong rational argument. Antony's funeral oration in *Julius Caesar* is based on a rational view of the situation. Brutus has acted wrongly; his predominantly rational defense of his behavior to the mourners has disguised the dishonorable motives of the conspirators. But Antony depends on irony and sarcasm which he uses *against* the crowd; for his purpose is to rouse them to fury. His appeal, then, is not to reason. Brutus, it should be noted, makes an ethical as well as a rational appeal; he presents himself as a good man whose motive in the conspiracy is an honorable one. Antony subtly attacks this presumption in his often-repeated, "And Brutus is an honorable man."

By contrast, King attacks the presumed ethical position of the clergymen, but he does so in a direct way. His appeal is not covert:

> I must make two honest confessions to you, my Christian and Jewish brothers. First, I must confess that over the past few years I have been gravely disappointed with the white moderate. I have almost reached the regrettable conclusion that the Negro's great stumbling block in his stride toward freedom is not the White Citizens' Counciler or the Ku Klux Klanner, but the white moderate, who is more devoted to "order" than to justice; who prefers a negative peace which is the absence of tension to a positive peace which is the presence of justice; who constantly says: "I agree with you in the goal you seek, but I cannot agree with your methods of direct action"; who paternalistically believes he can set the timetable for another man's freedom; who lives by a mythical concept of time and who constantly advises the Negro to wait for a "more convenient season." Shallow understanding from people of good will is more frustrating than absolute misunderstanding from people of ill will. Lukewarm acceptance is much more bewildering than outright rejection.

King identifies what he takes to be the real motives of the white moderate and asks him to examine these rationally. The emotional appeal is also a direct one. Implicit in this part of the refutation is his appeal to the clergymen to regard him as a man of good character and good will, open to reason and strong emotion both. In the next chapter we will consider the many ways ideas can be refuted logically.

CONCLUSION

An effective conclusion need not be long; a concise one is less likely to labor the obvious or repeat ideas unnecessarily. Certainly the emotional temperature of the essay must not be allowed to drop so markedly that anti-climax results, though the tautness of the argument may have been relaxed toward the end. The impression you give of yourself should be sustained and not altered unintentionally. In a complex discourse the chief arguments may be summarized—or perhaps the chief points on which the refutation depends, if these are taken to be more crucial. Here is the conclusion of King's letter, which achieves these aims effectively:

> If I have said anything in this letter that overstates the truth and indicates an unreasonable impatience, I beg you to forgive me. If I have said anything that understates the truth and indicates my having a patience that allows me to settle for anything less than brotherhood, I beg God to forgive me.
> I hope this letter finds you strong in the faith. I also hope that circumstances will soon make it possible for me to meet each of you, not as an integrationist or a civil rights leader but as a fellow clergyman and a Christian brother. Let us all hope that the dark clouds of racial prejudice will soon pass away and the deep fog of misunderstanding will be lifted from our fear-drenched communities, and in some not too distant tomorrow the radiant stars of love and brotherhood will shine over our great nation with all their scintillating beauty.

The formality of the writing situation permits the highly emotional conclusion, which would be out of place in a more informal one. One kind of effective conclusion is a reference to the ideas that open the essay; another, to the chief method of analysis or thesis. Here are two examples of this kind of reference. The procedure is especially useful when the essay or argument does not call for an extended recapitulation or emotional appeal.

BEGINNING	ENDING
The right of every newspaper publisher to decline advertising, with or without explaining his reasons for doing so, was recently upheld in a vital decision of the Supreme Court of the United States. Briefly, the Court ruled that a newspaper is not a common carrier, therefore does not have to sell its space to everyone who requests it. In other words, it's up to each individual publisher to print what *he* thinks is in the public interest and to be able to turn down advertisements unsuited to his audience, for all manner of reasons including libel, vulgarity, bad taste, or because they	Freedom of speech and freedom of the press include the right to refrain from speaking and publishing, to omit or turn down something for publication. If this were not the intent of the Bill of Rights, no newspaper could function since it would be forced to print everything anyone submitted to it. An editor (or publisher) would have no function in a society where everything submitted had to be put into type. Again, no editor exists in the true sense of the word on such totalitarian publications as *Izvestia* and *Pravda*. Mimics, yes; editors, no. And the Supreme Court is now

are misleading. *It is one of those milestone decisions that come out of the Supreme Court affecting the very innards of the newspaper business.* [thesis statement]

saying to us that this right to publish and to refuse to publish extends beyond news to the advertising content that helps keep every paper in business—*a milestone decision in every way.* [reiteration of the thesis]
—RICHARD L. TOBIN, "The Right to Turn Down Advertising," Saturday Review, June 12, 1971

BEGINNING

One of the greatest riddles of the universe is the uncanny ability of living things to carry out their normal activities with clocklike precision at a particular time of the day, month and year. Why do oysters plucked from a Connecticut bay and shipped to a Midwest laboratory continue to time their lives to ocean tides 800 miles away? How do potatoes in hermetically sealed containers predict atmospheric pressure trends two days in advance? What effects do the lunar and solar rhythms have on the life habits of man? Living things clearly possess powerful adaptive capacities—but the explanation of whatever strange and permeative forces are concerned continues to challenge science. Let us consider the phenomena more closely.

ENDING

Evidence suggests the primary timing system to be the movements of the sun, moon and earth. Nature provided means by which this timer could simultaneously serve the rhythmicalities of both living organisms and their environment. Ingeniously the timing bridge to living systems was fashioned, not in terms of such variable and biologically potent forces as light and temperature (to which organisms must respond in specifically adaptive fashions), but in terms of more stable forces demanding little or no specific adaptive response and simultaneously so pervasive that no living thing would ever normally be deprived of their influence. Only with such provisions could living clocks become the loyal servant rather than the domineering master of life.
—FRANK A. BROWN, JR., "Life's Mysterious Clocks"

THE ARGUMENTATIVE ESSAY

The points we have been making are illustrated in the following essay by Norman Cousins, former editor of *Saturday Review*. This weekly magazine devoted to cultural and political issues is addressed to an educated, general audience whose interests range from literature, music, films, and plays to communications, science, and social issues of national concern. Accordingly Cousins does not fit his argument to particular assumptions or ideas; instead he assumes in his reader a general knowledge of and concern about issues relating to the survival of civilization, but he is careful to state his premises fully. His introduction and conclusion are necessarily short, for, given the restrictions of an editorial page, there is little space for a recapitulation or the extended emotional appeal that we find in King's letter. The emotional appeal extends through the whole essay and is reiterated strongly in the brief final paragraph. It should be noted, too, that Cousins limits himself to a *specific point at issue*—whether we can safeguard civilization from impulsive and irrational acts of individuals rather than accidental explosions. In both the confirmation and refutation the focus of discussion is kept on this issue.

Can Civilization Be Assassinated?

by Norman Cousins

¶1 The instant reaction of most people to the assassination of the President was expressed in four words: "I can't believe it." This was not merely a sudden reflex response, like crying out in pain. It was a direct and accurate reflection of the inability of the human mind to deal with tragedy beyond a certain dimension. For man retains his sanity by assigning boundary lines to the range of improbables in life. He knows he may be confronted with accident, disaster, and death. But even this catalogue of horrors exists within a certain range of grim expectation. A tragedy may be stark, but as long as it is recognizable, the rational intelligence will try to cope with it.

¶2 But then the outermost limits of the improbables are violently punctured, and the mind turns blank. An embittered, unbalanced individual looks down a gun sight, squeezes a trigger, and the human intelligence staggers with the impact. When people say, therefore, that they still find it difficult to believe the President was murdered, what they are really saying is that it is virtually impossible to conceive that one sullen, warped mind could have produced such havoc all by itself.

¶3 Yet this is precisely the ultimate significance of the atomic age. Not just a President but all civilization is vulnerable to the weird turnings of a disturbed mind. It takes no more than a single individual to unhinge history. Consider the facts. Both the Soviet Union and the United States have placed in the hands of numerous individuals the power to start the chain reaction that could lead to the assassination of civilization. The Soviet Union operates submarines not far off the East and West coasts of the United States. These submarines are equipped with launching platforms for missiles with nuclear warheads. Every major city in the United States is within range. These missiles are subject to the decision of the submarine commanders. The United States, in addition to its Polaris fleet, maintains hundreds of jet

ANALYSIS

Introduction. This essay was published shortly after the assassination of President Kennedy. In a previous editorial Cousins had explored the character of Kennedy and the implications of his death; here he uses the tragedy as a frame of reference for an examination of a central issue. He thus builds to a statement of his thesis at the beginning of paragraph 3: "all civilization is vulnerable to the weird turnings of a disturbed mind." The appeal is an emotional one—a proper one in the circumstances.

Statement of facts. Though paragraphs 1–2 provide important information—in spite of the odds against it, a President can be assassinated —paragraph 3 constitutes the narration. Cousins reminds the reader of the enormous power the United States and the U.S.S.R. have invested

planes in the air on a twenty-four-hour basis not far from the borders of the Soviet Union. These planes are fully loaded with hydrogen explosives. The greatest possible care has been taken to ensure that the commanders of these planes will not be given irresponsible orders; but the central fact is that the orders are transmitted to human beings who have to carry them out. The power, therefore, is subject to individual decision and motivation.

¶4 It is to be assumed that every one of the hundreds of men on both sides who have been given access to the final button has been carefully screened. But no system has been devised that can penetrate fully the mysteries of human personality and motivation. No psychologist or psychiatrist can probe deeply enough into those remote pockets of a man's mind where bitterness or venom may be stored. No psychologist or psychiatrist can predict unfailingly when a sudden impulse will seize a man's mind. No psychologist or psychiatrist can certify absolutely how each of a large number of individuals will react under an almost limitless range of circumstances.

¶5 A man doesn't have to be deranged or go berserk in order to commit an act of catastrophic irresponsibility. He can be impelled by the noblest motives of duty or righteousness. Several years ago a French air force pilot, disgusted by what he believed to be the inadequacy and incompetence of his government, decided to bomb an Algerian village. He was motivated by what he considered the highest impulses of patriotism—much the way an American general recently decided to substitute his understanding of what was happening in the world for the understanding of the President and the Secretary of State. These experiences were exceptional. It was only one French pilot out of many thousands and it was only one American general

in individuals. The narration opens and closes with a statement of the problem:

It takes no more than a single individual to unhinge history.

The power, therefore, is subject to individual decision and motivation.

Confirmation. Cousins dispenses with a division of the arguments and proceeds to his argument, stating the problem forcefully in paragraph 4. The last three sentences of the paragraph are loosely balanced to emphasize the impossibility of penetrating the mysterious human brain.

In Paragraph 5 Cousins support his thesis, that civilization is vulnerable, with his *first argument*—that man is unpredictable. His *second argument*, developed in this paragraph, is that man need not be deranged to blow up the world: he may act from the highest motives. The point is developed by *example.*

At the end of paragraph 5 Cousins introduces a *third argument:* it

out of hundreds. But that is just the point. It takes only one man in our time to trigger the assassination of human society.

¶6 True, the most scrupulous safeguards have been established to guard against such a grisly event. Officials have painstakingly explained how extensive are the precautions and how small are the chances that these precautions might not work. But the danger, though small, is not nonexistent. The chances that a deranged assassin could penetrate the protective mechanism set up to safeguard the life of an American President were very small, but it happened. It was irrational. It was remote. It was most improbable. But it happened. In defense of the Secret Service, it is said that there was no way of X-raying the mind of every spectator in the line of march. Quite so. It is equally true that there is no way of X-raying the mind of every man in an atomic age who has the power to incinerate millions of human beings. The only possible defense is to take that power away from him. If the President's assassin had been unable to obtain the murder weapon, his bitterness would not have been lethal.

¶7 In any event, the key fact about the extensive precautions now taken against unintended nuclear war is that these safeguards are directed mainly to the danger of war through accident rather than to arbitrary decision by someone in a position to explode a bomb. The safeguards cannot possibly guard against the volatility, variability, and unpredictability of human personality.

¶8 It will be argued that only a few men possess the power to authorize a nuclear war. This is correct; but many men possess the power to detonate the bombs that could start a war without authorization. The proof of this fact resides in the very efforts taken by military officials to convince a pos-

takes only one man to blow up the world. The *principle of order* in paragraphs 4–5 is that of probability. The first argument is one with which no person would disagree; many *would* disagree with the third. Cousins is attacking the view that it is improbable a single person could assassinate civilization: the marshalling of evidence shows that one person could.

Refutation. Cousins begins his refutation in paragraph 6 by admitting that "the most scrupulous safeguards have been established to guard against such a grisly event." But he shows that these safeguards are inadequate by citing the assassination of the President and restating the arguments of paragraphs 4–5.

Paragraph 7 shows that the objection that there are extensive safeguards avoids the real issue—which is not the prevention of an accidental explosion but the prevention of an irrational and impulsive act.

Paragraph 8 takes up an *even stronger* objection, "that only a few men possess the power to authorize a nuclear war." In the absence of

sible enemy that no surprise attack, however vast, can destroy the certainty of retaliation. Even if the President, every one in line of Presidential succession, and the nation's top military commanders are all killed in the first wave of an attack, there will always be someone down the line to respond with nuclear force. This is what is meant by credibility. The enemy must believe there are literally hundreds of men in a position to punish him with devastating nuclear counterattack.

¶9 Few themes have challenged the thoughts of philosophers through the ages more than the idea of the fragility of human life. Even a drop of water, says Pascal, can suffice to destroy a man. But now, as the culmination of a century of science, man must also ponder the fragility of his civilization. Generally, a disaster had to be experienced before man developed the means to deal with it or prevent its recurrence. How does mankind protect itself against something that has never happened before? How does it protect itself against the supremely irrational, against something that lies far outside the range of the improbables? How can the same sense of biting reality that a man attaches to his next pay check be extended to questions concerning human destiny?

¶10 If human history is now drawing to a close, it is not because of any malevolence or incompetence deep within the species but because the human mind seems unable to convince itself that its own destiny is the issue.

—December 21, 1963

direct evidence to the contrary, Cousins depends on the *cause and effect* reasoning to answer this objection. The effect is the policy of "credibility"; a necessary condition of this policy (that is, a condition in the absence of which the policy could not exist) is that "many men possess the power to detonate the bombs that could start a war without authorization." (See pp. 200–01 for a discussion of necessary and sufficient condition.)

Paragraph 9 summarizes the argument and reviews obstacles that stand in the way of a solution. Cousins reserves discussion of the chief obstacle for the conclusion: modern man is not yet convinced that his survival is at stake. Cousins might have ended with his tentative solution, proposed briefly in paragraph 6: "The only possible defense is to take that power away from him." However, man's lack of insight into the crisis at hand is a more important consideration. The final paragraph thus refers back, indirectly, to the tragedy which introduces the essay.

THE EXPOSITORY ESSAY

The expository essay adapts the parts of the argumentative essay to its own uses. The purpose of the essay, the character of the audience, and the character of the writer are important in determining its structure. Before we analyze one such essay, we should say something about outlining. Three kinds of outline have proved useful—the paragraph outline, the topic outline, and the sentence outline. The first is merely a list of the topic ideas of the paragraphs; one of its uses is to work out relationships and possible rearrangements. The sentence outline states each idea fully, allowing you to clarify your wording before the actual writing begins. In such an outline the details that develop the ideas are usually omitted; however, classifications of detail may be shown. Outlines are chiefly means of working out the logical order of ideas; for this reason ideas may appear in a different order in the final essay. Here is a brief sentence outline of the Cousins essay:

Can Civilization Be Assassinated?

I. Civilization is vulnerable to the irrational acts of individuals (¶ 1–3).
- A. Wishing to believe that actions can be protected and controlled (¶1), people cannot conceive the meaning of the assassination of a President (¶2).
- B. But individual motivation makes it impossible to predict or control the fate of civilization (¶3).
  1. The U.S. and the U.S.S.R. possess fearsome weapons.
  2. These weapons must be operated by individuals.

II. No safeguards can protect civilization from the irrational individual (¶4–8).
- A. Screening men does not fully disclose their personality (¶4).
- B. An individual need not be insane to act irresponsibly (¶5).
- C. No safeguards are foolproof against irrationality (¶6).
  1. The only possible safeguard is to remove power

The opening statement—extracted from the thesis statement of ¶3—summarizes the ideas of the introductory paragraphs. A and B are coordinate ideas—equal in importance.

1 and 2 classify the detail of ¶3. The order of details in ¶3 need not correspond to the outline.

The heading is extracted from the first sentence of ¶6.
The details of ¶s4–5 need not be indicated.

from the individual
($\P$6).

2. Present safeguards are designed to prevent accidents ($\P$7).
   a. Many men have the power to detonate bombs ($\P$8).
   b. Our policy of "credibility" supports this fact ($\P$8).

In the actual essay ideas a and b are given special emphasis in a separate paragraph. They develop, however, the more important idea of $\P$7— and might have been included in that paragraph.

III. The solution must encompass immense problems ($\P$9–10).
   A. Disasters must occur to persuade people that civilization is fragile ($\P$9).
   B. People are incapable of believing that their personal survival is at stake.

The series of questions in $\P$9 might be classified and indicated in a breakdown of A.

A developed outline of this kind will help you to think out your ideas thoroughly. But if you wish merely to put down your topic ideas, a topic outline listing these according to their relative importance may be sufficient:

   I. The vulnerability of civilization
      A. The incredibility of wholly unpredictable acts
      B. The impossibility of controlling the fate of civilization
         1. The weapons of the U.S. and the U.S.S.R.
         2. The operation of these weapons by individuals
   II. The impossibility of foolproof safeguards
      A. The weakness of screening
      B. The various motives of irresponsible actions
      C. The absence of defense against irreason
         1. The solution of removing power from the individual
         2. Designing safeguards to prevent accidents
            a. The power of many men to detonate bombs
            b. The policy of "credibility"
   III. The immense problems that complicate solution
      A. The fragility of civilization
      B. The belief of people in their necessary survival

These outlines show that the logical and rhetorical structure of ideas may differ markedly. It is impossible to say which consideration —the logical or the rhetorical—is a prior one for the writer: sometimes they occur simultaneously. Indeed, as we have seen, the ideas themselves may be selected on the basis of rhetorical considerations, particularly if the argument is concerned with probable truth. For this reason, outlining is at best a preliminary procedure—open to revision in light of new thoughts and rhetorical considerations. Sticking closely to the outline can make the essay rigid if you forget that logical and rhetorical order are not synonymous.

The Keys to Dreamland

by Northrop Frye

¶1 I have been trying to explain literature by putting you in a primitive situation on an uninhabited island, where you could see the imagination working in the most direct and simple way. Now let's start with our own society, and see where literature belongs in that, if it does. Suppose you're walking down the street of a North American city. All around you is a highly artificial society, but you don't think of it as artificial: you're so accustomed to it that you think of it as natural. But suppose your imagination plays a little trick on you of a kind that it often does play, and you suddenly feel like a complete outsider, someone who's just blown in from Mars on a flying saucer. Instantly you see how conventionalized everything is: the clothes, the show windows, the movement of the cars in traffic, the cropped hair and shaved faces of the men, the red lips and blue eyelids that women put on because they want to conventionalize their faces, or "look nice," as they say, which means the same thing. All this convention is pressing toward uniformity or likeness. To be outside the convention makes a person look queer, or, if he's driving a car, a menace to life and limb. The only exceptions are people who have decided to conform to different conventions, like nuns or beatniks. There's clearly a strong force making toward conformity in society, so strong that it seems to have something to do with the stability of society itself. In ordinary life even the most splendid things we can think of, like goodness and truth and beauty, all mean essentially what we're accustomed to. As I hinted just now in speaking of female make-up, most of our ideas of beauty are pure convention, and even truth has been defined as whatever doesn't disturb the pattern of what we already know.

¶2 When we move on to literature, we again find conventions, but this time we notice that they are conventions, because we're not so used to them. These conventions seem to have something to do with making literature as unlike life as possible. Chaucer represents people as making up stories in ten-syllable couplets. Shakespeare uses dramatic conventions, which means, for instance, that Iago has to smash Othello's marriage and dreams of future happiness and get him ready to murder his wife in a few minutes. Milton has two nudes in a garden haranguing each other in set speeches beginning with such lines as "Daughter of God and Man, immortal Eve"—Eve being Adam's daughter because she's just been extracted from his ribcase.

ANALYSIS

Paragraphs 1–3. This essay is one of six Massey lectures delivered over the Canadian Broadcast Corporation. Though the ideas are abstract, they are presented in an informal style, with emphasis on examples. ¶1 introduces an unfamiliar idea—literary conventions—through a familiar idea—conventions of ordinary life (*topic of similarity*). ¶2 begins with discussion of an important difference between everyday

Almost every story we read demands that we accept as fact something that we know to be nonsense: that good people always win, especially in love; that murders are complicated and ingenious puzzles to be solved by logic, and so on. It isn't only popular literature that demands this: more highbrow stories are apt to be more ironic, but irony has its conventions too. If we go further back into literature, we run into such conventions as the king's rash promise, the enraged cuckold, the cruel mistress of love poetry—never anything that we or any other time would recognize as the normal behavior of adult people, only the maddened ethics of fairyland.

¶3 Even the details of literature are equally perverse. Literature is a world where phoenixes and unicorns are quite as important as horses and dogs— and in literature some of the horses talk, like the ones in *Gulliver's Travels.* A random example is calling Shakespeare the "swan of Avon"—he was called that by Ben Jonson. The town of Stratford, Ontario, keeps swans in its river partly as a literary allusion. Poets of Shakespeare's day hated to admit that they were writing words on a page: they always insisted that they were producing music. In pastoral poetry they might be playing a flute (or more accurately an oboe), but every other kind of poetic effort was called song, with a harp, a lyre or a lute in the background, depending on how highbrow the song was. Singing suggests birds, and so for their typical songbird and emblem of themselves, the poets chose the swan, a bird that can't sing. Because it can't sing, they made up a legend that it sang once before death, when nobody was listening. But Shakespeare didn't burst into song before his death: he wrote two plays a year until he'd made enough money to retire, and spent the last five years of his life counting his take.

¶4 So however useful literature may be in improving one's imagination or vocabulary, it would be the wildest kind of pedantry to use it directly as a guide to life. Perhaps here we see one reason why the poet is not only very seldom a person one would turn to for insight into the state of the world, but often seems even more gullible and simple-minded than the rest of us. For the poet, the particular literary conventions he adopts are likely to become, for him, facts of life. If he finds that the kind of writing he's best at has a good deal to do with fairies, like Yeats, or a white goddess, like Graves, or a life-force, like Bernard Shaw, or episcopal sermons, like T. S. Eliot, or bullfights, like Hemingway, or exasperation at social hypocrisies, as with the so-called angry school, these things are apt to take on a reality for him that seems badly out of proportion to his contemporaries. His life may imitate literature in a way that may warp or even destroy his social personality, as

conventions and those of literature: we notice the second kind because they are unfamiliar (*topic of difference*). The series of examples shows that Frye considers his audience to be educated, familiar enough with important works of literature to understand his references, but needing help in their interpretation. ¶3 contributes a new kind of example, stressing not merely the unreality of literary details but also their falseness to literal reality.

Paragraph 4. Frye is moving from simple to complex ideas. In ¶4 he

Byron wore himself out at thirty-four with the strain of being Byronic. Life and literature, then, are both conventionalized, and of the conventions of literature about all we can say is that they don't much resemble the conditions of life. It's when the two sets of conventions collide that we realize how different they are.

¶5 In fact, whenever literature gets too probable, too much like life, some self-defeating process, some mysterious law of diminishing returns, seems to set in. There's a vivid and expertly written novel by H. G. Wells called *Kipps,* about a lower-middle-class, inarticulate, very likeable Cockney, the kind of character we often find in Dickens. Kipps is carefully studied: he never says anything that a man like Kipps wouldn't say; he never sounds the "h" in home or head; nothing he does is out of line with what we expect such a person to be like. It's an admirable novel, well worth reading, and yet I have a nagging feeling that there's some inner secret in bringing him completely to life that Dickens would have and that Wells doesn't have. All right, then, what would Dickens have done? Well, one of the things that Dickens often does do is write *badly.* He might have given Kipps sentimental speeches and false heroics and all sorts of inappropriate verbiage to say; and some readers would have clucked and tut-tutted over these passages and explained to each other how bad Dickens's taste was and how uncertain his hold on character could be. Perhaps they'd be right too. But we'd have had Kipps a few times the way he'd look to himself or the way he'd sometimes wish he could be: that's part of his reality, and the effect would remain with us however much we disapproved of it. Whether I'm right about this book or not, and I'm not at all sure I am, I think my general principle is right. What we'd never see except in a book is often what we go to books to find. Whatever is completely lifelike in literature is a bit of a laboratory specimen there. To bring anything really to life in literature we can't be lifelike: we have to be literaturelike.

¶6 The same thing is true even of the use of language. We're often taught that prose is the language of ordinary speech, which is usually true in literature. But in ordinary life prose is no more the language of ordinary speech than one's Sunday suit is a bathing suit. The people who actually speak prose are highly cultivated and articulate people, who've read a good many books, and even they can speak prose only to each other. If you read the beautiful sentences of Elizabeth Bennett's conversation in *Pride and Prejudice,* you can see how in that book they give a powerfully convincing impression of a sensible and intelligent girl. But any girl who talked as co-

shows that literary conventions become for the poet as ordinary as those discussed in ¶1. The final sentence returns to the reader who, Frye indicates, notices the difference between the two kinds of convention. This difference, we discover, is the essential quality of literary experience.

Paragraphs 5–8. ¶5 develops this idea through a contrast between Wells and Dickens; the discussion focuses on the reader who, through

herently as that on a street car would be stared at as though she had green hair. It isn't only the difference between 1813 and 1962 that's involved either, as you'll see if you compare her speech with her mother's. The poet Emily Dickinson complained that everybody said "What?" to her, until finally she practically gave up trying to talk altogether, and confined herself to writing notes.

¶7 All this is involved with the principle I've touched on before: the difference between literary and other kinds of writing. If we're writing to convey information, or for any practical reason, our writing is an act of will and intention: we mean what we say, and the words we use represent that meaning directly. It's different in literature, not because the poet doesn't mean what he says too, but because his real effort is one of putting words together. What's important is not what he may have meant to say, but what the words themselves say when they get fitted together. With a novelist it's rather the incidents in the story he tells that get fitted together—as D. H. Lawrence says, don't trust the novelist; trust his story. That's why so much of a writer's best writing is or seems to be involuntary. It's involuntary because the forms of literature itself are taking control of it, and these forms are what are embodied in the conventions of literature. Conventions, we see, have the same role in literature that they have in life: they impose certain patterns of order and stability on the writer. Only, if they're such different conventions, it seems clear that the order of words, or the structure of literature, is different from the social order.

¶8 The absence of any clear line of connection between literature and life comes out in the issues involved in censorship. Because of the large involuntary element in writing, works of literature can't be treated as embodiments of conscious will or intention, like people, and so no laws can be framed to control their behavior which assume a tendency to do this or an intention of doing that. Works of literature get into legal trouble because they offend some powerful religious or political interest, and this interest in its turn usually acquires or exploits the kind of social hysteria that's always revolving around sex. But it's impossible to give legal definitions of such terms as obscenity in relation to works of literature. What happens to the book depends mainly on the intelligence of the judge. If he's a sensible man we get a sensible decision; if he's an ass we get that sort of decision, but what we don't get is a legal decision, because the basis for one doesn't exist. The best we get is a precedent tending to discourage cranks and pressure groups from attacking serious books. If you read the casebook on

the conventions of literature, discovers a reality not always obvious in life. The transitional sentence that opens the paragraph does double duty as a statement of the topic idea. The same is true of the opening sentence of ¶6, which explores the universal phenomenon of language. Language cannot be completely lifelike either, because the complex act of writing is controlled by the conventions of literature—conventions which Frye showed to be radically different from those of life and imposing their own order (¶7). Yet we have also seen that the

the trial of *Lady Chatterley's Lover*, you may remember how bewildered the critics were when they were asked what the moral effect of the book would be. They weren't putting on an act: they didn't know. Novels can only be good or bad in their own categories. There's no such thing as a morally bad novel: its moral effect depends entirely on the moral quality of its reader, and nobody can predict what that will be. And if literature isn't morally bad it isn't morally good either. I suppose one reason why *Lady Chatterley's Lover* dramatized this question so vividly was that it's a rather preachy and self-conscious book: like the Sunday-school novels of my childhood, it bores me a little because it tries so hard to do me good.

¶9 So literature has no consistent connection with ordinary life, positive or negative. Here we touch on another important difference between structures of the imagination and structures of practical sense, which include the applied sciences. Imagination is certainly essential to science, applied or pure. Without a constructive power in the mind to make models of experience, get hunches and follow them out, play freely around with hypotheses, and so forth, no scientist could get anywhere. But all imaginative effort in practical fields has to meet the test of practicability, otherwise it's discarded. The imagination in literature has no such test to meet. You don't relate it directly to life or reality: you relate works of literature, as we've said earlier, to each other. Whatever value there is in studying literature, cultural or practical, comes from the total body of our reading, the castle of words we've built, and keep adding new wings to all the time.

¶10 So it's natural to swing to the opposite extreme and say that literature is really a refuge or escape from life, a self-contained world like the world of the dream, a world of play or make-believe to balance the world of work. Some literature is like that, and many people tell us that they only read to get away from reality for a bit. And I've suggested myself that the sense of escape, or at least detachment, does come into everybody's literary experience. But the real point of literature can hardly be that. Think of such writers as William Faulkner or François Mauriac, their great moral dignity, the intensity and compassion that they've studied the life around them

writer comes to take them for life, as Frye reminds us at the beginning of ¶8.

In ¶8 the even more difficult problem of censorship is explored to show that no clear connection exists between literature and life. Frye would have had difficulty explaining at the beginning of the essay why literature is not in itself morally good or bad: the earlier exploration of the relationship of reader and writer to the work provides the basis for the distinctions of the paragraph.

Paragraphs 9–10. ¶9, which develops the idea that the connection cannot be a consistent one (an idea stated in another way in ¶4), depends on the *topic of contraries*. The contraries are imagination in the applied sciences and imagination in literature (the contrary qual-

with. Or think of James Joyce, spending seven years on one book and seventeen on another, and having them ridiculed or abused or banned by the customs when they did get published. Or of the poets Rilke and Valéry, waiting patiently for years in silence until what they had to say was ready to be said. There's a deadly seriousness in all this that even the most refined theories of fantasy or make-believe won't quite cover. Still, let's go along with the idea for a bit, because we're not getting on very fast with the relation of literature to life, or what we could call the horizontal perspective of literature. That seems to block us off on all sides.

¶11 The world of literature is a world where there is no reality except that of the human imagination. We see a great deal in it that reminds us vividly of the life we know. But in that very vividness there's something unreal. We can understand this more clearly with pictures, perhaps. There are trick-pictures—*trompe l'oeil,* the French call them—where the resemblance to life is very strong. An American painter of this school played a joke on his bitchy wife by painting one of her best napkins so expertly that she grabbed at the canvas trying to pull it off. But a painting as realistic as that isn't a reality but an illusion: it has the glittering unnatural clarity of a hallucination. The real realities, so to speak, are things that don't remind us directly of our own experience, but are such things as the wrath of Achilles or the jealousy of Othello, which are bigger and more intense experiences than anything we can reach—except in our imagination, which is what we're reaching with. Sometimes, as in the happy endings of comedies, or in the ideal world of romances, we seem to be looking at a pleasanter world than we ordinarily know. Sometimes, as in tragedy and satire, we seem to be looking at a world more devoted to suffering or absurdity than we ordinarily know. In literature we always seem to be looking either up or down. It's the vertical perspective that's important, not the horizontal one that looks out to life. Of course, in the greatest works of literature we get both the up and down views, often at the same time as different aspects of one event.

ity lies in the use of imagination). In ¶9 Frye continues the exploration of a misconception about literature begun in the previous paragraph; he proceeds to another misconception in ¶10–the assumption that literature is a make-believe world that offers an escape from life. But Frye is not prepared yet to define the nature of that peculiar make-believe. The reason is that he has been building to the central idea of the essay—the nature of imagination in literature.

Paragraph 11. In ¶5 Frye revealed the nature of this quality of imagination in his comment on the unreality of Dickens, but he did not define it. Pursuing a metaphor he introduced in an earlier lecture, he defines this imagination as the vehicle of a "vertical perspective." Literature cannot connect with life *directly* because it looks up and down rather than on a horizontal axis toward life.

¶12 There are two halves to literary experience, then. Imagination gives us both a better and a worse world than the one we usually live with, and demands that we keep looking steadily at them both. I said in my first talk that the arts follow the path of the emotions, and of the tendency of the emotions to separate the world into a half that we like and a half that we don't like. Literature is not a world of dreams, but it would be if we had only one half without the other. If we had nothing but romances and comedies with happy endings, literature would express only a wish-fulfilment dream. Some people ask why poets want to write tragedies when the world's so full of them anyway, and suggest that enjoying such things has something morbid or gloating about it. It doesn't, but it might if there were nothing else in literature.

¶13 This point is worth spending another minute on. You recall that terrible scene in *King Lear* where Gloucester's eyes are put on the stage. That's part of a play, and a play is supposed to be entertaining. Now in what sense can a scene like that be entertaining? The fact that it's not really happening is certainly important. It would be degrading to watch a real blinding scene, and far more so to get any pleasure out of watching it. Consequently, the entertainment doesn't consist in its reminding us of a real blinding scene. If it did, one of the great scenes of drama would turn into a piece of repulsive pornography. We couldn't stop anyone from reacting in this way, and it certainly wouldn't cure him, much less help the public, to start blaming or censoring Shakespeare for putting sadistic ideas in his head. But a reaction of that kind has nothing to do with drama. In a dramatic scene of cruelty and hatred we're seeing cruelty and hatred, which we know are permanently real things in human life, from the point of view of the imagination. What the imagination suggests is horror, not the paralyzing sickening horror of a real blinding scene, but an exuberant horror, full of the energy of repudiation. This is as powerful a rendering as we can ever get of life as we don't want it.

¶14 So we see that there are moral standards in literature after all, even though they have nothing to do with calling the police when we see a word in a book that's more familiar in sound than in print. One of the things Gloucester says in that scene is: "I am tied to the stake, and I must stand the course." In Shakespeare's day it was a favorite sport to tie a bear to a stake and set dogs on it until they killed it. The Puritans suppressed this sport, according to Macaulay, not because it gave pain to the bear but because it gave pleasure to the spectators. Macaulay may have intended his remark to be a sneer at the Puritans, but surely if the Puritans did feel this way they were one hundred per cent right. What other reason is there for abolishing public hangings? Whatever their motives, the Puritans and

---

Paragraphs 12–14. Frye uses ¶12 and ¶13 to clarify his metaphor and lead back to an uncompleted idea—the impact of literature on life. Gloucester's blinding shows us that imagination in literature judges as it depicts, thus its "exuberant horror, full of the energy of repudiation." Literature, in short, "refines our sensibilities"—the point of ¶14.

Shakespeare were operating in the same direction. Literature keeps presenting the most vicious things to us as entertainment, but what it appeals to is not any pleasure in these things, but the exhilaration of standing apart from them and being able to see them for what they are because they aren't really happening. The more exposed we are to this, the less likely we are to find an unthinking pleasure in cruel or evil things. As the eighteenth century said in a fine mouth-filling phrase, literature refines our sensibilities.

¶15 The top half of literature is the world expressed by such words as sublime, inspiring, and the like, where what we feel is not detachment but absorption. This is the world of heroes and gods and titans and Rabelaisian giants, a world of powers and passions and moments of ecstasy far greater than anything we meet outside the imagination. Such forces would not only absorb but annihilate us if they entered ordinary life, but luckily the protecting wall of the imagination is here too. As the German poet Rilke says, we adore them because they disdain to destroy us. We seem to have got quite a long way from our emotions with their division of things into "I like this" and "I don't like this." Literature gives us an experience that stretches us vertically to the heights and depths of what the human mind can conceive, to what corresponds to the conceptions of heaven and hell in religion. In this perspective what I like or don't like disappears, because there's nothing left of me as a separate person: as a reader of literature I exist only as a representative of humanity as a whole. We'll see in the last talk how important this is.

¶16 No matter how much experience we may gather in life, we can never in life get the dimension of experience that the imagination gives us. Only the arts and sciences can do that, and of these, only literature gives us the whole sweep and range of human imagination as it sees itself. It seems to be very difficult for many people to understand the reality and intensity of literary experience. To give an example that you may think a bit irrelevant: why have so many people managed to convince themselves that Shakespeare did not write Shakespeare's plays, when there is not an atom of evidence that anybody else did? Apparently because they feel that poetry must be written out of personal experience, and that Shakespeare didn't have enough experience of the right kind. But Shakespeare's plays weren't produced by his experience: they were produced by his imagination, and the way to develop the imagination is to read a good book or two. As for us, we can't speak or think or comprehend even our own experience except within the limits of our own power over words, and those limits have been established for us by our great writers.

Paragraphs 15–16. ¶15 extends this point by returning to the central metaphor of the essay; the top and bottom of the vertical axis are now complete. ¶16 returns to the more important consideration, the central concern of the essay—the nature of imagination in literature. The last sentence of the paragraph returns to the earlier point that literature is essentially an experience of language (¶s6–7).

¶17 Literature, then, is not a dream-world: it's two dreams, a wish-fulfillment dream and an anxiety dream, that are focused together, like a pair of glasses, and become a fully conscious vision. Art, according to Plato, is a dream for awakened minds, a work of imagination withdrawn from ordinary life, dominated by the same forces that dominate the dream, and yet giving us a perspective and dimension on reality that we don't get from any other approach to reality. So the poet and the dreamer are distinct, as Keats says. Ordinary life forms a community, and literature is among other things an art of communication, so it forms a community too. In ordinary life we fall into a private and separate subconscious every night, where we reshape the world according to a private and separate imagination. Underneath literature there's another kind of subconscious, which is social and not private, a need for forming a community around certain symbols, like the Queen and the flag, or around certain gods that represent order and stability, or becoming and change, or death and rebirth to a new life. This is the myth-making power of the human mind, which throws up and dissolves one civilization after another.

¶18 I've taken my title for this talk, "The Keys to Dreamland," from what is possibly the greatest single effort of the literary imagination in the twentieth century, Joyce's *Finnegans Wake*. In this book a man goes to sleep and falls, not into the Freudian separate or private subconscious, but into the deeper dream of man that creates and destroys his own societies. The entire book is written in the language of this dream. It's a subconscious language, mainly English, but connected by associations and puns with the eighteen or so other languages that Joyce knew. *Finnegans Wake* is not a book to read, but a book to decipher: as Joyce says, it's about a dreamer, but it's addressed to an ideal reader suffering from an ideal insomnia. The

Paragraphs 17–20. ¶17, returning to the uncompleted idea that literature is a kind of make-believe, now states fully what kind it is. The two kinds of dreams are related to two kinds of subconscious language, dream-symbol and myth. The difference is illustrated in ¶18 through James Joyce who used a public language whose meanings are available to everyone. The example is a good one because it allows Frye to drive home another idea, introduced earlier in the essay.

That idea is the role of the reader in the total literary experience. His contribution to the experience is a result of his power to understand: the more sensitive the response to the work and the more acute

reader or critic, then, has a role complementing the poet's role. We need two powers in literature, a power to create and a power to understand.

¶19 In all our literary experience there are two kinds of response. There is the direct experience of the work itself, while we're reading a book or seeing a play, especially for the first time. This experience is uncritical, or rather pre-critical, so it's not infallible. If our experience is limited, we can be roused to enthusiasm or carried away by something that we can later see to have been second-rate or even phony. Then there is the conscious, critical response we make after we've finished reading or left the theater, where we compare what we've experienced with other things of the same kind, and form a judgment of value and proportion on it. This critical response, with practice, gradually makes our pre-critical responses more sensitive and accurate, or improves our taste, as we say. But behind our responses to individual works, there's a bigger response to our literary experience as a whole, as a total possession.

¶20 The critic has always been called a judge of literature, which means, not that he's in a superior position to the poet, but that he ought to know something about literature, just as a judge's right to be on a bench depends on his knowledge of law. If he's up against something the size of Shakespeare, he's the one being judged. The critic's function is to interpret every work of literature in the light of all the literature he knows, to keep constantly struggling to understand what literature as a whole is about. Literature as a whole is not an aggregate of exhibits with red and blue ribbons attached to them, like a cat-show, but the range of articulate human imagination as it extends from the height of imaginative heaven to the depth of imaginative hell. Literature is a human apocalypse, man's revelation to man, and criticism is not a body of adjudications, but the awareness of that revelation, the last judgment of mankind.

the judgment, the greater the power of the imagination which, Frye indicated earlier, judges as it depicts. ¶20, the final paragraph of the essay, states the thesis fully—in the concluding definition of literature in relation to the imagination.

The lucidity of the essay owes much to the extreme economy of exposition, an economy made possible by the movement from the simple to the complex and by the *restatement* of earlier ideas in light of new examples and their interpretation. Throughout the essay Frye keeps his general audience in mind, developing abstract ideas through concrete instances and depending on familiar contexts for ideas of the imagination and the like.

THE AUTOBIOGRAPHICAL ESSAY

The Holborn

by Arturo Vivante

On a moonless, starless night in London in December, 1939, my father, my mother, my two brothers, my sister, and I advanced along the sidewalk warily, a tight-knit little group. No chink of light showed from door or window. Sometimes a car went by with covered, slitted headlights. We grazed the walls and shopwindows, and groped at each doorway, hoping one might open into a restaurant.

We were staying in a hotel near Russell Square, in three little rooms at the end of a long, long corridor. The hotel was so huge one could nearly always get a room. That, I think, was its main advantage, and the reason we had gone there. Murky and dimly lit, it provided little contrast to the black-out outside. Rather, it seemed to partake of it. The lampshades in the lobby were like hoods. Only directly under them was there sufficient light to read a paper by. The darkness from the street entered as you entered, weaved its way around the heavy lampshades, and, hardly mitigated, spread along corridors and halls into the rooms. It was the sort of hotel refugees go to, and that was what we were. We had left Italy earlier that year at different times. My younger brother and I were going to one boarding school, my sister to another, my elder brother was living in the home of an old friend, my parents, who had spent the summer and fall in a country cottage, were looking for a house in which to settle, and now we had all convened in London for a family reunion.

The hotel must have had a restaurant, but we certainly didn't want to eat there, so we had gone out. We had walked around a great deal. I think we were quite lost. But we weren't so much trying to find our way as a place to eat. How different this town was from Rome, where practically every other doorway was a café or a *trattoria* that, war or no war, stayed open late

ANALYSIS

The qualities of a good autobiographical essay can be stated briefly, with reference to Arturo Vivante's account of an episode in his life.

1. Vivante *focuses* on a single episode that reveals a number of important qualities: his sensitivity as a boy to experience, his background, his relation to members of his family, his values and interests—in short, the important elements of a vivid impression of character. Vivante *shows* the kind of person he is.

2. The single episode *organizes* the detail and determines its selection. Vivante need not dwell on his family's history or his father's personal fortunes or character: we are told as much about the family as we

into the night. Here everything was closed, or seemed to be. We stopped a passerby and asked him if he knew of a restaurant.

"I'm afraid you won't find anything open at this time here," he said.

My father drew a tiny flashlight and a watch from his pocket. It wasn't even eight. My God, there must be something. We moved along from door to door. Suddenly one gave. I remember the feel of it. It was a leather-covered door, fat and cushiony. It swung open as we pressed it, and it disclosed light. Light refracted by crystal chandeliers. Light broken up and shining. Rivulets of light. It lit us up. It bathed us. We looked at each other and felt we were really seeing each other now. We were in a restaurant—the Holborn.

I don't think I have ever seen a restaurant quite like it. The place had a glow the chandeliers couldn't account for. It came from a fire—a robust flame that rose from an open burner in full view of the tables. With its wavering light, it lit our faces orange and made the shadows dance. A white-bonneted cook busied himself about it. And there were copper pans so highly polished they brought the shield of Achilles to my mind. The tables were beautifully laid with white linen cloths, fine dishes, long-stemmed slender goblets, silver, napkins folded in the shape of cones. The waiters plied between the tables, carrying full platters high on their palms. Although the room did not appear crowded, there were a great many guests, some of them lovely women with bare shoulders, long gowns, and hats with sweeping curves. And there were wreaths of smoke, like lightest clouds unfolding, and a mingled sound of voices—almost tuneful—and warmth, and softness, and an undefinable perfume in the air. The atmosphere was dreadfully inviting. So inviting it seemed almost forbidden.

We stood at the threshold, looking at my father. Would he really let us eat here? Wasn't this a bit too good for us? He didn't seem to think so—without the slightest hesitancy, he brought us in toward the headwaiter, who was coming over.

Waiters, especially headwaiters in black ties and dinner jackets, have always made me feel uneasy. As they come to meet me, I half expect them

need to understand what happened; the episode reveals qualities of family and particularly of his father that no amount of direct commentary could have made as vivid. The father's behavior in the restaurant and his attitude toward the experience (in contrast to his children's) reveal more about him than the information about his past indicates. His final comment, "Poor boy," underscores an ironic contrast that is a chief device of characterization in the whole essay.

3. Each detail is *relevant* to the impression Vivante wishes to convey. The contrasts of light and dark in the opening paragraphs are relevant to the contrasts evident in the experience in the restaurant (contrasts whose implications are not fully disclosed until the end when we discover that the restaurant was not fine enough to make an impression on the father). The final comment, however, though focusing on the

either to refuse to seat me or to seat me at a table near the door. Once seated and presented with a menu, lest my choice meet with a supercilious frown I often find myself ordering an expensive dish—one that will meet with their approval and not one I really want, like eggs fried in olive oil or a Welsh rabbit. Not so my father. He was quite rich when he was a young man—went to the Ritz in Paris, climbed the Alps, took private dancing lessons. He seemed perfectly at home here. A slightly built man in a blue suit, he moved nimbly, and the waiter didn't so much lead as accompany him to a table—the one my father wanted, central, near the fire. He ordered wine with our meal, and soon it was being poured from a bottle wrapped in a napkin and resting in a wicker cradle. My brothers and I had never seen such niceties. We laughed. Our table was round—about the size and shape of the one we had at home in Italy. The wine, too, was about the same —Chianti. It might have been from our own vineyard. As for the food, it seemed perfectly grand to me, used as I was at school to eating only bread, margarine, and jam for supper.

"When the English set themselves to it, they can cook as well as anybody," one of us said.

"Better," my younger brother said, finishing his Yorkshire pudding.

"And you get dessert every day," I said.

The waiter, who kept refilling our water glasses, suggested plum pudding,

---

ironic difference in response and attitude, heightens our impression of the boy whose sense of isolation (suggested but not stressed in the opening paragraphs) is now underscored.

4. The style of the essay is appropriate to the treatment and subject. Vivante writes with an eye to the mood and details of the experience, depending on simple, concrete words and figures ("The lampshades in the lobby were like hoods") that convey the impressions of the boy. At the same time we know through the mature vocabulary and sentence construction that the experience has been remembered, felt

and soon, with a flaming blue halo and the smell of spirits hovering around it, a plum pudding was brought in.

Later, after coffee, the check came. We felt apprehensive round the table. Did my father have enough money? He had. He produced a strange white bill such as I had never seen before—a five-pound note—and got some change, which he left on the table. He made no comment on the price. He just smoked a cigarette and watched the smoke, contemplatively. When we left, the headwaiter gave us good directions. It wasn't very far to Russell Square.

Soon after that, the war, suddenly flaring, scattered us, and not till many years later, when we had all returned home to Italy, did we sit together again around a table. I mentioned the restaurant to my family then, but the memory of it had faded from their minds. "Don't you remember?" I said. "We were groping our way along the sidewalk in the dark, when we came into this place all brightly lit and glowing. A flame was blazing on a grill; the chef wore a white bonnet; they served the wine from a bottle in a wicker cradle. . . . Surely you remember."

No, they didn't. Obviously, the Holborn hadn't made the impression on them it had made on me—the night not seemed so dark, the lights so bright.

"Strange," I said. "For me it was the best restaurant, ever."

"Poor boy," my father said, quite touched.

---

again, and expressed by the grown man who invests the experience with the irony of his later perception. The sentences are occasionally broken into phrases ("Light refracted by crystal chandeliers. Light broken up and shining. Rivulets of light") and short clauses ("It lit us up. It bathed us"), to suggest a succession of intense impressions; other sentences linger on an aspect of the experience ("And there were wreaths of smoke, like lightest clouds unfolding, and a mingled sound of voices—almost tuneful—and warmth, and softness, and an indefinable perfume in the air"). The style reveals the mind of the grown man and the boy simultaneously.

THE MEANING OF STYLE

The Roman rhetorician Quintilian distinguished three styles and their uses. Writers have transmitted these styles with modifications fitted to new uses and conventions in language. The three are the *plain*, best fitted for instruction and statement of fact, usually bare of developed figures of speech; the *florid*, best fitted for delighting the audience and winning its favor, and dependent on metaphor and other figures of speech, but quietly rhythmic and generally reflective; the *grand*, best fitted for moving the audience, and dependent on amplification and forceful figures of speech. We recognize these styles in the levels of diction distinguished earlier, though there is no obvious or strict correspondence between the plain and informal, for example. Formal English may encompass all three of the styles.

This conception of style implies that the writer and speaker chooses how he wishes to express and arrange his ideas in their final form. We see this kind of choice in a gifted speaker and writer like Winston S. Churchill, who could rise to the grand style when the occasion called for it and was a master of the plain style in exposition:

> I do not grudge our loyal, brave people, who were ready to do their duty no matter what the cost, who never flinched under the strain of last week—I do not grudge them the natural, spontaneous outburst of joy and relief when they learned that the hard ordeal would no longer be required of them at the moment; but they should know the truth. They should know that there has been gross neglect and deficiency of our defenses; they should know that we have sustained a defeat without a war, the consequences of which will travel far with us along our road. . . .
>
> —Speech to the House of Commons
> in October 1938, following the Munich Conference

No case of this kind can be judged apart from its circumstances. The facts may be unknown at the time, and estimates of them must be largely guesswork, colored by the general feelings and aims of whoever is trying to pronounce. Those who are prone by temperament and character to seek sharp and clear-cut solutions of difficult and obscure problems, who are ready to fight whenever some challenge comes from a foreign Power, have not always been right. On the other hand, those whose inclination is to bow their heads, to seek patiently and faithfully for peaceful compromise, are not always wrong. On the contrary, in the majority of instances they may be right, not only morally but from a practical standpoint. . . . There is, however, one helpful guide, namely, for a nation to keep its word and to act in accordance

with its treaty obligations to allies. This guide is called *honor*.
[commenting on the Munich conference]
—*The Gathering Storm* (1948)

Though each writer adjusts his style to the purpose of his discourse, he exhibits his own personal or characteristic style of thought and expression. The two are not always obviously connected, however. The person whose thoughts and speech ramble on may write that way; or his thinking may become more orderly when he writes, and perhaps only then. There is no obvious or necessary relation between the shape of sentences and paragraphs and the shape of experience itself, though sentences may occasionally *imitate* the shape of experience, as a strongly periodic sentence may imitate the movement of waves building to a crash. Most of the time, our sentences reflect the rhythms and the emphasis we give to our ideas in speech. Churchill's sentences frequently build to a climax in familiar ways; these ways are familiar, in part, because we associate them with recurring ideas and attitudes. It is the characteristic idea that suggests a characteristic mode of expression, and not the reverse.

Two examples of curt style in contemporary prose show this clearly. Consisting of short balanced phrases and clauses, curt style may give the impression of what Walker Gibson calls "tough talk." Here is an example:

> Sooner or later, fight metaphors, like fight managers, go sentimental. They go military. But there is no choice here. Frazier was the human equivalent of a war machine. He had tremendous firepower. He had a great left hook, a left hook frightening even to watch when it missed, for it seemed to whistle; he had a powerful right.
> —NORMAN MAILER, "Ego," *Life Magazine*, March 19, 1971

Used in another context, it may express a wholly different tone, as the following critical comment on Mailer's book on Apollo 11, *Of a Fire on the Moon*, shows:

> His mind is full of dartings, feints, freak hobbyhorses, amateur virtuoso bits. The head scutters about, linking the moonshot with cancer, with the hard clear face of black poverty, with a revolution in capitalism and in styles of consumption, with the exacerbation (for Aquarius's own party) produced by a new triumph of the Squares.
> —BENJAMIN DE MOTT, *Saturday Review*, January 16, 1971

The impression created in each passage depends on the attitude each writer implies; we get the impression of a personal style, usually not in single sentences such as these, but through characteristic attitudes and ideas we recognize in the whole paragraph or essay—attitudes we come to associate with characteristic ways of expressing ideas.

At a far point on the spectrum of style we have a modification of the florid, tending almost to the grand, in William Faulkner. At this point on the spectrum personal style is often easier to recognize. In the following passage from a work of fiction, Faulkner depends on sentences of inordinate length and strongly rhythmic phrases to convey a sixteen-year-old boy's impression of a large destructive bear:

> It ran in his knowledge before he ever saw it. It loomed and towered in his dreams before he even saw the unaxed woods where it left its crooked print, shaggy, tremendous, red-eyed, not malevolent but just big, too big for the dogs which tried to bay it, for the horses which tried to ride it down, for the men and the bullets they fired into it; too big for the very country which was its constricting scope.   —"The Bear"

The following sentence from one of Faulkner's essays exhibits the same rhythms and amplification:

> [The American Dream] It abandoned us, which had supported and protected and defended us while our new nation of new concepts of human existence got a firm enough foothold to stand erect among the nations of the earth, demanding nothing of us in return save to remember always that, being alive, it was therefore perishable and so must be held always in the unceasing responsibility and vigilance of courage and honor and pride and humility.   "On Privacy"

Faulkner's Nobel Prize acceptance speech contains another example of this pattern:

> I believe that man will not merely endure: he will prevail. He is immortal, not because he alone among creatures has an inexhaustible voice, but because he has a soul, a spirit capable of compassion and sacrifice and endurance.

The characteristics of personal style differ from writer to writer. Some develop an argument chiefly through refutation of their opponents' views; others dispense with the refutation altogether. Some prefer highly developed introductions and conclusions, others extremely short ones. Some build long paragraphs that constitute short essays, others think of paragraphs as spoken thoughts and punctuate them according to the breaks in conversation. Some punctuate to mark the pauses and stops of speech, others to clarify words as they appear in print. Not all aspects of a piece of writing will be revealing of personal style, at least at first sight. We discover new characteristics the longer we read.

Style in writing is ultimately the reflection of a style of thought. An effective style is arrived at through practice and self-discovery. In developing your personal style, you will occasionally imitate the styles of other writers to sharpen your own handling of language. But imitation should never be a thoughtless mimicking. Your eye should be on the object you are describing, your concern with your own feeling for the fact and the idea. What you gain through thoughtful imitation and your continuously growing sense of the original and expressive should serve your own ends. "The chief stimulus of good style," the English writer Walter Pater suggests, "is to possess a full, rich, complex matter to grapple with."

EXERCISES

1. Write a short autobiographical essay centering on an episode in your childhood that led to an unexpected truth. Do not comment directly on your character. Let the details of the episode reveal your character to the reader.

2. Develop one of the following statements from the Frye essay on the basis of your own experience. Direct your exposition to a particular audience—for example, high school English students—and give consideration to your tone and style:

   a. "In ordinary life even the most splendid things we can think of, like goodness and truth and beauty, all mean essentially what we're accustomed to."

   b. "When we move on to literature, we again find conventions, but this time we notice that they are conventions, because we're not so used to them."

   c. "It's when the two sets of conventions [those of life and literature] collide that we realize how different they are."

   d. "What we'd never see except in a book is often what we go to books to find."

3. Northrop Frye states: "Imagination gives us both a better and a worse world than the one we usually live with, and demands that we keep looking steadily at them both." Write a short essay showing how the essay "The Keys to Dreamland" illuminates this idea.

4. Write an analysis of a newspaper or magazine editorial, distinguishing its parts (introduction, confirmation, refutation, etc.) and discussing the uses to which these are put.

5. Using the Cousins essay as a model, write an argumentative essay that develops a thesis relating to one of the following:

   a. the role of college students in planning curriculum

   b. the role of newspapers in local elections

   c. the role of parents in shaping the political beliefs of their children

6. Compare a writer's essay with one of his stories or novels—for example, George Orwell's "Politics and the English Language" and 1984—and write an analysis of notable similarities or differences in style.

7. Compare two stories of a writer for evidence of personal style. The stories of Thomas Wolfe, J. D. Salinger, and I. B. Singer are particularly useful for this assignment.

8. Analyze the use made of *similarity, difference, degree,* and the like, in an essay by a contemporary writer or a recent opinion of a Supreme Court justice. Write a summary of your findings.

9. Write an analysis of the use Northrop Frye makes of the common topics in his essay "The Keys to Dreamland."

10. Compare two speeches of a congressman or officials of the administration to discover differences in the rhetoric. Explain these differences on the basis of evidence in the speeches themselves. Then comment on the rhetorical features common to both.

THE
LOGIC
OF THE
ESSAY

THE MEANING OF LOGIC

The world challenges us to use our reason—if we are prepared to recognize that challenge. We need only recall Orwell's comment on the indefensible language of politics to understand how easily we lose sight of reason. The empty slogans and confused appeals of small-minded politicians and advertisers are so common that we learn to close off our attention. We may read the newspaper thoughtlessly. A reader probably would pass over the following statement in an article on experiments with injections of brain tissue into rats:

> Other scientists at the meeting were concerned about the potential application of this technique—most scientists seem to fear all governments—and insisted such research must be accompanied, rather than followed by the development of strong ethical guidelines.
> —FRASER KENT, "Brain Injection Used to Alter Instinct in Rat," Cleveland *Plain-Dealer*, December 31, 1970

If he is reading attentively, however, he may ask himself whether the columnist is expressing his own opinion about the attitude of "most" scientists toward government or is paraphrasing the statements of scientists at the meeting. He will be aware that the qualifiers *most* and *seem* do not make the statement less categorical (an absolute assertion is being made about most scientists); the statement remains unsupported, regardless of the qualification. Statements of this sort present more of a challenge to critical reason than blatant overstatements often made in letters to the editor.

Our impulse is to brand such statements as illogical. We may assume mistakenly, though, that a statement we believe untrue is for this reason illogical. This equation of falsehood and illogicality is much too simple and, unfortunately, inaccurate; for patently untrue statements may occasionally *seem* logical. Why this is so needs explanation.

Logic, defined rather loosely, is the science of correct reasoning. It is concerned with truth but in special ways. How can patently untrue statements be thought logical? Consider the following propositions:

All men are immortal.
Cleopatra is a man.
Cleopatra is immortal.

This argument is *valid* in the sense that the process of reasoning is correct: if the first two propositions are true and are arranged in the manner indicated, the conclusion must be true also. Here is the reason untrue statements seem logical; we are attending to the process of reasoning.

The following argument is *invalid* even though the propositions are obviously true:

Some men are vegetarians.
Some plumbers are vegetarians.
Therefore some plumbers are men.

That is, here the process of reasoning is incorrect, as we shall explain later in this chapter.

Logicians indicate that a satisfactory argument must be both valid and sound, that is, the process of reasoning must be correct and the premises from which conclusions are derived must be true. But can we always be certain that our assumptions or premises are true? Euclidean geometry and Newtonian physics were based on assumptions that non-Euclidean geometricians in the nineteenth century and Einstein in the twentieth century showed to be, in some circumstances, inapplicable or wrong. Einstein himself revised his thinking on relativity and cosmology during the course of his life. The English mathematician and philosopher Alfred North Whitehead comments that scientists since at least the Middle Ages have proceeded on unexamined assumptions:

The truth is that science started its modern career by taking over ideas derived from the weakest side of the philosophies of Aristotle's successors. In some respects it was a happy choice. It enabled the knowledge of the seventeenth century to be formularized so far as physics and chemistry were concerned, with a completeness which has lasted to the present time. But the progress of biology and psychology has probably been checked by the uncritical assumption of half-truths.

—*Science and the Modern World* (New York: New American Library, 1948), p. 18.

The relation of logic to "truth" is thus a complex one. In the sections that follow we will explore this relation in a number of ways: we will see that arguments are classified as inductive or deductive according to the kind of truth that is claimed for their conclusions. We will also consider ways to avoid illogical statements in our writing. We will see that an argument may be judged illogical on grounds other than validity or soundness: illicit appeals to the audience also make statements illogical.

We will begin with the various illicit appeals to the audience.

THE APPEAL TO EMOTION

Aristotle recognized that the appeal to reason is only one of a number of appeals the speaker makes to his audience. He distinguished two others—the appeal to emotion and the appeal by the speaker for respect for his character. Antony in his funeral oration, in Shakespeare's *Julius Caesar*, makes both of these appeals inseparably; in his oration Brutus appeals directly to reason and asks the audience to respect his motives:

> Romans, countrymen and lovers! hear me for my cause, and be silent, that you may hear; believe me for mine honor, and have respect to mine honor, that you may believe; censure me in your wisdom, and awake your senses, that you may the better judge. If there be any in this assembly, any dear friend of Caesar's, to him I say, that Brutus' love to Caesar was no less than his. If then that friend demand why Brutus rose against Caesar, this is my answer: Not that I lov'd Caesar less, but that I lov'd Rome more. Had you rather Caesar were living and die all slaves, than that Caesar were dead, to live all free men? As Caesar lov'd me, I weep for him; as he was fortunate, I rejoice at it; as he was valiant, I honor him; but, as he was ambitious, I slew him.

Though this statement is not without emotion, the appeal is directly to reason; Brutus also appeals to the crowd to believe that his motives are honorable.

To a man like Brutus for whom emotion is at best an unreliable guide to conduct, the appeal to reason is the only ethical one. But the relation between reason and emotion is complex, as Cardinal Newman suggests:

> . . . deductions have no power of persuasion. The heart is commonly reached, not through the reason, but through the imagination, by means of direct impressions, by the testimony of facts and events, by history, by description.
>
> —*The Tamworth Reading Room*

The ethical use of emotional appeals depends on circumstances. In a political campaign the character of a candidate may be a legitimate issue; indeed, his character may be *the* issue if an opponent establishes facts that call into doubt his capacity for office.

Antony's attack on the character of Brutus would have been legitimate had it been open to examination by reason. The issue he raises in the following passage about Caesar's ambition is a legitimate one:

> When that the poor have cried, Caesar hath wept;
> Ambition should be made of sterner stuff:
> Yet Brutus says he was ambitious,
> And Brutus is an honorable man.
> You all did see that on the Lupercal
> I thrice presented him a kingly crown,
> Which he did thrice refuse. Was this ambition?
> Yet Brutus says he was ambitious,
> And, sure, he is an honorable man.
> I speak not to disprove what Brutus spoke,
> But here I am to speak what I do know.
> You all did love him once, not without cause;
> What cause withholds you then to mourn for him?
> O judgment! thou art fled to brutish beasts
> And men have lost their reason.

But the appeal to reason masks a covert attack—covert because of the implication that Brutus has *lied* about Caesar and therefore is a dishonorable man. Antony does not allow the crowd to consider the possibility that Brutus was *wrong* about Caesar and acted from honorable motives. Covert attacks of this sort are frequent because they are so often successful. Antony's oration allows us to define the relation between reason and emotion in logical discourse with some precision. The appeal to emotion must not cloud the specific point at issue or weaken the power of the listener to pass rational judgment on it. But these words of Shaw are worth remembering: "We still have a silly habit of talking and thinking as if intellect were a mechanical process and not a passion." Men can and do become passionate about ideas, but at the same time the ideas must stand the test of reason.

ATTACKING AN OPPONENT

We have indicated under what circumstances an attack on the character of an opponent is illicit. A proposal to ban billboards along highways deserves to be considered on its merits—even if the proposal is made by an individual or group that stands to profit by such a ban. Serious discussion of issues is crippled when appeals to emotion load the argument against one of the participants. The writer of the following statement says what he means, but the epithets will surely not encourage an opponent to consider his ideas dispassionately:

> The science of penology, in these days, is chiefly in the hands of sentimentalists, and in consequence it shows all the signs of glycosuria. The idea seems to be to turn the dungeons and bullpens of the law into laboratories of the uplift, so that the man who goes in a burglar will come out a Y.M.C.A. secretary. To this end all harsh handling of the felon is frowned upon, and on the slightest showing of renascent piety in him he is delivered from his cage, almost with apologies.
> —H. L. MENCKEN, "The Criminal Law" [written in 1922]

Mencken is attacking the character of his opponents in calling them "sentimentalists." In later paragraphs, he softens his tone (in the succeeding paragraph he recognizes that underlying this "softness" is revulsion against cruel punishments), but the argument remains a loaded one because of his introduction.

THE APPEAL TO PREJUDICE

Related to attacks on the opponent is the appeal to prejudice for or against a person or issue. Such appeals may be open or covert. Mencken's passage appeals to feelings about do-gooders that will dispose some readers toward the writer's viewpoint. Antony's funeral oration is a famous example of the appeal to prejudice. A difficult question arises over direct appeals to patriotic feeling in deliberative and ceremonial oratory—for example, King Henry V's appeal to his soldiers before the battle of Agincourt in Shakespeare:

> For he today that sheds his blood with me
> Shall be my brother; be he ne'er so vile,
> This day shall gentle his condition . . . .

The militarist and the pacifist will disagree sharply over the ethics of this appeal. The first may argue that the king is not asking his soldiers to make up their minds about the justice of the war; their presence on the field is warrant of their purpose, and the intention of the speech is to rouse them. The pacifist may object to the nature of the personal appeal, with its stress on honor rather than on the morality of war. One critic at least has taken the morality of war to be a theme of the play, with King Henry implicitly condemned for his war-mongering and cruelty. The validity of the appeal depends obviously on what the participants in the argument consider the purpose of the speech.

A more subtle form of the appeal to prejudice occurs when assumptions are introduced without defense, because they conform to the opinions of the reader. Newsmagazines, when charged with this practice, argue that any news report is bound to reflect a viewpoint. Clearly, however, columnists and reporters do succeed in identifying their special viewpoint and in interpreting events in direct terms, in defensible language.

THE APPEAL TO FORCE

Threatening physical harm is another illicit appeal. We will not be surprised that it is a common one. Thucydides, the Greek historian of the long and fateful war between Athens and Sparta, reports the following words of Athenian envoys to the people of Melos who had refused to side with them:

> Well, then, we Athenians will use no fine words; we will not go out of our way to prove at length that we have a right to rule, because we overthrew the Persians; or that we attack you now because we are suffering any injury at your hands. . . . But you and we should say what we really think, and aim only at what is possible, for we both alike know that into the discussion of human affairs the question of justice only enters where the pressure of necessity is equal, and that the powerful exact what they can, and the weak grant what they must.   —The History of the Peloponnesian War

Thucydides uses the episode to reveal the cynical expediency that had overcome Athens in the course of the war. The episode has numerous counterparts in modern history, chief among them Hitler's famous words to the Austrian Chancellor Schuschnigg at Berchtesgaden in 1938, before the seizure of Austria:

> You have done everything to avoid a friendly policy . . . . The whole history of Austria is just one uninterrupted act of high

treason. That was so in the past and is no better today. This historical paradox must now reach its long-overdue end. And I can tell you right now . . . that I am absolutely determined to make an end of all this. The German Reich is one of the great powers, and nobody will raise his voice if it settles its border problems. [Schuschnigg's report]

—WILLIAM L. SHIRER,
The Rise and Fall of the Third Reich, p. 326.

Related to the three kinds of appeal just noted are the appeal to pity and the appeal to authority. The first is sometimes the reverse of the attack on the opponent, for it asks for a dismissal of the issue on the ground that a defendant is deserving of pity. He may deserve pity and the mercy of the court, but the two considerations need to be separated if the proceeding is to conform to reason. The second occurs when a respected person is cited in support of or in opposition to an issue *merely* on the basis of his reputation. Citing the opinion of a distinguished jurist or scientist is entirely legitimate when the issue is within his area of competence. A football player's opinion on shaving cream, however, is worth no more than another man's.

THE APPEAL TO IGNORANCE

It is illogical to assert that life exists on Mars on the ground that no one has proved the reverse. It is also illogical to assert that it does not exist for the reverse reason. This does not mean that we are obligated to presume guilt or draw no conclusion whatever in the absence of firm evidence; a man's reputation could be quickly destroyed if this were the case. An interesting example of this argument occurs in Oswald Spengler's *The Decline of the West*, published in Germany in 1918:

Every critical science, like every myth and every religious belief, rests upon an inner certitude. Various as the creations of this certitude may be, both in structure and in repute, they are not different in basic principle. Any reproach, therefore, levelled by Natural science at Religion is a boomerang. We are presumptuous and no less in supposing that we can ever set up "the Truth" in the place of "anthropomorphic" conceptions, for no other conceptions but these exist at all. Every idea that is possible at all is a mirror of the being of its author. The statement that "man created God in his own image," valid for every historical religion, is not less valid for every physical theory, however firm its reputed basis of fact.

The statement amounts to the following: since no one has shown ideas of God to be more than mere reflections of their originators, no idea of God can be other than an anthropomorphism, nor can any natural science do more than mirror its creator. The statement that it is "presumptuous" to think that anthropomorphic conceptions can be surpassed, "for no other conceptions but these exist at all," is a *tautology*, an instance of circular reasoning in which a premise is restated as a conclusion.

DEDUCTION

In deductive reasoning the premises of the argument—the assumptions or propositions on which the reasoning is grounded—are presented as certain and decisive evidence for the truth of the conclusion, when they are arranged in a valid way:

> All men are mortal beings.
> The plumbers in this union are men.
> Therefore the plumbers in this union are mortal beings.

The predicate of the conclusion (mortal beings) is the *major term*; the subject of the conclusion, the *minor term* (plumbers). The premise that contains the major term is called the *major premise*; the premise that contains the minor term is called the *minor premise*. The term that appears in the two premises but not in the conclusion is the *middle term*. The two premises and the conclusion constitute a syllogism—in the example cited, a deductive syllogism in which the conclusion is assumed to be certain in light of its premises. That is, if the premises are true, the conclusion must be true. We have seen, though, that the deductive argument can be valid even if the premises and conclusion are false.

The most common form of the syllogism consists of categorical propositions—those that make positive or negative assertions about classes. Four kinds of categorical propositions may be distinguished on the basis of whether they are positive or negative in their assertion (quality) and whether the subject term refers to some or all members of a class (quantity):

> All plumbers are mortal beings (*universal affirmative:* the premise makes a positive assertion about all plumbers)
>
> No plumbers are mortal beings (*universal negative:* the premise makes a negative assertion about all plumbers)
>
> Some plumbers are mortal beings (*particular affirmative:* the premise makes a positive assertion about part of a class)
>
> Some plumbers are not mortal beings (*particular negative:* the premise makes a negative assertion about part of a class)

A few of the more simple tests of validity may be cited. The most common source of invalid reasoning, perhaps, is an undistributed middle term. In the following syllogism the middle term is undistributed in the premises:

> All men are mortal beings.
> All plumbers in this union are mortal beings.
> Therefore all plumbers in this union are men.

The middle term *mortal beings* includes more than men; for this reason plumbers, included in the class *mortal beings*, need not be men. In the syllogism

> All men are mortal beings.
> The plumbers in this union are men.
> Therefore the plumbers in this union are mortal beings.

the middle term *men* is distributed: the minor term *plumbers* clearly refers to the whole of the class *men* and not to a part of the class. In the faulty syllogism above, the premises do not provide conclusive evidence that all plumbers are men. The statement that follows exposes this kind of invalid reasoning. A reader of *Saturday Review* wrote the magazine concerning Charles Reich's *The Greening of America:*

> I think Mr. Reich assigns too much blame to the corporate state for what he calls the schizoid quality of contemporary American life (the split between the public man and the private man). Does he intend us to believe that the restrictions put on the worker by the corporate state are largely responsible for the generally sad condition of family life in this country, for the unsatisfactory relationships between husbands and wives, between parents and children? If this is so, shouldn't there be a great difference in the quality of the lives of these workers and the more independent professionals, such as doctors, lawyers, and college professors? I see no evidence that this latter group has been spared from the malaise that grips most of our society today.
>
> —a letter from Rene J. Muller in "Book Forum,"
> *Saturday Review*, March 13, 1971

The writer suggests in the remainder of his letter that the corporate state is blamed disproportionately for the ills noted and that the American university is perhaps more to blame because of its failure to promote liberal education and teach men how to "achieve a balance between the interior and the exterior worlds." The argument in the passage quoted shows that the class of people who are not under the control of the corporate state suffers from the same ills as the workers who are; in other words, the qualities Reich attributes to the influence of the corporate state are distributed among all members of the class *Americans*.

The following additional tests of validity can be briefly stated:

1. The conclusion of the syllogism must not assert more than the premises assert:

> All men are mortal beings.
> No plumbers are men.
> Therefore no plumbers are mortal beings.

The premises do not assert that mortal beings are all men (the same problem encountered with the undistributed middle term). Some of the plumbers may be women who are also mortal beings.

2. One of the premises must be positive:

> No Martians are mortal beings.
> No Venusians are Martians.
> Therefore no Venusians are mortal beings.

As in the previous example, the premises do not claim that the class *mortal beings* excludes Venusians. No conclusion whatever can be drawn if no positive assertion is made about any class. Notice, though, that if one premise is negative the conclusion must be too. The premise *All Venusians are Martians* will correct the syllogism.

3. Universal premises cannot lead to a particular conclusion because universal propositions do not necessarily imply that real members of the class exist. Particular propositions do imply that at least one real member of the class exists. A particular conclusion thus would imply more than its premises do:

> All Martians are mortal beings.
> All two-headed vertebrates are Martians.
> Therefore *some* two-headed vertebrates are mortal beings.

4. A syllogism must not contain more than three terms. If it does contain more, terms must be reworded to achieve the required three. The reason for this requirement is that ambiguity or unintended implication may result; if the terms *teacher* and *professor* were used in the premises to refer to the same people, it might be thought they referred to different classes of people. This problem must not be confused with *sorites* in which the conclusion of a syllogism serves as the major premise of a succeeding one, so that the argument is continuous:

> All registered voters are public spirited people.
> All concerned citizens are registered voters.
> *All concerned citizens are public spirited people.*
> Active supporters of the school levy are concerned citizens.
> Active supporters of the school levy are public spirited people.

The Aristotelian sorites is a familiar one in argument:

American high schools are obsessed with discipline.
Institutions obsessed with discipline are little concerned with intellectual achievement.
Institutions that are little concerned with intellectual achievement stress frill courses and sports.
Institutions that stress frill courses and sports do not face the realities of modern life.
American high schools do not face the realities of modern life.

This series of propositions reminds us of an important point: a deductive argument may be valid in its reasoning without being sound. The person who finds himself upset by any or all of the statements in the sorites above would feel uneasy if he knew that the process of reasoning was correct and thought he was for this reason obliged to accept the argument. We need to remember that a sound argument must be valid in its reasoning and true in its premises. Another important qualification must be made. In a paragraph or an essay the premises and conclusion need not be stated in the order they appear in the syllogism; the rhetoric of a paragraph or essay may require that the minor premise—perhaps the least controversial—precede the major—the most controversial. Or one of the premises may not be stated explicitly. These problems are evident in the following passage:

> [1]Any crossing of two beings not at exactly the same level produces a medium between the level of the two parents. [2]This means: the offspring will probably stand higher than the racially lower parent, but not as high as the higher one. [3]Consequently, it will later succumb in the struggle against the higher level. [4]Such mating is contrary to the will of Nature for a higher breeding of all life. [5]The precondition for this does not lie in associating superior and inferior, but in the total victory of the former. [6]The stronger must dominate and not blend with the weaker, thus sacrificing his own greatness. [7]Only the born weakling can view this as cruel, but he after all is only a weak and limited man; for if this law did not prevail, any conceivable higher development of organic living beings would be unthinkable.   —ADOLF HITLER, *Mein Kampf*

The argument is deductive because the premises are presented as givens—as certain and decisive evidence. Hitler explains his premises, but explanation is not intended as proof. The argument in part is enthymemic (an enthymeme is a syllogism in which one of the premises is implied). Thus the third sentence may be restated formally (and somewhat inexactly):

In the struggle for survival offspring on a lower racial level will succumb to offspring on a higher racial level.

The offspring of two parents from different racial levels will
be on a lower racial level. [that is, lower than the parent
on the higher level]
Therefore the offspring of parents from different racial levels
succumb to offspring on a higher racial level.

The implied major premise is actually the conclusion of a series of
other arguments whose premises are only partly stated in sentences
1 and 4 (one important premise implied by sentence 4 is that the
course of evolution is inherently a progression toward physically and
mentally stronger characteristics). The argument actually illustrates a
sorites in which a number of premises are implied, among those later
in the passage, that nature is never cruel and that only the weak individual will view his extinction as cruel (sentences 6 and 7). Arguments
tend to be enthymemic because a full statement of all premises would
occupy at least six times the length of the statement Hitler makes and
a full statement of the terms of each premise would further increase
the length. Premises may be left to inference because they cannot
withstand rational examination. Hitler conceals nothing because he
is absolutely convinced of his ideas: he opens the chapter of *Mein
Kampf* in which the statement appears, as follows: "There are some
truths which are so obvious that for this very reason they are not seen
or at least not recognized by ordinary people."

Hitler's illogical reasoning is plain. First, the premises are unsound
in part because essential terms (*level, medium, lower, higher, superior,
inferior*) are vague and undefined. It is impossible, also, on the basis
of the statement, to know whether Hitler is speaking figuratively in
attributing will to Nature. Second, sentences 6 and 7 are circular:
only the weak will consider their extinction cruel because it is a characteristic of the weak to consider their extinction cruel. (We will
consider circular statements in more detail shortly.) Third, the premises are unsound because they are factually absurd. The question of
what constitutes a "race" remains an open one. The historian Arnold
Toynbee points out in *A Study of History* that classifications of racial
characteristics can be based arbitrarily on color or hairiness or smell
which all excite race-feeling and are all equally suitable, or unsuitable,
for being taken as bases for racial classifications. Jacques Barzun, in
his study of superstitions about race, points out that mankind is not
divided into unchanging types, "recognizable by physical features";
that mental and moral behavior cannot be related to physical characteristics; that the "social entities variously termed race, nation, class,
family" have not been studied sufficiently to produce reliable knowledge. Barzun draws this conclusion:

. . . a satisfactory definition of race is not to be had. The
formulas in common use do not really define or do not accord
with the facts, so that a prudent man will suspend judgment

until genetics can offer a more complete body of knowledge. But to expect prudence in thinking about subjects charged with political emotion is folly too; and so we find the racists of the past 150 years leaping over the initial obstacle of race-theorizing, making assumptions to suit their object and failing to define their terms, just like the man in the street who borrows their language without questioning its validity.

—*Race: A Study in Superstition*
(New York: Harper and Row, 1965), p. 16

SPECIFIC POINT AT ISSUE

What premises we decide to present and discuss depends on the specific point at issue. Hitler's assumption that history is moving in a certain direction (implied in the phrase "the will of Nature") might have to be identified and discussed if the specific issue were the determination of national policy according to a reading of history. An important step in argumentation, the statement of the proposition, may require isolating the specific issue, as in the following comment:

> The question is not whether we should or should not send a manned rocket ship to the moon, but whether the project is so vital and so urgent as to warrant the indefinite postponement of other national efforts. This question has been debated at length, both in the Congress and in various publications. I have heard nothing to persuade me that it would be a national calamity if the landing on the moon were delayed until 1980 or 1990. I have heard and seen a great deal which persuades me that our continuing neglect of deteriorating schools and rising unemployment *would* be a national calamity.—J. WILLIAM FULBRIGHT, *Old Myths and New Realities*

In exposition, distinguishing the relative importance of issues can serve as a tool of analysis (here we have an adaptation of argumentative form to the uses of exposition). Isolating the specific issue is one way of limiting the subject in the light of the particular interests and attitudes of your audience.

"RED HERRING"

Throwing in the proverbial "red herring" is a way of directing attention away from the specific issue. Asserting that manned space exploration has had the support of Congress through the sixties is irrelevant to the issue Fulbright raises. (Congress may have been in error in appropriating large sums for space exploration instead of increasing the appropriations for education.) The specific issue, notice, is not the desirability of space exploration but rather the determination of national priorities. In the following passage the writer dismisses an argument as irrelevant to the specific point at issue:

> ... the deeper assumption in the charge that higher education is "exploitative" is that it trains students for work which is frivolous or harmful, not useful. The basic purposes of the society are wicked, and its fundamental arrangements misconceived. But we need not examine that very large proposition here. True or not, it cannot be used to indict universities. For the universities are themselves the major centers in which that proposition, in its extreme or more moderate forms, flourishes. They shelter the teachers and students who express and propagate this view of American society. That in itself makes it impossible to denounce universities as unequivocal instruments of the status quo. At any rate, it makes it impossible if one respects facts.
> —CHARLES FRANKEL, *Education and the Barricades*

Statements of this sort are designed to clarify the true grounds of a larger argument. You will find the procedure particularly useful in building to a statement of your thesis.

COMPLEX QUESTION

Frequently a proposition offered for discussion contains a presumption of fact that needs to be examined; we discover that in being asked to assent to the proposition as stated we are obliged to assent to a presumed fact ("Why did you cheat on the examination?"). In retort, we may ask that the question be simplified, that is, that the specific point at issue be clarified or isolated from the presumption of fact. Frequently defining terms is a way of simplifying the question:

> A skid-row drunk lying in a gutter is crime. So is the killing of an unfaithful wife. A Cosa Nostra conspiracy to bribe public officials is crime. So is a strong-arm robbery by a 15-year-old boy. The embezzlement of a corporation's funds by an executive is crime. So is the possession of marihuana cigarettes by a student. These crimes can no more be lumped together for purposes of analysis than can measles and schizophrenia, or lung cancer and a broken ankle. As with disease, so with crime: if causes are to be understood, if risks are to be evaluated, and if preventive or remedial actions are to be taken, each kind must be looked at separately. Thinking of "crime" as a whole is futile.—The President's Commission on Law Enforcement and Administration of Justice

Related to the problem of specific issue is that of identifying an important underlying premise. In the following passage the writer builds a case against government censorship involving prior restraint by identifying one unstated premise underlying an argument in its favor:

> The freedom toward which the American people are fundamentally orientated is a freedom under God, a freedom that knows itself to be bound by the imperatives of the moral law. Antecedently it is presumed that a man will make morally and socially responsible use of his freedom of expression; hence there is to be no prior restraint on it. However, if his use of freedom is irresponsible, he is summoned after the fact to responsibility before the judgment of the law. There are indeed other reasons why prior restraint on communications is outlawed; but none are more fundamental than this.
> —FATHER JOHN COURTNEY MURRAY, *We Hold These Truths*

The underlying premise is that "a man will make morally and socially responsible use of his freedom of expression." Since the presumed "imperatives of the moral law" are sometimes cited in support of "prior restraint," Father Murray shows that the idea of moral imperatives implies a prior freedom of expression.

NON SEQUITUR

When the conclusion does not appear to follow from the premises, an argument is sometimes considered a *non sequitur* (literally "does not follow"). Supplying an unstated premise will usually reveal either the logical sequence of ideas or the illogicality of the argument. The person who announces that he is a doctor because his father was assumes that the unstated reason is self-evident; and it *will* be self-evident to many people. But the statement will seem absurd to another person for whom the desires and choices of parents are not imperatives. An example from Adolf Hitler, an artist of the non sequitur, is worth citing:

> The artist does not create for the artist: he creates for the people and we will see to it that henceforth the people will be called in to judge its art. No one must say that the people has no understanding for a really valuable enrichment of its cultural life. . . . When we know today that the development of millions of years repeats itself in every individual compressed into a few decades, then this art ["modern art"], we realize, is not "modern"; it is on the contrary in the highest degree "archaic," far older probably than the Stone Age. The people when it passes through these galleries will recognize in me its

own spokesman and counselor: it will draw a sigh of relief and express its glad agreement with this purification of art. And that is decisive: an art which cannot count on the readiest and most intimate agreement of the great mass of the people, an art which must rely upon the support of small cliques, is intolerable. Such an art does but endeavor to confuse, instead of gladly reinforcing, the sure and healthy instinct of a people. [from a speech delivered in 1937]

The passage is logically disconnected throughout. The progression from the people as the *consumers* of art to the people as the intuitive, infallible *judges* of great art is one non sequitur; another is the progression from the people as *judges* to Adolf Hitler as their "spokesman and counselor" (Hitler suppresses the missing link in the argument: the intuitive genius of the people accounts for their recognition of him as supreme art critic).

It is worth noting, incidentally, that the non sequitur is a powerful device of advertising because it leaves the premise unstated. A hair shampoo may be advertised as beneficial because it contains protein, and this is all that is said. The statement assumes that an effective shampoo necessarily contains the same substance found in hair. Providing the scientific basis underlying the claim may deprive the statement of its feeling of certainty. A different advertising strategy is employed if the shampoo is accompanied by a pamphlet offering scientific proof for the claim. A non sequitur is often used in advertising when the underlying assumption needs to be disguised.

DISJUNCTION

A disjunctive argument offers two alternatives. One kind suggests that both disjuncts or alternatives are possibly true:

Tooth decay is caused by mouth acids or viruses.

If we can show that tooth decay is not caused by mouth acids, then we have shown that it *is* caused by viruses. But if we show merely that it is caused by viruses, we have not shown that it is not caused by mouth acids: both can be the cause. Additional evidence is needed to eliminate this possibility. A second kind of disjunction suggests that only one alternative can be true:

Hitler is either alive or dead.

If we can show that Hitler is alive, then we have shown the alternative to be false. A difficulty arises when, in this second kind of disjunction, the alternatives are not actually exclusive of each other but are stated as if they were:

We must choose between high unemployment or inflated prices.

There are, of course, other possible choices: those offered seem to exhaust the possibilities because we are not invited to consider others.

THE DILEMMA

A particular disjunction may present a dilemma which seems to offer no apparent third possibility or solution. Here, again, is Adolf Hitler:

> One is either the hammer or the anvil. We confess that it is our purpose to prepare the German people again for the role of the hammer. For ten years we have preached, and our deepest concern is: How can we again achieve power? We admit freely and openly that, if our Movement is victorious, we will be concerned day and night with the question of how to produce the armed forces which are forbidden us by the peace treaty. We solemnly confess that we consider everyone a scoundrel who does not try day and night to figure out a way to violate this treaty, for we have never recognized this treaty.
> [a statement in Munich, March 15, 1929]

The dilemma presented is that we must be the attacker (the hammer) or the attacked (the anvil). Two strategies may be employed in dealing with such an argument: we may "go between the horns" of the dilemma by showing that a third possibility exists(for example, negotiation) or by "grasping the dilemma by the horns," that is, showing that one of the disjuncts is false or that both are. Senator Fulbright employs the second strategy in the following passage. The dilemma presents a choice between a crash program in space and a Russian "first" in lunar exploration:

> The argument most frequently heard in support of Project Apollo, the moon shot program, is that if we do not pursue a crash program in space the Russians will get to the moon ahead of us. This argument can be challenged on two grounds: first, it is not at all clear that the Russians are *trying* to beat us to the moon; secondly—and more important—it is even less clear that it would be an irretrievable disaster if they did.
> —*Old Myths and New Realities*

Fulbright goes between the "horns" by showing that the assumptions underlying one of the disjuncts are false.

HYPOTHETICAL ARGUMENTS

A hypothetical statement raises a possibility ("If"); a categorical statement makes an absolute assertion. An argument may contain one or more hypothetical statements in its premises. The following contains one only:

> If he graduates with honors, he will be at the top of his class.
> He graduated with honors.
> Therefore he is at the top of his class.

The argument is valid because the categorical premise affirms the antecedent (*If he graduates with honors*) and the conclusion, the consequent (*then he will be at the top of his class*). If the categorical premise affirms the consequent, the argument is invalid:

> If he graduates with honors, he will receive an assistantship.
> He received an assistantship.
> Therefore he graduated with honors.

Clearly, he may have received the assistantship for a reason not cited. The following hypothetical argument is valid:

> If he graduated with honors, then his transcript will state this fact.
> His transcript does not state this fact.
> Therefore he did not graduate with honors.

The categorical premise here denies the consequent and the conclusion, the antecedent of the hypothetical premise. The argument would be invalid, however, if the categorical premise denied the antecedent:

> If he graduated with honors, then he is worthy of praise.
> He did not graduate with honors.
> Therefore he is not worthy of praise.

AMBIGUITY AND EQUIVOCATION

We have already discussed imprecise or ambiguous definition in premises. Stuart Chase criticizes a definition by Harold Laski, the English political economist, on this ground. Laski wrote:

> I suggest the conclusion that Fascism is nothing but monopoly capitalism imposing its will on the masses which it has deliberately transformed into slaves. The ownership of the instruments of production remains in private hands.

Chase comments:

> Meaning in the form of a row of abstractions does not satisfy him [the student of semantics]. He finds three high-order terms equated and an inference applied to one or all of them:

private ownership=capitalism=fascism. He is immediately suspicious of the identification of three timeless, spaceless, descriptionless entities. He never saw an "ism" imposing its will. He asks what are the referents for "private ownership," "monopoly capitalism," and "fascism." He wonders what is meant by "capitalism imposing its will on the masses," remembering that this is a stock phrase in socialist propaganda. He thinks of chain gangs, galley slaves, Negroes on plantations before the Civil War. "Ownership of the instruments of production" troubles him as another stock phrase. He recalls how Berle and Means in their *Modern Corporation and Private Property* show that many legal "owners" of large corporations have nothing to say about their "property." They collect dividends, if any, and drop their proxies in the wastebasket. "Private hands" worries him more. He knows that whatever titles private persons may hold to property in Germany or Italy, the Government jolly well tells them when, where, and how much to let go of.   —*The Tyranny of Words*

Equivocation, a related fallacy, is the confusion in premises of different meanings of a word (or relative meanings, as in the application of the term *competent* to both a plumber and an argument, in the same context). Here is an astonishing example:

We now have 160,000 engineers graduate from our universities each year, which is three times more than this country [the U.S.]. Some say that the more scientists we have, the sooner will communism collapse. Then we seem to be working to our own end, but that is not the case. We regard communism as a science.—NIKITA KHRUSHCHEV, replying to a question at the National Press Club in Washington, September 17, 1959

Deliberate restrictions may be put on words—resulting in the same kind of effect as equivocation. In the following statement of the Nazi writer Alfred Rosenberg, the words *opportunities* and *possibilities* are severely restricted by the concluding statement:

The woman belongs deeply to the total life of the people. All educational opportunities must remain open to her. Through rhythmics, gymnastics, and sport the same care must be given to her physical training as is the case with men. Nor should any difficulties be created for her in the vocational world under present-day social conditions . . . . Hence all possibilities for the development of a woman's energies should remain open to her. But there must be clarity on one point: only man must be and remain a judge, soldier, and ruler of the state.   —*The Myth of the Twentieth Century*

This passage reminds us of the need to examine our words not only for possible connotations, but also for loose or vague meanings.

BEGGING THE QUESTION

A question is begged when it assumes as true what it is trying to prove is true: "Should we allow the courthouse gang to run the city?" This question is complex and needs to be broken down. The following argument for "iron discipline" in the Communist state begs a serious question.

> The achievement and maintenance of the dictatorship of the proletariat is impossible without a party which is strong by reason of its solidarity and iron discipline. But iron discipline in the Party is inconceivable without unity of will, without complete and absolute unity of action on the part of all members of the Party. This does not mean, of course, that the possibility of contests of opinion within the Party is thereby precluded. On the contrary, iron discipline does not preclude but presupposes criticism and contest of opinion within the Party. Least of all does it mean that discipline must be "blind." On the contrary, iron discipline does not preclude but presupposes conscious and voluntary submission, for only conscious discipline can be truly iron discipline. But after a contest of opinion has been closed, after criticism has been exhausted and a decision has been arrived at, unity of will and unity of action of all Party members are the necessary condition without which neither Party unity nor iron discipline in the Party is conceivable.
>
> —JOSEPH STALIN, *The Foundations of Leninism* (1924)

The statement implies that once a decision has been arrived at, there is no possibility of future error and therefore no need of future criticism or dissent. The question begged is whether there is any way to guarantee the success of a policy or to arrive at final truth.

One other example deserves to be cited:

> What should our policy be toward non-Marxist ideas? As far as unmistakable counter-revolutionaries and wreckers of the socialist cause are concerned, the matter is easy; we simply deprive them of their freedom of speech. But it is quite a different matter when we are faced with incorrect ideas among the people. Will it do to ban such ideas and give them no opportunity to express themselves? Certainly not. It is not only futile but very harmful to use crude and summary methods to deal with ideological questions among the people, with questions relating to the spiritual life of man. You may

ban the expression of wrong ideas, but the ideas will still be there. On the other hand, correct ideas, if pampered in hot-houses without being exposed to the elements or immunized against disease, will not win out against wrong ones. That is why it is only by employing methods of discussion, criticism and reasoning that we can really foster correct ideas, overcome wrong ideas and really settle issues.—MAO TSE-TUNG, from a speech delivered in Peking to the Supreme State Conference, February 27, 1957

The question begged is why the ideas of "counter-revolutionaries and wreckers of the socialist cause" are not also permitted to flourish and be exposed to criticism and reasoning. The illogic of both statements is clothed in bad rhetoric in the form of seemingly bland abstractions.

ARGUING IN A CIRCLE

The circular argument returns to where it starts, or restates its premise (in different words) in its conclusion. As such it is a form of begging the question. The following specimen from an Italian Fascist engages in tautology (repetitious statements, one of which is taken to prove the other) as it moves from the idea that Fascism is "action and sentiment" to a virtual restatement in the concluding sentence:

It is true that Facism is, above all, action and sentiment and that such it must continue to be. Were it otherwise, it could not keep up that immense driving force, that renovating power which it now possesses and would merely be the solitary meditation of a chosen few. Only because it is feeling and senti-ment, only because it is the unconscious reawakening of our profound racial instinct, has it the force to stir the soul of the people, and to set free an irresistible current of national will. Only because it is action, and as such actualizes itself in a vast organization and in a huge movement, has it the con-ditions for determining the historical course of contemporary Italy.
—ALFREDO ROCCO, The Political Doctrine of Fascism (1925)

The second and third sentences are intended as proof ("Were it other-wise"), yet they merely restate the first and concluding sentences in the same, or similar, words (feeling, sentiment, force) and with a mere rearrangement of ideas.

ACCIDENT

The fallacy of accident is the application of a maxim or principle to an instance whose special circumstances make the application irrelevant. In concurring with the majority opinion in *Alberts* v. *California* and dissenting in *Roth* v. *California* (1957), two cases that caused a reexamination of the nature of obscenity, Justice Harlan implicitly calls attention to this fallacy:

> In final analysis, the problem presented by these cases is how far, and on what terms, the state and federal governments have power to punish individuals for disseminating books considered to be undesirable because of their nature or supposed deleterious effect upon human conduct. Proceeding from the premise that "no issue is presented in either case, concerning the obscenity of the material involved," the Court finds the "dispositive question" to be "whether obscenity is utterance within the area of protected speech and press," and then holds that "obscenity" is not so protected because it is "utterly without redeeming social importance." This sweeping formula appears to me to beg the very question before us. The Court seems to assume that "obscenity" is a peculiar *genus* of "speech and press," which is as distinct, recognizable, and classifiable as poison ivy is among other plants. On this basis the *constitutional* question before us simply becomes, as the Court says, whether "obscenity," as an abstraction, is protected by the First and Fourteenth Amendments, and the question whether a *particular* book may be suppressed becomes a mere matter of classification, of "fact," to be entrusted to a fact-finder and insulated from independent constitutional judgment. But surely the problem cannot be solved in such a generalized fashion. Every communication has an individuality and "value" of its own. The suppression of a particular writing or other tangible form of expression is, therefore, an *individual* matter, and in the nature of things every such suppression raises an individual constitutional problem in which a reviewing court must determine for *itself* whether the attacked expression is suppressible within constitutional standards. Since those standards do not readily lend themselves to generalized definitions, the constitutional problem in the last analysis becomes one of particularized judgments which appellate courts must make for themselves.

Harlan objects to applying a generalized definition of obscenity to books as "a mere matter of classification," without regard to their special values. The pertinent issue for Harlan is whether obscenity is an "abstraction" that subsumes various written and spoken statements or is a quality peculiar to and inseparable from a particular statement. The special circumstances of the book may make the application of an "abstraction" irrelevant.

INDUCTION

Induction is usually understood to be the process of generalizing from particular instances. By this definition, induction can sometimes be perfect: "Each adult on my block is registered to vote." This statement cannot, however, be used to predict that each of these men *will* vote. If each of them voted in every past election, it is probable but not certain that each will vote in succeeding elections. A perfect induction is, in effect, an instance of deduction because it makes a verifiable claim about a class, that is, it presumes to know what each member of the class has done. Since few inductions can be perfect, inductive arguments—unlike deductive ones—present evidence from which only limited generalizations may be drawn. In this kind of argument, the evidence may provide strong support for the conclusion, but it is not taken to be certain and decisive, as are the premises of a deductive argument. Arguments that cite cause on the basis of repeated experiments and many arguments from analogy are inductive on the assumption that the evidence increases the probability of the generalization. We have noted that should an induction be taken as certain and decisive it may become one of the premises in a deductive argument.

Because of the difficulties involved in arriving at premises, a writer's chief concern is frequently with establishing and defending premises, and attacking the soundness of other premises, rather than with the *form* of the argument, that is, with the process of reasoning. We noted earlier that many deductive arguments in the history of science, constructed on premises thought to be certain and decisive, have been proven unsound. New systems of geometry provide new premises for thinking about the universe. In other words, neither deductive nor inductive arguments can have any *final* guarantee of certainty: the difference between the two lies in the *presumed* certainty and decisiveness of the premises.

To state the difference in another way, the deductive argument is not concerned with the truth or falsity of its premises, primarily because these are assumed to be materially true or self-evident. The inductive argument is primarily concerned with the material truth of its premises and the basis on which this truth is established.

THE "INDUCTIVE LEAP"

When an argument moves too quickly from particular experiences to a generalization about them, when we jump to a conclusion before we have enough evidence for it, an "inductive leap" is said to occur. Usually the more evidence we provide, the more probable the generalization. The qualification "usually" is made because a few well-chosen instances (like a single good example) may be sufficient to establish the generalization. The evidence cited must, however, exhaust the possibilities that affect the generalization; it must also be typical of the situation under analysis (if it is not typical, we may have the fallacy of accident). The limits of the generalization must also be indicated. Thus, in trying to prove that the Vietnam war is responsible for the increasing drug use among college students, a writer first must explain and justify his procedures: He may be offering a hypothesis based on careful observation and verifiable details, or merely summarizing the research and expert testimony of others. Or he may be doing both. If he is gathering the evidence himself, he must base his conclusions on the behavior of individuals differing in background, interests, and emotional maturity in order to show that concern about the war is one constant element in the experience of these drug users. The more instances he can cite, the more certainly he will be able to establish a pattern of behavior, and the more probable and convincing his argument.

Many so-called inductive arguments go wrong because they are based on hearsay and idle speculation rather than on personal observation grounded in common sense. The statement "People on welfare are lazy and dishonest" will seem obvious to those who want to believe it. They will cite newspaper accounts of "welfare chisellers" and the like to support their belief; they will not consider the probability that these are exceptions. But they would laugh at the statement "Blondes like to play the piano." Statements like "French is easier to learn than English" may be based on personal observation yet are hard to verify because of the difficulty in defining terms and establishing a basis for testing the experience of people learning languages. Usually statements of this sort are mere personal judgment. The following passage discusses the danger of generalizing on the basis of seemingly obvious but actually mistaken connections among words:

> Let us consider a few examples. In English we divide most of our words into two classes, which have different grammatical and logical properties. Class 1 we call nouns, e.g., "house, man"; class 2, verbs, e.g., "hit, run." Many words of one class can act secondarily as of the other class, e.g., "a hit, a run," "to man (the boat)," but, on the primary level, the division between the classes is absolute. Our language thus gives us a bipolar division of nature. But nature herself is not thus polarized. If it be said that "strike, turn, run," are verbs because they denote temporary or short-lasting events, i.e., actions, why then is "fist" a noun? It also is a temporary event. Why are "lightning, spark, wave, eddy, pulsation, flame,

storm, phase, cycle, spasm, noise, emotion" nouns? They are temporary events. If "man" and "house" are nouns because they are long-lasting and stable events, i.e., things, what then are "keep, adhere, extend, project, continue, persist, grow, dwell," and so on doing among the verbs? If it be objected that "possess, adhere" are verbs because they are stable relationships rather than stable percepts, why then should "equilibrium, pressure, current, peace, group, nation, society, tribe, sister," or any kinship term be among the nouns? It will be found that an "event" to us means "what our language classes as a verb" or something analogized therefrom. And it will be found that it is not possible to define "event, thing, object, relationship," and so on, from nature, but that to define them always involves a circuitous return to the grammatical categories of the definer's language.

—BENJAMIN L. WHORF, *Language, Thought, and Reality*

Whorf presents contrary evidence from two American Indian languages:

In the Hopi language, "lightning, wave, flame, meteor, puff of smoke, pulsation" are verbs—events of necessarily brief duration cannot be anything but verbs. "Cloud" and "storm" are at about the lower limit of duration for nouns. Hopi, you see, actually has a classification of events (or linguistic isolates) by duration type, something strange to our modes of thought. On the other hand, in Nootka, a language of Vancouver Island, all words seem to us to be verbs, but really there are no classes 1 and 2; we have, as it were, a monistic view of nature that gives us only one class of word for all kinds of events. "A house occurs" or "it houses" is the way of saying "house," exactly like "a flame occurs" or "it burns." These terms seem to us like verbs because they are inflected for durational and temporal nuances, so that the suffixes of the word for house event make it mean long-lasting house, temporary house, future house, house that used to be, what started out to be a house, and so on.

We are talking here really about the need to qualify the statements we make—even when the evidence for them seems highly probable or decisive.

SAMPLING

Statistical arguments are so full of pitfalls that, if they are to be used at all, they must be used with extreme caution. The statistical evidence should be well established and, if possible, be supported by other compelling evidence. Only that statistical evidence cited in scholarly sources should be used, not that in popular magazines and newspaper columns unless these report authorities on the subject accurately. Even this evidence demands caution. The statement, "X City, which last year had 50 felonious crimes per thousand population, is safer than Y City, which had 100 felonious crimes per thousand," is virtually meaningless; for a city with an efficient police force will report a higher number of felonious crimes. A revealing use of statistical evidence occurred recently in the conclusion drawn by a group of Democrat congressmen that a liberal trend was evident in the 1970 elections. *The New York Times* political writer Tom Wicker, in commenting on this conclusion, first states the evidence cited for the conclusion, then reports the finding of the Field poll in California that personality and age often seem more important to voters than issues:

> [The Study Group conclusion] was based on a finding that 49 of 58 incumbent members of the House, highly rated as liberals on the ADA voting scale, gained support over their 1968 showing, while 80 of 129 members at the bottom of that scale lost support from 1968. The post-election Field analysis of California voting shows how such generalized statistics can mislead. They do not take into account the relative advantages of the personalities involved. They do not necessarily consider specific matters—like [Senator George] Murphy's age—having nothing to with ideology. And they obscure the difference in presidential and mid-term elections.

Wicker also warns against drawing the opposite conclusion:

> On the other hand, the Study Group figures provide one more argument against last fall's confident thesis that the country was "swinging to the right." Those who believe that are being reduced again to the old Goldwater thesis that Americans are just waiting for a "real conservative" to come along.
> — Cleveland *Plain Dealer*, December 31, 1970

Two writers on ecology have attacked a prevalent assumption that the poor are mainly responsible for the population explosion. The writers indicate that "In reality, fewer than one-third of the babies in the U.S. each year belong to the poor, and fewer than 20 per cent to the non-white." It is the non-poor who exert the greatest pressure on resources and the environment (the per capita consumption of energy in the U.S. is 56 times greater than that of India):

> Similar arguments, applied within the boundaries of the United States, indicate that a poor person in our population has far less opportunity to loot and pollute than does the

average American. Thus the slightly higher birth rate among U.S. poor is more than compensated for, in terms of stress on resources and environment, by their lower per capita impact (and the fact that they comprise a relatively small fraction of the population). The higher birth rate is of course a liability, but its consequences are most serious for the poor themselves. Statistically, not only are large families more likely to be poor, they are also more likely to *remain* poor. It is also worth noting that, although the poor have had relatively little to do with generating our environmental deterioration, they are often disproportionately its victims. The urban poor are confined to the cores of cities where air pollution is heaviest and urban decay and overcrowding are worst. Migrant farm workers may be spared the evils of modern urban life, but they suffer directly from agricultural pollution, especially misuse of pesticides.

—PAUL R. EHRLICH AND JOHN P. HOLDREN,
"Who Makes the Babies?"
Saturday Review, February 6, 1971

It should be noted that these writers themselves make statements that assume facts not in evidence:

Evidently . . . the backbone of our population growth is supplied by the parents of "Middle America," many of whom assure themselves that having a third or fourth child is reasonable because they can "afford" it.

The generalization about parents of Middle America is a form of sampling—of stating as a fact what "many" people think. The basis of the sample is not given. Compare the following argument based on a different assumption concerning pressure on resources:

"There is no population bomb! Industrialization is the answer to the population problem. In colonial times, the average American family had 13 children, but now that we can count on the little ones growing up healthy, the average is about two. That's evolution working—where industrialization occurs, the birth rate simply goes down. Now, of course, you have the environmentalists telling you that you can't industrialize any further because of pollution, which is more nonsense. Pollution is nothing but resources we're not harvesting. We allow them to disperse because we've been ignorant of their value.

—R. BUCKMINSTER FULLER, in *Life Magazine*,
February 26, 1971

Notice that this writer also bases his interpretation of a statistical fact on an unverified sampling of views.

CAUSE AND EFFECT

Cause and effect reasoning is a difficult form of analysis and takes different forms. Actually the word *cause* has different meanings. We sometimes mean by it a *necessary condition* without which the effect cannot occur. In this limited sense, the cause of frostbite is freezing temperature: frostbite cannot occur unless the temperature is freezing. And sometimes we mean a condition that is sufficient to produce the effect (*sufficient condition*): the effect must always occur in its presence. Thus, freezing temperature may be a necessary condition for the occurrence of frostbite, but it is not sufficient to produce the effect: other necessary conditions must also be present for frostbite to occur. "It is obvious that there may be several *necessary* conditions for the occurrence of an event, and that they must all be included in the *sufficient* condition."[1] When we wish to single out one prominent cause that we are certain has led to the effect, we are speaking of a *necessary condition* (we may warn someone not to expose his fingers or to avoid staying out too long in a freezing temperature). Other times we speak of cause as the sum of *necessary* conditions *sufficient* to produce the effect. Thus, the cause of frostbite would be the sum of conditions (freezing temperature, prolonged exposure, and so forth) which must produce the effect. We can never, of course, be certain that we have discovered all of the necessary conditions: cause and effect reasoning can be only more or less probable.

Sound cause and effect reasoning will show that the conditions cited are necessary and the sum of them sufficient to produce the effect. It will *not* assume that a condition is a cause *merely because* it preceded the effect (striking a match precedes the phenomenon of fire but is not for that reason the cause). This is called the *post hoc ergo propter hoc* fallacy (after this, therefore because of this).

We also may refer to the *proximate* and *remote causes* of an event when these occur in a chain. Thus, the proximate cause of hunger is no intake of food, and the cause of *that* deprivation may be poverty or famine. The social worker will be concerned with proximate causes in this situation, a government commission with the remote.

Loose cause and effect reasoning makes bad writing. We come back to the point that limiting the subject of your essay properly will help you avoid such common faults in reasoning as "accident" and ambiguity. The tighter the subject, the less opportunity for misleading or circular definition or unintentionally throwing in the "red herring." Limiting your topic will force you to scale down your generalizations, particularly those that make broad assertions about causes and effects. If you limit yourself to pollution control in your city—indeed, to one aspect of this problem—you are less likely to generalize about world-

[1] Irving M. Copi, *Introduction to Logic* (Macmillan: New York, 1961), p. 356.

wide causes of pollution, the evils of overconsumption, the basic qualities of human nature, the thinking of people about pollution since Christopher Columbus.

Bold assertions about cause and effect, without a careful marshalling of evidence, persuade no one except those already committed to your proposition. As soon as you take on the job of proving what "most" people in the world, in the United States, in Cleveland, Ohio, or even in your neighborhood think, your statements become vague, your essay becomes formless. Bold assertions often hide uncertainty and confusion about one's experience and ideas. Your reader will be convinced, finally, by your evidence and not by the mere assertion that evidence for your ideas does exist.

ANALOGY

An applicant for a job might argue that he will make a good salesman because he learned on the football field how to feint and deceive and seize the initiative. The prospective employer may agree or disagree depending on what he thinks of the analogy. Is his store a playing field and are his customers the "enemy"? If he lines up his salesmen in the morning for instructions, does he imagine himself to be a coach inspecting his team?

The probability of an argument from analogy depends on the number of relevant points of similarity and the relative insignificance of the points of dissimilarity. A young man may argue that he will make a competent supervisor in a large factory because he ran a large section of a discount store for a year; he will cite relevant points of similarity—supervising a number of employees, negotiating with managers, looking into complaints. He will have to show that points of dissimilarity—such as a difference in the number and kind of employees—do not weaken his argument.

In arguments concerning issues and ideas, analogy may support an argument. The rhetorical use of analogy should be distinguished from the logical: analogies are frequently introduced for their strong emotional appeal, without regard to logic. The amusing analogy at the end of the following passage is introduced for its rhetorical force:

> The popular belief in athletics is grounded upon the theory that violent exercise makes for bodily health, and that bodily health is necessary to mental vigor. Both halves of this theory are highly dubious. There is, in fact, no reason whatever for believing that such a game as, say, football improves the health of those who play it. On the contrary, there is every reason for believing that it is deleterious. The football player is not only exposed constantly to a risk of grave injury, often of an irremediable kind; he is also damaged in his normal

physiological processes by the excessive strains of the game, and the exposure that goes with playing it. If it were actually good for half-grown boys to wallow for several hours a day in a muddy field, with their heads bare and the bleak autumnal skies overhead, then it would also be good for them to be sprayed with a firehose before going to bed. And if it were good for their nonplaying schoolmates to sit watching them on cold and windy bleachers then it would also be good for those schoolmates to hear their professors in the same place.
—H. L. MENCKEN, "The Striated Muscle Fetish"

This passage reminds us that, though logical and rhetorical considerations are often parallel and often intersect, a logical argument may not always be sufficient to make an essay convincing.

An argument will be weakened if it stands on the analogy alone. The two applicants cited earlier probably will be asked to present other evidence of their qualifications, for example, letters of recommendation. Certain popular writers on men and animals depend chiefly on analogy in drawing conclusions about human behavior. Here is an example from a widely read book: that man descended from a line of killer apes and thus is "naturally aggressive." Toward the end of the book the following passage occurs:

West Side Story is a supreme work of art for many reasons not the least of which is truthfulness. The authors treat the romantic fallacy as if it did not exist. On a stage laid bare, and in young hearts laid naked, we watch our animal legacy unfold its awful power. There is the timeless struggle over territory, as lunatic in the New York streets as it is logical in our animal heritage. There is the gang, our ancestral troop. There is the rigid system of dominance among males within the gang, indistinguishable from that among baboons. There is the ceaseless individual defense of status. There is the amity-enmity code of any animal society: mercy, devotion, and sacrifice for the social partner; suspicion, antagonism, and unending hostility for the territorial neighbor. And there is the hunting primate contribution, a dedication to the switch-blade knife as unswerving as to the antelope bone.
—ROBERT ARDREY, African Genesis

The analogies have seemed persuasive to many. But why? Together they do not, and cannot, prove that man inherited the instincts of his animal forebears. Indeed, other conclusions have been drawn from different analogies. Another popular writer on the subject states:

It has been suggested that because we evolved as specialized prey-killers, we automatically became rival-killers, and that there is an inborn urge within us to murder our opponents.

The evidence, as I have already explained, is against this. Defeat is what an animal wants, not murder; domination is the goal of aggression, not destruction, and basically we do not seem to differ from other species in this respect. There is no good reason why we should.

—DESMOND MORRIS, *The Naked Ape*

Notice the method of reasoning by analogy: "Defeat is what an animal wants." Here, in part, is how Morris reasons about animal and human aggression:

Animals fight amongst themselves for one of two very good reasons: either to establish their dominance in a social hierarchy, or to establish their territorial rights over a particular piece of ground. Some species are purely hierarchal with no fixed territories. Some are purely territorial, with no hierarchy problems. Some have hierarchies on their territories and have to contend with both forms of aggression. We belong to the last group: we have it both ways. As primates we were already loaded with the hierarchy system. This is the basic way of primate life. The group keeps moving about, rarely staying anywhere long enough to establish a fixed territory. Occasional inter-group conflict may arise, but it is weakly organized, spasmodic and of comparatively little importance in the life of the average monkey. . . .

These examples show that the analogies in themselves will not tell us which analogies to choose. We must make a number of assumptions about men and animals before the analogies can be reasoned. It is also worth noting that other explanations for juvenile gangs and war have been offered without resorting to a theory of instincts, even when the writer believes men share qualities with other primates. Here is the reasoning of one anthropologist:

The "innate pugnacity" of which [William] James speaks is often conspicuously lacking in the human species. Warfare is virtually non-existent among many primitive tribes. And in many instances where fighting does take place, the contestants do not meet each other face to face and slug it out man to man so that their "military instincts and ideals" can be exercised to the full. Instead, they resort to ambush, killing their victims before they have a chance to defend themselves. To slaughter helpless sleeping victims is quite sufficient to feed the "love of glory" of most peoples. And when free and open conflict does take place among primitive peoples, their pugnacity is often more vocal than military—as is usually the case among the lower primates.

—L. A. WHITE, *The Science of Culture*

Notice that the reference to the behavior of the lower primates is not presented as evidence for a psychological attitude, as a later statement shows:

> Warfare is a struggle between social organisms, not individuals. Its explanation is therefore social or cultural, not psychological. —*Ibid.*

The point we are making is that evidence from analogy, like statistical evidence, has inherent weaknesses and should not be presented without other compelling evidence if this exists. If the writer wishes his analogy to gain in force, he will do well to introduce his assumptions and argue them cogently. For analogies take on force only when writer and reader agree to the assumptions underlying their use.

EXERCISES

1. Evaluate the following arguments after analyzing the nature of the reasoning:

a. Sirs: Next month I will expect to see an article in your magazine warning people against skiing, skating or sledding. I just wonder why you chose to condemn snowmobiles, or aren't you aware that all winter sports produce casualties or death?—a letter to *Life Magazine*, March 19, 1971.

b. In our society, the traditional controls have been unable to cope with the continued deterioration of our environment basically because of our failure to recognize pollution for what it is: a form of aggression against society as a whole and our neighbors in particular. Existing or possible control methods are of three types: informal (our mores), formal or legal, and economic. The informal controls are those most capable of producing a high general level of conformity to the demands of society, while legal controls operate primarily to establish a minimum standard of acceptable conduct. Economic controls hardly exist. The informal controls are the most effective, as the regulated individual conforms as a result of his ingrained socialization. Ultimately, in a democratic society, all control should be based upon this societal consensus of what is permissible conduct.—Arnold W. Reitze, Jr., an excerpt from "Pollution Control: Why Has It Failed?"

c. Theology teaches that the sun has been created in order to illuminate the earth. But one moves the torch in order to illuminate the house, and not the house in order to be illuminated by the torch. Hence it is the sun which revolves around the earth, and not the earth which revolves around the sun.—Besian Array, 1671 (cited in Morris R. Cohen and Ernest Nagel, *An Introduction to Logic and Scientific Method*)

d. There is nothing new, of course, about the New Morality. One would have to cut a lot of history classes to imagine that humankind had not attempted to find happiness in utter animalism. Or that they would not attempt to rationalize misbehavior by claiming lofty, even spiritual motives.

The temple prostitutes of Astarte 3,500 years ago expressed a philosophy which *Playboy* seems to have just rediscovered. The hashish-maddened Thugs of India went through elaborate religious rites before they set forth to rob and strangle travelers.

But none of these noble experiments produced workable societies. Nations that wallowed in corruption found commercial strength hard to achieve, for you can't build bankable credits where bribery is the norm and graph and short-weight the custom. And where moral standards were abysmal there occurred, paradoxically, an emasculation of the male, for irresponsibility produces the incompetence to cope and it leads to the matriarchy which is the chief social headache of America's current ghetto societies.

Some people never recovered. Much of our foreign aid has sunk without a trace in social systems that cannot organize themselves for any degree of success. Other civilizations, more happily, eventually became nauseated and went through puritan renaissances, some of them carried to ridiculous extremes.—Jenkin L. Jones, an excerpt from "Let's De-Kookify the Media," reprinted in *Congressional Record*, October 28, 1969

e. Mr. Speaker, yesterday, a coalition of southern Democrats, reactionary Republicans, and the Attorney General worked their will in the House. For the first time since the Congress began passing civil rights legislation in 1957, a giant step backward was taken in guaranteeing constitutional rights to all its citizens.

No one is fooled by the sanctimoniousness of the Attorney General's stated objectives in his substitute bill—to assure the right to vote to all persons in every State of the Union. The essence of the Attorney General's approach to voter's rights for all citizens is easily equated with the administration's political "southern strategy."

The right to vote for black Americans who live in the South has been a hard-fought battle against every conceivable obstruction put in their path by a highly developed, skilled "southern strategy" long before the present administration decided where to look for future votes.

This country has just begun—and I repeat—has just begun to see real progress in race relations. The Voting Rights Act of 1965 was fundamental to this progress. Almost one million southern Negro citizens, for the first time, were permitted under its provisions to register and to vote in local, State, and National elections. The guarantee of the right to vote is the most basic protection every American—black and white —must have if we are to remain a democracy. But, yesterday, erosion of this progress began here on the floor of the House.

The Southern States should not be permitted to engage in their old tactics of denying the right to vote to their Negro citizens—and this is what is being permitted by the acceptance in the House yesterday of the Attorney General's substitute bill.

One wonders how the Attorney General of the United States, with the power and the responsibility of his high office, can justify an action that would in effect destroy one of the most fundamental rights the Constitution has guaranteed to all Americans because of his desire to strengthen his party's political base in the South.

The most succinct and clear interpretation of the Attorney General's substitute bill was stated yesterday by the ranking Republican on the Judiciary Committee, the gentleman from Ohio [Mr. McCulloch] when he said that the Attorney General's bill "creates a remedy for which there is no wrong and leaves grievous wrongs without adequate remedy." And he then asked, as he did of the Attorney General when he testified before the committee, "What kind of civil rights bill is that?"—Representative James C. Corman of California, an excerpt from *Congressional Record*, December 12, 1969

f. I believe that the answer to this chaos lies in the legislation which I introduce today which would clearly outlaw most wiretapping and legitimize necessary wiretapping while subjecting it to rigid controls and procedures.

I know there are many who would go much further and abolish all wiretapping. It would perhaps be exhilarating to mount the hobbyhorse of unrestricted individual rights and demand an end to all wiretapping on the ground that the right of privacy is so sacred as to be inviolate; or upon the ground that the power to tap wires is so dangerous to freedom that it cannot be entrusted to anyone.

But before we go too far in pressing the claims of inalienable rights, we must remember that many of what we popularly call individual rights are not inherent rights at all, not natural rights that man possesses as a human being but instead are limited rights, derived from society itself, rights which are products and growths of society, which have meaning only within a social context.

The right to use a telephone in absolute secrecy is certainly not an inherent right of man. The telephone is a product of a highly developed, cooperative, social existence. Therefore, man's rights with respect to the telephone may be properly limited by the needs of the society which developed it, which has a stake in its use and which suffers grievously from its abuse by criminals.

As to the second objection, that the power to authorize wiretapping is too dangerous to be entrusted to any man, I say this: Almost every action of our lives involves the placing of trust in someone. If we are not to be paralyzed completely as a people, we must repose somewhere the authority to act and we must assume that the highest officials in the land can be safely entrusted with that authority.—Senator Thomas Dodd, an excerpt from *Congressional Record*, March 30, 1961

g. Mr. President, I have been concerned for some time that the U.S. Supreme Court has, through its decisions in the criminal justice area, been seriously weakening the Government's effort to combat the growing menace of crime in the United States. On several occasions I have spoken on the floor of the Senate on this subject. The statistics that are available dramatically portray the source of my concern.

Since 1960, the Supreme Court has reviewed 112 Federal criminal cases and 144 State criminal cases in which it has handed down written opinions. The Supreme Court has chosen to reverse 60 percent of the Federal convictions it has considered, and 80 percent of the State convictions it has considered. In addition, it has granted 85 percent of the habeas corpus petitions presented to it in which it chose to hand down written decisions.

It has been suggested in some quarters that the Court has merely been enforcing the law and that if blame is to be assigned, it should be assigned to the police for bringing about these reversals. What this position ignores is that the Supreme Court has not only been enforcing the law, but it has been making it, too. Indeed, since 1960, in the criminal justice area alone, the Supreme Court has specifically overruled or rejected the reasoning of 25 of its own precedents—often by the narrowest of 5-to-4 margins. Seventeen of these decisions involved a change in constitutional doctrine—without the intervention of a constitutional convention. Seven of these decisions represented a new interpretation of statutory language—without intervening congressional action. Only one of these decisions may be classified as modifying the common law, an area in which the Court traditionally has had freer reign in developing the law.

It has also been contended by some that these reversal decisions are having no adverse impact on law enforcement and on the rising incidence of crime. This contention is not supported by the facts. Indeed, since 1960, while our population has increased 11 percent, serious crime has overall increased 122 percent. Robbery alone has increased 142 percent; burglary, 104 percent. Operating under the new standards and requirements imposed by recent Supreme Court decisions, moreover, police clearance—solving—of serious crimes has experienced a steady, across-the-board decline. For example: The clearance for robbery has dropped 25.9 percent and the clearance for burglary 38.8 percent. Verdicts of not guilty in robbery cases have increased 23 percent and in burglary cases 53 percent.—Senator John McClellan, an excerpt from *Congressional Record*, October 23, 1969

2. Identify the assumptions or premises in the following passages and the conclusions derived from them:

a. In like manner the best government rests on the people and not on the few, on persons and not on property, on the free development of public opinion and not on authority; because the munificent Author of our being has conferred the gifts of mind upon every member of the human race without distinction of outward circumstances. Whatever of other possessions may be engrossed, mind asserts its own independence. Lands, estates, the produce of mines, the prolific abundance of the seas, may be usurped by a privileged class. Avarice, assuming the form of ambitious power, may grasp realm after realm, subdue continents, compass the earth in its schemes of aggrandizement, and sigh after other worlds; but mind eludes the power of appropriation; it exists only in its own individuality; it is a property which cannot be confiscated and cannot be torn away; it laughs at chains; it bursts from imprisonment; it defies monopoly. A government of equal rights must, therefore, rest upon mind; not wealth, not brute force, the sum of the moral intelligence of the community should rule the State.—George Bancroft, *The Office of the People*

b. Government is not made in virtue of natural rights, which may and do exist in total independence of it; and exist in much greater clearness, and in a much greater degree of abstract perfection: but their abstract perfection is their practical defect. By having a right to everything they want everything. Government is a contrivance of human wisdom to provide for human wants. Men have a right that these wants should be provided for by this wisdom. Among these wants is to be reckoned the want, out of civil society, of a sufficient restraint upon their passions. Society requires not only that the passions of individuals should be subjected, but that even in the mass and body, as well as in the individuals, the inclinations of men should frequently be thwarted, their will controlled, and their passions brought into subjection. This can only be done *by a power out of themselves*; and not, in the exercise of its function, subject to that will and to those passions which it is its office to bridle and subdue. In this sense the restraints on men, as well as their liberties, are to be reckoned among their rights. But as the liberties and the restrictions vary with times and circumstances, and admit of infinite modifications, they cannot be settled upon any abstract rule; and nothing is so foolish as to discuss them upon that principle. . . . —Edmund Burke, *Reflections on the Revolution in France*

c. First of all, as regards the future development of mankind,—and quite apart from all present political considerations—Fascism does not, generally speaking, believe in the possibility or utility of perpetual peace. It therefore discards pacifism as a cloak for cowardly supine renunciation in contra-distinction to self-sacrifice. War alone keys up all human energies to their maximum tension and sets the seal of nobility on those peoples who have the courage to face it. All other tests are substitutes which never place a man face to face with himself before the alternative of life or death. Therefore all doctrines which postulate peace at all costs are incompatible with Fascism. Equally foreign to the spirit of Fascism—even if accepted as useful in meeting special political situations—are all internationalistic or League superstructures which, as history shows, crumble to the ground whenever the heart of nations is deeply stirred by sentimental, idealistic or practical considerations. Fascism carries this anti-pacifistic attitude into the life of the individual. "I don't care a damn" *(me ne frego)*—the proud motto of the fighting squads scrawled by a wounded man on his bandages—is not only an act of philosophic stoicism, it sums up a doctrine which is not merely political: it is evidence of a fighting spirit which accepts all risks. It signifies a new style of Italian life. The Fascist accepts and loves life; he rejects and despises suicide as cowardly. Life as he understands it means duty, elevation, conquest; life must be lofty and full, it must be lived for oneself but above all for others, both near by and far off, present and future.—Benito Mussolini, *Fascism: Doctrine and Institutions*

THE
RESEARCH
PAPER

THE NATURE OF RESEARCH

The many kinds of research or library papers draw on a wide variety of material, ranging from critical biographies, journal and magazine articles, newspapers, historical studies, and theoretical books to private diaries, letters, memoirs, and official documents. How you will use these depends on your purpose. If you are writing the paper merely to acquaint yourself with a portion of the literature on a famous man, without reading extensively in it, it may be enough to examine critical biographies and sample works. But if you wish to draw your own conclusions, you will want to examine the man's own writings (diaries, letters, memoirs, essays, books), as well as statements made about him by friends and relatives, for the purpose of determining the authenticity and relative importance of primary sources. In his account of conflicting images of Daniel Boone in the essay that follows, Henry Nash Smith draws on the extensive literature on Boone to demonstrate that images of him reveal conflicting cultural attitudes toward the West.

The inexperienced researcher will depend on both kinds of material, not knowing enough about his subject to discover the important primary sources and not being certain of the reliable texts or editions. The experienced researcher like Smith may refer to secondary sources to confirm his conclusions; if he wishes, he can rely on primary sources almost entirely, because he has studied documents of the period long and intensively and is competent to authenticate them. He is able to distinguish the relative worth of secondary works, which may not agree on fundamental points or interpretation of evidence. To verify the conclusions of other writers and his own views, he will examine statements in their original context and in light of other statements by the writer; for writers do not always quote the full context on which so much can depend. This independent examination of sources is absolutely essential to the independent judgment he wants to make in his paper.

These points suggest again that you will not be able to state your ideas with absolute certainty. Not only will you have to qualify and support them in some instances with the opinion of scholars, but you will also have to indicate where differences in interpretation exist in secondary sources and what limits the available materials have imposed (for you may not be able to find all the books and articles needed for an exhaustive treatment of the subject). This limitation should not lead to overdependence on secondary sources. At all stages of work you should keep in mind that contributions to knowledge are made only after a long period of study and thought and not after a week of reading in the library. Remember that your effort must be modest in scope, and that you will do a better job if you do not try to deal with all aspects of the problem and to solve it once and for all. Your first job, then, is to find a limited topic which can be investigated fully and about which you can write something interesting and important. If, for example, you want to write on Jefferson's attitude toward democracy, you will do better to limit the topic to a subordinate consideration—Jefferson's attitude toward the Federalists, or the French Revolution, or perhaps the implications of his correspondence with John Adams. The card catalog of the library will indicate whether the essential materials are available for research.

You are more likely to find something interesting and perhaps original to say if you follow your curiosity in choosing a topic and avoid short-cuts that will use more of your time than will orderly procedures. Taking the first topic or materials that come to hand can produce bizarre and hackneyed topics, as stacks of papers on the Blarney Stone testify. A seemingly bizarre topic (the interior heat of distant stars) can lead, however, to unexpected discoveries (ways of measuring the size of the universe, the nature of quasars) if you are interested enough in the topic to be imaginative.

How limited or broad should the topic be? Jacques Barzun and Henry F. Graff offer an answer that is worth quoting: "your subject is defined by that group of associated facts and ideas which, when clearly presented in a prescribed amount of space, leave no questions unanswered, *within* the presentation, even though many questions could be asked outside it."[1]

We commented in the last section on the frequent disagreements of historians over the interpretation of evidence. Such disagreements may suggest a research topic. To cite one example, historians disagree over the significance of Jefferson's various statements on slavery. Some argue that Jefferson was in advance of his time in his proposals to abolish it. Yet one historian makes this challenging statement:

> Much has been made by rapt biographers of Jefferson's interest in abolishing slavery at this time. As a member of a committee to revise the legal code, he did draft a law for gradual emancipation, but never presumed to introduce it. "It was found," he explained, "that the public mind would not bear the proposition. . . . Yet the day is not distant when it must bear and adopt it, or worse will follow." Trying to force through any law, however desirable, which "the public mind would not bear" would have been thoroughly uncharacteristic of Jefferson's pragmatic political temperament.

And this historian adds in a footnote:

> Jefferson was characteristically circumspect about attacking slavery in his own state, but more aggressive in intercolonial affairs when he could expect Northern backing.
> —RICHARD HOFSTADTER, *The American Political Tradition*

Hofstadter's statement might encourage you to investigate at first-hand not only what Jefferson said about slavery but also what he did about it, and to see whether he ever contradicted himself, as some have maintained.

Such a study must, however, be limited in scope: you can come only to a *tentative* understanding of this complex problem. Still, the problem is worth exploring because Jefferson's attitude toward slavery goes to the heart of his character, over which writers differ. Yet so much evidence exists and so many writers have dealt with the subject, that you must center on one aspect of the total problem, perhaps Jefferson's effort to abolish slavery in Virginia, or his pronouncements against slavery in his correspondence, or differences in the interpretation of evidence—though these other aspects might be introduced as *subordinate* considerations. The more limited the topic, the more concentrated the discussion will be. A short research paper would have to be restricted to a narrow topic; a long paper could combine two of these considerations: for example, Jefferson's efforts to abolish slavery

[1]*The Modern Researcher*, 2nd ed., (New York: Harcourt Brace Jovanovich, 1970), p. 21.

and interpretations made of these efforts, the former subordinate to the latter. Of course, your topic may change as you become familiar with the material and discover that one problem is more crucial than another, or that the crux of the controversy lies in the interpretation of one or two letters or public statements. The evidence and state of the controversy must be your guide. And you must be ready to revise your topic as well as your outline as you proceed.

Let us follow the course of research a little further. You may begin with Hofstadter's statement, and because you know something—but not a great deal—about Jefferson's attitude toward slavery, you do a little reading in a biography of Jefferson to discover the controversies he was involved in. You will discover four or five prominent ones, among these (1) Jefferson's statement against slavery in the Declaration of Independence and the subsequent deletion of this statement from the final draft, and Jefferson's discussion of this deletion in his autobiography; (2) his efforts to have slavery abolished in Virginia in the revision of the Virginia statutes between 1776 and 1779; (3) his efforts in Congress to prevent slavery in the Western territories; and (4) his later amendment to a bill before the Virginia Assembly governing slaves. In addition, you will find many statements about slavery in Jefferson's letters and public writings. Once you have acquired the basic facts, you may want to read the documents in collections of Jefferson's papers and writings to form an impression of your own before you find out what others think. Having done this preliminary reading, you must decide on which aspects to center. Your reading will suggest numerous possibilities.

It cannot be repeated too often that a research paper of this kind is only a beginning, an opportunity to learn something new. It may open the way to a fuller investigation based on more intensive study. To many students, the research paper has unexpectedly suggested a promising field of concentration.

THE MATERIALS OF RESEARCH: REFERENCE BOOKS

In collecting materials, many researchers never get beyond the card catalog or the periodical indexes. Even these will produce relatively few books and articles if you do not know how to check cross-references or investigate alternate subject headings. In compiling a bibliography, reference books are indispensable. They are also difficult to use unless you are aware of pitfalls they present.

You first should know well both Constance Winchell's *Guide to Reference Books*, which lists important and reliable reference books according to subject and field, and the special bibliographies in your particular field of research. R. D. Altick and Andrew Wright's *Selective Bibliography for the Study of English and American Literature* (fourth edition, 1971) and Donald F. Bond's *A Reference Guide to English Studies* (1962; a revision of Tom Peete Cross's *Bibliographical Guide to English Studies*) are nearly exhaustive compilations of important reference works and individual bibliographies, for example, Lewis Leary's *Articles on American Literature, 1900–1950,* which lists materials not to be found in the restricted periodical indexes (*Reader's Guide to Periodical Literature, International Index to Periodicals*) and provides invaluable information on the articles. Bibliographies of this sort supplement the annual bibliographies published in *PMLA* (the journal of the Modern Language Association) and in *American Literature;* these bibliographies do not cover all periodicals (for example, *The New Yorker*) in which important discussions of writers appear. Thus Anthony West's important discussions of twentieth-century British writers in *The New Yorker* in the fifties and sixties are listed in the bibliographies on single British writers that appear in special numbers of *Modern Fiction Studies.* Such special bibliographies as Tannenbaum's *Elizabethan Bibliographies,* Blanck's *Bibliography of American Literature,* Stratman's *Bibliography of Medieval Drama,* and *Articles on American Studies* (printed annually in *American Quarterly* since 1955) may provide additional valuable material. The *Essay and General Literature Index* is valuable for its citations of individual essays in collections and book-length studies of periods, literary movements, and the like. Another important source is the bibliographies in such collections and studies. Footnotes may also provide extensive information, particularly those in journal articles and monographs.

The titles of reference works are sometimes unreliable indications of the contents: Uden's *They Looked Like This* does not reproduce pictures and photographs of famous people, as you might think, but instead gives us descriptions of them by their contemporaries (useful information in a study of their fictional counterparts). Briggs' *A Dictionary of British Folk-Tales* not only classifies folk materials by motif but indicates the uses that writers have made of them (useful information in studying the plays of William Butler Yeats and John Synge). The date of the reference work is obviously important. Brandon's *A Dictionary of Comparative Religion* was published recently enough to contain information on the Black Muslims; Hastings' *Encyclopedia of Religion and Ethics* was published before the founding of the sect. Allibone's *Critical Dictionary of English Literature and British and American Authors,* published in the later nineteenth century, has been superseded by twentieth-century reference works but is indispensable in securing information on writers forgotten today and seldom or never mentioned in literary histories and compilations. Many older dictionaries and encyclopedias, incidentally, have supplements or appendices that bring entries up to date.

It should be mentioned that some reference works are plainly unreliable or confusing in their classifications: the index of one reference work on poetry lists *The Castle of Indolence* and "The City of Dreadful Night" under the heading *James Thomson*, though the text correctly identifies the first as the work of James Thomson (1700–48), and the second as that of James Thomson (1834–82). A much quoted collection of speeches and documents, James D. Richardson's *Messages and Papers of the Presidents* (1897), alters the punctuation of some of the original documents, with resulting changes in nuance and perhaps meaning. Richardson, for example, edits a portion of Jefferson's First Inaugural Address as follows:

> But every difference of opinion is not a difference of principle. We have called by different names brethren of the same principle. We are all Republicans, we are all Federalists. If there be any among us who would wish to dissolve this Union or to change its republican form, let them stand undisturbed as monuments of the safety with which error of opinion may be tolerated where reason is left free to combat it.

The manuscript of the address, reproduced in Lipscomb and Bergh's edition of Jefferson's writings, indicates that Jefferson wrote the following:

> but every difference of opinion(,) is not a difference of principle. we have called by different names brethren of the same principle. we are all republicans: we are all federalists. if there be any among us who would wish to dissolve this Union or to change it's republican form, let them stand undisturbed as monuments of the safety with which error of opinion may be tolerated, where reason is left free to combat it.

It will be noted that Jefferson here does not distinguish capital letters (his periods, however, are clear). His care with "Union" suggests he may have intended to write "republicans" and "federalists" in lower case. Yet Lipscomb and Bergh print the passage as follows:

> But every difference of opinion is not a difference of principle. We have called by different names brethren of the same principle. We are all republicans—we are all federalists. If there be any among us who would wish to dissolve this Union or to change its republican form, let them stand undisturbed as

monuments of the safety with which error of opinion may be tolerated where reason is left free to combat it.
—*The Writings of Thomas Jefferson*, ed. A. A. Lipscomb and A. E. Bergh (Washington, D.C., 1905), III, 319

To account for these changes, you would have to find out whether Richardson, and Lipscomb and Bergh, used a version of the address different from the manuscript reproduced in the volume cited above. The authoritative edition of Jefferson's papers, edited by Julian P. Boyd and published by Princeton University Press, when completed will provide scholars with a wholly reliable text (the volumes are in continuous publication). The possible change in the meaning of *republicans* and *federalists* remains a matter of concern, as two recent books on Jefferson show:

> In viewing the last sentence of this famous passage, one should observe that Jefferson did not capitalize the key words and thus turn them into unquestionable party names, as later editors of this address took the liberty of doing. Allowance may be made for his characteristic dislike for capitals, and also for his failure to use terms with the precision of an academic philosopher, but his thought can be best understood if the words are left just as he wrote them. From other things he said about this time, it is evident that he regarded the hard core of the Federalists as unyielding and irreconcilable. He could only have meant that nearly all Americans favored a republic rather than a monarchy and accepted the federal system of government, as contrasted with consolidation on the one hand and full state sovereignty on the other. In this sense, he had used almost the same language several years earlier. —DUMAS MALONE, *Jefferson the President* (Boston: Little, Brown and Company, 1970), p. 20.

> The statement was as baffling as it was startling. Jefferson was always stingy with capital letters, otherwise he might have written, "We are all Republicans: we are all Federalists," which was the way many heard it and nearly everyone read it, usually with capitals, in the newspapers. In this sense it was a bold appeal for reconciliation of parties or, more accurately, a converting ordinance for erring Federalists. But erasing imaginary fears of Republicanism, the new President hoped to draw over the mass of Federalists to his cause.
> —MERRILL D. PETERSON, *Thomas Jefferson and the New Nation* (New York: Oxford University Press, 1970), p. 656

You can be certain of one point at least: the manuscript reproduced by Lipscomb and Bergh is not the original version since the final sentence quoted is known to be a revision (Peterson indicates this fact). Examples of such fundamental disagreements over the meaning of famous passages would fill many books.

THE MATERIALS OF RESEARCH: PERIODICALS

In examining reference books, you should watch for others on the subject, shelved under the same or similar call numbers. You should also learn the difference between the Dewey and the Library of Congress classifications. (Many libraries are in the process of changing from the Dewey to the Library of Congress classification, and books on a single writer or subject may be shelved under both classifications.) You will want to consult all periodicals which contain materials on your subject, but you should be careful to distinguish scholarly publications from popular magazines and monthlies, which vary in the quality of their writing and documentation. *Harper's Magazine* and *The Atlantic* contain articles by recognized authorities, though not necessarily professional scholars or teachers; newspaper articles and articles in magazine supplements are often derivative and careless accounts, without documentation or even a summary indication of sources (the articles in *The New York Times Magazine* are sometimes exceptions to this generalization). Newsmagazines should be used with the utmost caution. Information from these sources should be verified from scholarly sources or *The New York Times;* in the finished paper it should be presented with suitable qualifications. The *Congressional Record* is an invaluable source for statements of congressmen which are almost always abbreviated in newspaper and magazine stories.

If your library does not subscribe to a periodical, you may find articles in it abstracted in *Abstracts of English Studies* (1958—) and similar publications, for example, the annual bibliography of articles drawing upon psychology in literary analysis, in *Literature and Psychology.* Sometimes the format and even the title of these publications change: *Abstracts of English Studies* has been published by subject in a new format since 1969; the journal *University Review* was formerly published as the *University of Kansas City Review;* the *Journal of English Literary History* is now published as *ELH* and libraries shelve it under different alphabetical classifications. If a library does not hold a particular journal, offprints usually can be secured through the interlibrary loan service. It may be pointed out that the *Library of Congress Author Catalog* and its supplements (from July 31, 1942 to the present) and the *National Union Catalog* provide a nearly exhaustive listing of books, with an indication of libraries in the United States containing copies. (Your library proba-

bly contains a subject index to the Library of Congress Catalog.)
Here is a brief list of indexes that you may find useful:

Annual Magazine Subject-Index (1909—49)
Art Index (1929—)
Bibliographic Index (1937—)
Biography Index (1946—)
Dramatic Index (1909—)
Education Index (1929—)
Short Story Index (1953—)
United States Catalog: Books in Print (1899–1934)
Cumulative Book Index (1898—), supplement to *United States Catalog*
Poole's Index to Periodical Literature (1802–1906) [superseded by the *Reader's Guide*]

NOTE CARDS

The work of gathering materials will go for nothing if you are not careful to take notes that will be meaningful a month or a year later and are complete enough so that you need not return to your sources. A common and sometimes costly mistake is to combine notes or slips under one card that gives complete information about the source, instead of identifying the author and title on each card. You will not be able to rearrange your cards if you do this, and you will not remember how to arrange them if they fall. Each card should indicate the author and title of the book, in short form once the full title has been recorded on the first card for a book or in a separate bibliography. And each card should contain the page number in a prominent place. It is extremely important, also, to write in complete sentences and not in phrases, because phrases that mean something when recorded become meaningless days or weeks later (you will almost certainly not remember the context of the idea which the phrase suggests). It also helps to jot at the bottom of the card (not on the back) the significance of the material or the use intended for it. Ideally, you should not have to return to the books you consulted; they may not be available when you need them again. And this means, too, that you must check your cards carefully against the original to be certain you copied quotations or paraphrased ideas correctly. Proofreading will seem laborious after the first few cards, but it is absolutely essential. Incidentally, it is also essential to indicate with a slant line where the page break occurs in a quotation that runs into a second page, in case only part of the quotation is used. The material recorded should be selective: it is not necessary to record every idea or illustration. Too much material is as undesirable as too little.

Here are good and bad note cards for a paper on Jefferson:

BAD

G. Bowers

    death of father   30 slaves   increased
      after his death

    couldnt end slavery   reason   couldn't
      afford it he sold them rather than treatm
      bad

    Don Quix?   TJ?

Here is the original passage, carefully recorded:

GOOD

Claude G. Bowers, The Young Jefferson: 1743-1789
Boston: Houghton Mifflin Company, 1945

"On the death of his father, he had come into possession of thirty slaves, and in the succeeding years the number had augmented. The economic system of the State was based on slavery, and, while he would have gladly joined all others in the freeing and colonization of the slaves, he alone could not do so and compete with slave labor. Such action, on his part alone, would have been Quixotic and destructive of his own economic life." (p. 174)

Bowers emphasizes the economic difficulties.

The phrases on the first note card mean nothing set down as they are; and the abbreviations may be meaningless a week after the material is recorded. The second note card provides the entire quotation and complete information about author, title, publisher, and date of publication. However, the passage would be better paraphrased (put in your own words), with only a highly significant phrase or sentence quoted. And if another card already contains complete information on the source, a short title is preferable:

Bowers, Young J, p. 174

J inherited 30 slaves from his father. This number increased. Though he wanted to free and colonize them, he couldn't have competed in a slave economy. "Such action, on his part alone, would have been Quixotic and destructive of his own economic life."

Bowers emphasizes the economic problem.

QUOTING AND CITING SOURCES

You may needlessly copy an entire paragraph when your discussion requires only a few sentences from it, without loss of context. The solution is to use ellipsis: three periods or, infrequently, asterisks, to indicate the omission of a word, phrase, clause, or sentence. The omissions must not, however, alter the meaning of the original passage. How much of the following passage can be omitted without altering the meaning?

> Every man being, as has been shown, naturally free, and nothing being able to put him into subjection to any earthly power but only his own consent, it is to be considered what shall be understood to be a sufficient declaration of a man's consent to make him subject to the laws of any government. There is a common distinction of an express and a tacit consent which will concern our present case. Nobody doubts but an express consent of any man entering into any society makes him a perfect member of that society, a subject of that government. The difficulty is, what ought to be looked upon as a tacit consent, and how far it binds—i.e., how far anyone shall be looked upon to have consented and thereby submitted to any government, where he has made no expressions of it at all. And to this I say that every man that has any possessions or enjoyment of any part of the dominions of any government

does thereby give his tacit consent, and is as far forth obliged to obedience to the laws of that government, during such enjoyment, as anyone under it; whether this his possession be of land to him and his heirs forever, or a lodging only for a week, or whether it be barely traveling freely on the highway; and, in effect, it reaches as far as the very being of anyone within the territories of that government.

—JOHN LOCKE, *Second Treatise of Civil Government* (1690)

How much can safely be omitted depends on how much of the *particular* context is indicated in the introduction to the passage. If the introduction indicates that Locke is dealing with the difference between an expressed or explicit consent and a tacit or implicit one, the passage could be reduced in length as follows:

Every man being . . . naturally free, and nothing being able to put him into subjection to any earthly power but only his own consent, it is to be considered what shall be understood to be a sufficient declaration of a man's consent to make him subject to the laws of any government. . . . Nobody doubts but an express consent of any man entering into any society makes him a perfect member of that society, a subject of that government. The difficulty is, what ought to be looked upon as a tacit consent, and how far it binds—i.e., how far anyone shall be looked upon to have consented and thereby submitted to any government, where he has made no expressions of it at all. And to this I say that every man that has any possessions or enjoyment of any part of the dominions of any government does thereby give his tacit consent, and is as far forth obliged to obedience to the laws of that government, during such enjoyment, as anyone under it . . . .

The passages omitted are important clarifications of the ideas but unessential to the definitions of two kinds of consent. Note that the explanation of "bind" is essential and cannot be omitted. Depending on what is omitted, ellipses may be used alone or in combination with the natural period of a sentence. In the first ellipsis above, the periods indicate that the omission has come in the middle of the sentence. In the second ellipsis, the first period is the natural period of the sentence; the reader knows that at least one sentence has been omitted since the first word of the following sentence is capitalized. The final ellipsis indicates that the end of the sentence has been omitted.

Normally, ellipsis is not used at the beginning or end of a self-contained quotation (the reader knows that the quotation has been taken from a larger context); ellipsis may, however, be used in this way to indicate that what precedes or what follows is more than usually significant but has been omitted of necessity. If a large number of sentences has been omitted *within* a long quotation, the usual practice is to separate the divisions of the quotation with a row of spaced periods running from margin to margin. And if the original passage contains an error, the error should remain in the quotation—immediately followed by [sic] within brackets to indicate that the passage has been reproduced exactly as found. *Sic* means *thus* or *as I found it.*

It must be remembered that no quotation carries its full context. You must indicate enough of this context in your discussion so that the quotation carries approximately the same emphasis and accent of meaning. No quotation can stand alone without discussion or interpretation, nor can the quotation make a point in itself; it should be used as illustration of an idea you have explained, or will explain in the course of the paper. As a rule, the less you quote, the more effective are the passages quoted, assuming of course that they are pertinent to the discussion.

One additional point needs to be made concerning omissions. The general rule governing omissions is often difficult to apply when nonrestrictive material such as that discussed above implies an interpretation or point of view. Consider the following paragraphs from a news report on the possibility of a federal grand jury investigation of the deaths at Kent State University on May 4, 1970:

> A special Ohio grand jury, ordered by former Gov. James A. Rhodes, indicted 25 persons, mostly students and faculty at Kent State, and exonerated the [Ohio National] Guard last Oct. 16.
>
> In a report later called unconstitutional by a federal district court, the Grand Jury found that the slayings and the wounding of nine were justified. It also excoriated the university administration for fostering "an attitude of laxity, overindulgence and permissiveness."
>
> The jury, made up of persons from the predominantly rural area around KSU, said the Guardsmen had fired "in the honest and sincere belief . . . they would suffer bodily injury had they not done so."
>
> —Akron *Beacon-Journal*, March 21, 1971

If you wanted to omit the statement in the final paragraph indicating the make-up of the jury, you would have to decide whether the information merely *identifies* the jury or, additionally, is intended as a *judgment* on their findings. If you are in doubt, a careful reading of the whole news report may provide other indications of a point of view or implicit attitude. In the absence of a decisive indication, you will do best to quote the entire passage and, if necessary, tell the reader that a problem of interpretation exists.

Concerning the quotation of remarks of individuals, the words of Jacques Barzun and Henry F. Graff are important enough to cite here. Having indicated the importance of determining the exact statement a person made (the example is Lord Acton's "Power tends to corrupt and absolute power corrupts absolutely"), they comment:

> Having secured the author's very words, the reporter scans them for what they say, scans the neighboring words, the author's other works on the same subject, and gradually acquires familiarity with the natural movement of the man's thought. It is at this point that Literalism would be misplaced if it reentered. Its most obvious form would be to quote a remark such as Lord Acton's as if its being in print automatically gave it the same weight as every other by the same author. It may have more or less, depending on place and circumstance. Is the idea expressed the conclusion of a piece of reasoning in, say, an essay? Or is it a notion struck off in a letter to a friend? Or, conversely, is it an improvised retort to an opponent? It is the critic's duty to *judge* importance and value in the light of his wider knowledge. If he remains baldly literal and contents himself with quoting extracts, he invariably ends by showing his human subject to have been a mass of contradictions.—*The Modern Researcher*

FOOTNOTES

Latin abbreviations to indicate previous references are going out of style (the possible exception is *Ibid.*). Most writers use a short, simple reference to the author or title (or both) to keep the reader from flipping pages. The first reference to a book should be complete; succeeding references need cite only the author, if one book has been cited, or the author and a short form of the title, if two books or selections by the same author have been used. Footnotes that refer to journal articles should include complete information about the author, title of the article, journal, volume number and issue or date of publication—in addition to the page reference. It is essential to include this information even though the bibliography following the paper includes it. All quotations, material in paraphrase, and important ideas should be footnoted. Here are possible footnotes for a paper on Jefferson:

[1] Claude G. Bowers, *The Young Jefferson: 1743–1789* (Boston: Houghton Mifflin Co., 1945), p. 174.
[2] *Ibid.*, p. 182.   OR   [2] *Young Jefferson*, p. 182.
[3] Claude G. Bowers, *Jefferson in Power* (Boston: Houghton Mifflin Co., 1936), p. 36.

4 Bowers, *Young Jefferson*, p. 194.

5 Bowers, *Jefferson in Power*, p. 38.   OR   5 *Jefferson in Power*, p. 38.

6 J. Leslie Hall, "The Religious Opinions of Thomas Jefferson," *The Sewanee Review*, XXI (1913), p. 165.

Some writers include the documentation in the text itself (particularly when only a few sources are being used):

> Some commentators emphasize the economic difficulties Jefferson would have met if he had freed his slaves: "The economic system of the State was based on slavery, and, while he would have gladly joined all others in the freeing and colonization of the slaves, he alone could not do so and compete with slave labor" (Claude G. Bowers, *The Young Jefferson: 1743–1789*, Boston: Houghton Mifflin Co., 1945, p. 174).

The footnote, incidentally, is the place for important information that helps to illuminate the topic but does not strictly and logically belong in the paper itself. Footnotes should not be used to unload material in note cards that cannot be used in the paper.

BIBLIOGRAPHY

The following bibliography of selected articles and books on rhetoric conforms to that recommended by *The MLA Style Sheet*, Second Edition (1970).

Booth, Wayne C. "The Rhetorical Stance," *College Composition and Communication*, 14 (1963), 139–45.

———. *The Rhetoric of Fiction*. Chicago: The University of Chicago Press, 1961.

Brooks, Cleanth and Warren, Robert Penn. *Modern Rhetoric*, 3rd ed. New York: Harcourt Brace Jovanovich, 1970.

Burke, Kenneth. *A Rhetoric of Motives*. Englewood Cliffs, N.J.: Prentice-Hall, Inc., 1950.

———. "Rhetoric Old and New," rpt. in *New Rhetorics*. Ed Martin Steinmann, Jr. New York: Charles Scribner's Sons, 1967. [Burke's article first appeared in *Journal of General Education*, V (1951), 203–209. This entry shows how to list an article reprinted in a collection of essays.]

Corbett, Edward P. J. *Classical Rhetoric for the Modern Student*, 2nd ed. New York: Oxford University Press, 1971.

———. ed. *Rhetorical Analyses of Literary Work*. New York: Oxford University Press, 1969.

Crane, R. S., ed. *Critics and Criticism*. Chicago: The University of Chicago Press, 1952.

Sledd, James. *A Short Introduction to English Grammar*. Chicago: Scott, Foresman and Company, 1959.

Weaver, Richard. *The Ethics of Rhetoric*. Chicago: Henry Regnery Company, 1953.

Young, Richard E., Becker, Alton L., and Pike, Kenneth L., *Rhetoric: Discovery and Change*. New York: Harcourt Brace Jovanovich, 1970.

THE RESEARCH PAPER

DANIEL BOONE: EMPIRE BUILDER
OR PHILOSOPHER OF PRIMITIVISM?

by Henry Nash Smith

([1During the summer of 1842, following his sophomore year
at Harvard, Francis Parkman made a trip through northern
New York and New England. After spending several days
admiring the scenery along the shores of Lake George, he
noted in his journal: "There would be no finer place of
gentlemen's seats than this, but now, for the most part,
it is occupied by a race of boors about as uncouth, mean,
and stupid as the hogs they seem chiefly to delight in."[1]
The tone is even blunter than that of Timothy Dwight's
famous description of backwoodsmen in this area a generation earlier, but it embodies a comparable aristocratic
disdain. Observers from Eastern cities made similar comments about uncultivated farmers along every American
frontier. The class bias underlying the judgment was one
of the dominant forces shaping nineteenth-century attitudes
toward the West.
([2When Parkman got away from farms and hogs, out into the
forest, his tone changed completely. He wrote, for example,
that a woodsman named James Abbot, although coarse and
self-willed was "a remarkably intelligent fellow; has
astonishing information for one of his condition; is

[1] The Journals of Francis Parkman, ed. Mason Wade, 2 vols.
(paged continuously); (New York, 1947), p. 53.

ANALYSIS

Paragraphs 1–7. Smith introduces his subject—stated fully in ([6—
through an extended discussion of Parkman's attitude toward the
West. Parkman's two views represent, however, one of two conflicting
attitudes in the general culture—"primitivism" and belief in "manifest

resolute and independent as the wind." [2]   The young Brahmin's
delight in men of the wilderness comes out even more
forcibly in the journal of his Far Western trip four years
later.   The Oregon Trail presents the guide Henry Chatillon,
a French-Canadian squaw man, as a hero of romance—hand-
some, brave, true, skilled in the ways of the plains and
mountains, and even possessed of "a natural refinement and
delicacy of mind, such as is rare even in women." [3]
¶[3 Parkman's antithetical attitudes toward backswoods farmers
and the hunters and trappers of the wilderness illustrate
the fact that for Americans of that period there were two
quite distinct Wests: the commonplace domesticated area
within the agricultural frontier, and the Wild West beyond
it.   The agricultural West was tedious; its inhabitants be-
longed to a despised social class.   The Wild West was by
contrast an exhilarating region of adventure and comrade-
ship in the open air.   Its heroes bore none of the marks of
degraded status.   They were in reality not members of society at all, but noble anarchs owning no master, free
denizens of a limitless wilderness.
¶[4 Parkman's love of the Wild West implied a paradoxical rejection of organized society.   He himself was the product
of a complex social order formed by two centuries of
history, and his way of life was made possible by the
fortune which his grandfather had built up as one of the
great merchants of Boston.   But a young gentleman of leisure
could afford better than anyone else to indulge himself in
the slightly decadent cult of wildness and savagery which
the early nineteenth century took over from Byron.   Historians call the mood "primitivism."   Parkman had a severe
case.   In later life he said that from his early youth "His
thoughts were always in the forest, whose features possessed
his waking and sleeping dreams, filling him with vague

[2] Ibid., p. 77.
[3] The Oregon Trail, rev. ed. (New York, 1872), pp. 12-13.

destiny." The second of these attitudes, briefly outlined in ¶[5, is
explored in detail in ¶ 7. The extreme economy of this exposition is
evident in the careful selection of a few, brief revealing details drawn
from such primary sources as Parkman's journals and his The Oregon
Trail. Smith need not name the historians who have commented on
the primitivist mood or quote from their writings: the book Virgin
Land, in which this discussion of Boone appears, amply documents
these views. Had the essay appeared alone and been directed to a
general audience unfamiliar with these ideas, additional discussion

cravings impossible to satisfy."⁴   And in a preface to
The Oregon Trail written more than twenty years after the
first publication of the book he bewailed the advance of
humdrum civilization over the wide empty plains of Colorado
since the stirring days of 1846. ⁵
⟦⁵Such a mood of refined hostility to progress affected a
surprising number of Parkman's contemporaries.   Nevertheless, it could hardly strike very deep in a society committed to an expansive manifest destiny.   A romantic love
of the vanishing Wild West could be no more than a self-
indulgent affectation beside the triumphant official cult
of progress, which meant the conquest of the wilderness by
farms and towns and cities.   If there was a delicious melan-
choly for sophisticated and literary people in regretting
the destruction of the primitive freedom of an untouched
continent, the westward movement seemed to less imaginative
observers a glorious victory of civilization over savagery
and barbarism.   For such people—and they were the vast
majority—the Western hunter and guide was praiseworthy not
because of his intrinsic wildness or half-savage glamor,
but because he blazed trails that hard-working farmers
could follow.
⟦⁶One of the most striking evidences of the currency of these
two conflicting attitudes toward the westward movement is
the popular image of Daniel Boone.   The official view was
set forth in a greatly admired piece of allegorical sculp-
ture by Horatio Greenough in the National Capital, which
depicted the contest between civilization and barbarism as
a fierce hand-to-hand struggle between Boone and an Indian
warrior. ⁶ George C. Bingham's painting "The Emigration of
Daniel Boone" (1851) showed the celebrated Kentuckian
leading a party of settlers with their wives and children

⁴Journals, p. 3.
⁵The Oregon Trail, pp. [vii]-viii.
⁶The work is described in Ballou's Pictorial Drawing-Room
  Companion, IX (1855), 284.

might be provided in the *footnotes*. In introductory paragraphs of
this length, the focus must not be permitted to shift from the single
idea—the antithetical attitudes toward the West—that Smith uses as
a lead into his main subject.

Paragraph 4. The details of Parkman's life are undocumented because
they are not crucial to the argument and are well-known. An unfamiliar detail, drawn from an inaccessible primary source, is usually
documented.

and livestock out into a dreamily beautiful wilderness which they obviously meant to bring under the plow. [7]

([7] These empire-building functions were amply documented by the facts of history. Boone had supervised the Treaty of Sycamore Shoals which extinguished the Indian claim to much of Kentucky, he had blazed the Wilderness Trail through the forest, and after leading the first settlers to Boonesborough in 1775, he had stoutly defended this outpost of civilization against the Indians during the troubled period of the Revolution. [8] His functions as founder of the commonwealth of Kentucky had been celebrated as early as 1784 by John Filson, first architect of the Boone legend, in The Discovery, Settlement and Present State of Kentucke. Filson represents Boone as delighting in the thought that Kentucky will soon be one of the most opulent and powerful states on the continent, and finding in the love and gratitude of his countrymen a sufficient reward for all his toil and suffering. [9] The grandiose epic entitled The Adventures of Daniel Boone, published in 1813 by Daniel Bryan, a nephew of the hero, is even more emphatic concerning his devotion to social progress. Complete with Miltonic councils in Heaven and Hell, the epic relates how Boone was chosen by the angelic Spirit of Enterprise to bring Civilization to the trans-Allegheny wilderness. [1] When he is informed of his divine election for this task, Boone's kindling fancy beholds Refinement's golden file smoothing the heathen encrustations from the savage mind, while Commerce, Wealth, and all the brilliant Arts spread over the land. [2] He in-

[7] The painting is in the possession of Washington University, St. Louis. It was reproduced in The Magazine of Art, XXXII, 330 (June, 1939).

[8] John E. Bakeless, Daniel Boone, Master of the Wilderness (New York, 1939), pp. 85, 89, 144-145. The Port Folio mentioned Boone in 1814 as an example of American "enterprize" (Third [Fourth] Series, IV, 337).

[9] The Discovery, Settlement and Present State of Kentucke (Wilmington, Delaware, 1784), pp. 81-82.

[1] Daniel Bryan, The Mountain Muse: Comprising The Adventures of Daniel Boone; and The Power of Virtuous and Refined Beauty (Harrisonburg, Virginia, 1813), pp. 42-43.

[2] Ibid., p. 54.

Paragraphs 6–7. The details in ([6 are documented because their sources are unfamiliar. The opening sentence of ([7 indicates why the many facts presented in that paragraph need not be fully documented. It should be noted that Smith draws his most important evidence from primary sources which shed new light on Boone. The view of Boone's nephew is especially revealing because it constitutes *positive*

forms his wife in a Homeric leave-taking that the sovereign
law of Heaven requires him to tread the adventurous stage
of grand emprise, scattering knowledge through the heathen
wilds, and mending the state of Universal Man.[3] Faithful
to his mission even in captivity among the Indians, he
lectures the chief Montour on the history of the human race,
concluding with reflections on

> How Philanthropy
> And social Love, in sweet profusion pour
> Along Refinement's pleasure-blooming Vales,
> Their streams of richest, life-ennobling joy.[4]

[8]By the side of Boone the empire builder and philanthropist,
the anonymous popular mind had meanwhile created an entirely different hero, a fugitive from civilization who
could not endure the encroachment of settlements upon his
beloved wilderness. A dispatch from Fort Osage in the
Indian territory, reprinted in Niles' Register in 1816,
described an interview with Boone and added: "This singular
man could not live in Kentucky when it became settled.
. . . he might have accumulated riches as readily as any
man in Kentucky, but he prefers the woods, where you see him
in the dress of the roughest, poorest hunter."[5]
[9]Boone's flight westward before the advance of the agricultural frontier—actually dictated by a series of failures
in his efforts to get and hold land—became a theme of
newspaper jokes. The impulse that produced Western tall
tales transformed him into the type of all frontiersmen who
required unlimited elbow room. "As civilization advanced,"
wrote a reporter in the New York American in 1823, "so he,
from time to time, retreated"—from Kentucky to Tennessee,
from Tennessee to Missouri. But Missouri itself was filling
up: Boone was said to have complained, "I had not been two
years at the licks before a d—d Yankee came, and settled
down within an hundred miles of me!!" He would soon be driven
on out to the Rocky Mountains and would be crowded there in

[3] Ibid., p. 59.
[4] Ibid., pp. 184-185.
[5] Niles' Register, X, 361 (June 15, 1816).

---

supporting evidence (it shows that even a close relative was prepared
to countenance the image of Boone as empire builder).

Paragraphs 8–9 relate the second view of Boone—based on primary
journalistic sources—to one general feeling about the frontier, identified earlier.

eight or ten years. [6] Edwin James, chronicler of the Stephen H. Long expedition, visiting Fort Osage in 1819, heard that Boone felt it was time to move again when he could no longer fell a tree for fuel so that its top would lie witih a few yards of the door of his cabin. This remark set James, a native of Vermont, to thinking about the irrational behavior of frontiersmen. He had observed that most inhabitants of new states and territories had "a manifest propensity, particularly in the males, to remove westward, for which it is not easy to account." There was an apparently irresistible charm for the true Westerner in a mode of life "wherein the artificial wants and the uneasy restraints inseparable from a crowded population are not known, wherein we feel ourselves dependent immediately and solely on the bounty of nature, and the strength of our own arm. . . ."[7] The Long party came upon a man more than sixty years old living near the farthest settlement up the Missouri who questioned them minutely about the still unoccupied Platte Valley. "We discovered," noted James with astonishment, "that he had the most serious intention of removing with his family to that river."[8]

¶[10] Seizing upon hints of Boone's flight before the advance of civilization, Byron paused in his description of the siege of Ismail in the eighth canto of Don Juan to insert an extended tribute to him. Although Byron's Boone shrank from men of his own nation when they built up unto his darling trees, he was happy, innocent, and benevolent;

[6] Niles' Register, XXIV, 166 (May 17, 1823); American Monthly Magazine and Critical Review, III, 152 (New York, June, 1818). Niles' Register picked up a similar remark from the St. Louis Enquirer, XV, 328 (December 26, 1818).
[7] Edwin James, ed., Account of an Expedition from Pittsburgh to the Rocky Mountains, Performed in the Years 1819 and '20 . . . under the command of Major Stephen H. Long, 2 vols. and atlas (Philadelphia, 1823), I, 105.
[8] Ibid., I, 106.

Paragraph 10 presents even more conclusive evidence of the second view—evident in Byron's view of Boone in Don Juan. Smith documents the fact that these verses were known in the United States, in part through Boone's own Life and Adventures which most certainly was read widely. The choice of detail in the footnotes is as selective as that in the text.

Paragraphs 11–12. Smith explores conflicting attitudes toward Boone in single works, one by an anonymous kinsman, another by the most

simple, not savage; and even in old age still a child of
nature, whose virtues shamed the corruptions of civilization. Americans quoted these stanzas eagerly.⁹
〖¹¹Which was the real Boone—the standard-bearer of civilization and refinement, or the child of nature who fled into
the wilderness before the advance of settlement? An
anonymous kinsman of Boone wrestled with the problem in a
biographical sketch published a few years after the famous
hunter's death in 1820. It would be natural to suppose, he
wrote, that the Colonel took great pleasure in the magnificent growth of the commonwealth he had founded in the
wilderness. But such was not the case. Passionately fond
of hunting, "like the unrefined Savage," Boone saw only that
incoming settlers frightened away all the game and spoiled
the sport. He would "certainly prefer a state of nature to
a state of Civilization, if he were obliged to be confined
to one or the other."¹
〖¹²Timothy Flint's biography, perhaps the most widely read
book about a Western character published during the first
half of the nineteenth century, embodies the prevalent confusion of attitudes. Flint says that Boone delighted in
the thought that "the rich and boundless valleys of the
great west—the garden of the earth—and the paradise of
hunters, had been won from the dominion of the savage
tribes, and opened as an asylum for the oppressed, the
enterprising, and the free of every land." The explorer of
Kentucky

> had caught some glimmerings of the future, and saw with
> the prophetic eye of a patriot, that this great valley

⁹ They were reprinted, for example, in Life and Adventures of
Colonel Daniel Boone, the First White Settler of the State
of Kentucky . . . Written by Himself . . . Annexed Is a
Eulogy on Col. Boone and Choice of Life, by Lord Byron
(Brooklyn, 1823), reprinted in The Magazine of History,
Extra No. 180 (Tarrytown, New York, 1932), pp. 226-227.
¹ Ibid., pp. 217-221.

widely read biographer of the early nineteenth century. Smith quotes
extensively because these passages convey feelings about Boone not
easily paraphrased. The fewer the passages quoted, the more effective
and memorable each of them is. No research paper should be a tissue
of long quotations interlaced with connecting commentary.

Paragraph 12. Smith is careful to supply the context of the passages
he quotes. He knows that the quotation does not carry its context.

must soon become the abode of millions of freemen; and his heart swelled with joy, and warmed with a transport which was natural to a mind so unsophisticated and disinterested as his. 2

Yet we learn only a few pages later that he was driven out of Kentucky by "the restless spirit of immigration, and of civil and physical improvement." 3 Even in Missouri, "the tide of emigration once more swept by the dwelling of Daniel Boone, driving off the game and monopolizing the rich hunting grounds." In despair,

> he saw that it was in vain to contend with fate; that go where he would, American enterprize seemed doomed to follow him, and to thwart all his schemes of backwoods retirement. He found himself once more surrounded by the rapid march of improvement, and he accommodated himself, as well as he might, to a state of things which he could not prevent. 4

On yet other occasions Flint credits Boone with a sophisticated cult of pastoral simplicity greatly resembling his own, which he had imitated from Chateaubriand. When the frontiersman seeks to induce settlers to go with him into the new land, he is represented as promising them that the original pioneers, in their old age, will be surrounded by

> consideration, and care, and tenderness from children, whose breasts were not steeled by ambition, nor hardened by avarice; in whom the beautiful influences of the indulgence of none but natural desires and pure affections would not be deadened by the selfishness, vanity, and fear of ridicule, that are the harvest of what is called civilized and cultivated life. 5

2 The Life and Adventures of Daniel Boone, the First Settler of Kentucky, Interspersed with Incidents in the Early Annals of the Country (first published 1833); (Cincinnati, 1868), pp. 226-227. According to the Dictionary of American Biography, this work went through fourteen editions.
3 Ibid., pp. 229-230.
4 Ibid., p. 246.
5 Ibid., p. 41.

He does this economically: he does not have to summarize the whole book to present these ideas.

Paragraphs 13–14 extend the discussion by showing in historians and writers of the time an awareness of Boone's conflicting motives. The implications for the general cultural situation are indirectly suggested

◖[13The debate over Boone's character and motives lasted into
the next decade. The noted Western Baptist minister and
gazetteer, John M. Peck, prepared a life of Boone for Jared
Sparks's Library of American Biography in 1847 which
repeatedly attacked the current conception of the hero as a
fugitive from civilization. Peck says that Boone left
North Carolina for the Kentucky wilderness because of the
effeminacy and profligacy of wealthy slaveowners who scorned
the industrious husbandman working his own fields. But by
the time the biographer interviewed the aged hero in Missouri in 1818, Boone had become aware of an imposing historical mission. Although he had not consciously aimed to
lay the foundations of a state or nation, he believed that
he had been "a creature of Providence, ordained by Heaven
as a pioneer in the wilderness, to advance the civilization
and the extension of his country."6
◖[14James H. Perkins of Cincinnati, writing in 1846 in the
North American Review, was equally interested in the problem
of Boone's motives, but inclined to a more modest interpretation. Boone, he said, was a white Indian. Although he
and his companions were not at all like the boasting, swear-
ing, drinking, gouging Mike Finks of the later West, they
were led into the wilderness not by the hope of gain, nor
by a desire to escape the evils of older communities, nor
yet by dreams of founding a new commonwealth, but simply by
"a love of nature, of perfect freedom, and of the adven-

6Lives of Daniel Boone and Benjamin Lincoln, The Library of
American Biography, ed. Jared Sparks, Second Series, XIII
(Boston, 1847), pp. 186-189. Peck's characterization of
Boone exhibits a number of parallels with the character of
Leatherstocking. He was one of Nature's noblemen—benevolent, rigidly honest, reluctant to shed blood. Although
he never joined any church, he had received religious instructions in his youth, and "was a believer in Chris-
tianity as a revelation from God in the sacred scriptures."
The character of Boone in James Hall's "The Backwoodsman"
also strongly suggests Leatherstocking, although Hall
develops the functions of the hunter in rescuing a heroine
rather than his ethical nobility (Legends of the West,
"second edition," Philadelphia, 1833, pp. [1]-40).

in the interpretation given to Boone's motives. It should be noted
that the information provided in footnote 6 concerning parallels between Boone and characters in fiction might have been introduced in
these paragraphs if their sole purpose were to provide additional evidence confirming the conflicting views of Boone. The shift in focus

turous life in the woods." Boone "would have pined and
died as a nabob in the midst of civilization. He wanted a
frontier, and the perils and pleasures of a frontier life,
not wealth; and he was happier in his log-cabin, with a
loin of venison and his ramrod for a spit, than he would
have been amid the greatest profusion of modern luxuries."[7]
(¶15 If one detects a patronizing note in this account, it goes
along with greater respect for the simple, hearty virtues
that are left to the frontiersman. Such a view seems to
have become general in the 1840's. William H. Emory of the
Army of the West which invaded New Mexico in 1846 invoked
the figure of the Kentuckian to convey his impression of an
American settler in the Mora Valley northeast of Santa Fé:
"He is a perfect specimen of a generous openhearted adven-
turer, and in appearance what, I have pictured to myself,
Daniel Boone, of Kentucky, must have been in his day."[8]
(¶16 Yet the issue long remained unsettled. As a character in
fiction Boone could still be made the spokesman of a stilted
primitivism. Glenn, the young Eastern hero of John B.
Jones's shoddy Wild Western Scenes, published in 1849, is
traveling in the vicinity of Boone's last home in Missouri,
and there encounters the venerable pioneer. The highly
implausible conversation between the two men indicates to
what unhistorical uses the symbol of Boone could be put.
The Westerner asks Glenn whether he has become disgusted
with the society of men. Glenn, who happens to be just such

[7] North American Review, LXII, 97, 86-87 (January, 1846).
[8] Notes of a Military Reconnoissance from Fort Leavenworth
. . . to San Diego (1848), 30 Cong., 1 Sess. House Executive Document No. 41, in Vol. IV, p. 25.

to the cultural situation is most evident in ¶15 which is solely concerned with the changing attitude toward the frontiersman.

Paragraph 16 cites one extended example of the second view of Boone.
The date of the book Smith quotes from indicates the extent to which
Boone had become a legend on which hack writers could draw. Smith

a rhetorical misanthrope as the question implies, welcomes
the opportunity to set forth his views:

> I had heard [he declares] that you were happy in the
> solitude of the mountain-shaded valley, or on the inter-
> minable prairies that greet the horizon in the distance,
> where neither the derision of the proud, the malice of
> the envious, nor the deceptions of pretended love and
> friendship, could disturb your peaceful meditation; and
> from amid the wreck of certain hopes, which I once thought
> no circumstances could destroy [it is a matter of disap-
> pointment in love], I rose with a determined vow to seek
> such a wilderness, where I would pass a certain number
> of my days engaging in the pursuits that might be most
> congenial to my disposition. Already I imagine I ex-
> perience the happy effects of my resolution. Here the
> whispers of vituperating foes cannot injure, nor the
> smiles of those fondly cherished, deceive.

Boone clasps the young coxcomb's hand in enthusiastic agreement. [9] If Daniel Bryan's epic represents the limit of possible absurdity in making Boone the harbinger of civilization and refinement, this may stand as the opposite limit
of absurdity in making him a cultural primitivist. The
image of the Wild Western hero could serve either purpose.

[9] Wild Western Scenes: A Narrative of Adventures in the
Western Wilderness, the Nearest and Best California.
Wherein the Exploits of Daniel Boone, the Great American
Pioneer, Are Particularly Described, by Luke Shortfield
(pseud.); (Philadelphia, 1849), p. 22. Since Boone plays
but a negligible part in the story, the exploitation of his
name in the title suggests the currency of the Boone
legend.

comments on the significance of his example in his footnote. The concluding statement indicates that the purpose of the essay is not to settle the dispute (a different kind of evidence would have to be introduced for this purpose), but to explore the implications of the Boone
legend for changing attitudes toward the frontier (the subject of the
introductory paragraphs).

INDEX

A 2
B 3
C 4
D 5
E 6
F 7
G 8
H 9
I 0
J 1